I0411230

# The Johannesburg Formula
# PART ONE:

## *AFTER FEBRUARY 2013*

1st edition

First published in 2015

Copyright

©2015 The Johannesburg Formula

All Rights Reserved

ISBN 978 150 860 6031

# The Johannesburg Formula

## SPECIAL PROJECTS

### inewshare™

NB! Proceeds from the sale of this book and the series will go towards the establishment of an Economic Equality Fund: inewshare™... . ...inewshare™ is an innovative solution and novel global methodology that is based on the principle of eradicating economic inequality, by introducing more than 7 billion people across the world to a common purpose and common outcome of eradicating inequality. For the first time inewshare™ aims to give access to 7 billion people across the world, a platform of economic equity and an initiative to push the frontiers of poverty back through innovation, equal access and ownership in the Fund. As an unconventional economic experiment of its kind, inewshare™ will be registered, formalised and capitalised as and when funds from sales of products reach the requisite amounts to enable requirements. The fund currently has an account with Capitec, a bank in South Africa. inewshare™ operates on a principle of funding through innovation to capitalise the fund. For example the sale of *The Johannesburg Formula* series is an example of the funding model.

For more details see:

www.Youtube/inewshare

www.blogspot.com/inewshare

# The Johannesburg Formula

Graham Hancock, your quest has awoken an inquiry that deserves answers.

*ALSO*

TO THE VOICELESS...

THROUGH YOU WE ALL SPEAK, through us you all speak...the future is void without the relics of the past that speak truth to us though we embark on a future THAT IS unknown.

# CONTENTS

## PART ONE - AFTER FEBRUARY 2013

# ACKNOWLEDGEMENTS

To family, for tolerating maverick tendencies at the risk of being labelled, in a society that is still coming to terms with *observing without judging* as a common protocol of a mobile society.

To the people at the Constitutional Court of South Africa who even though did not get to hear the matter in court, never denied the application callously, but instead recognised that the application was what may be termed "irregular". This means that if I would file a "regular" application it would be eligible for a fair case management process.

To the many South Africans and journalists, radio presenters and television teams who ran the story after it broke and did not retract from professional obligation for any reason.

# INTRODUCTION

The Constitutional Court of South Africa (SA) is an esteemed institution that is a bastion of all that is desirable in a newly ushered society, straddling between development and idealism, where many of the desirable outcomes are yet to come 'off the wall' of the documents wherein they are written and benefit the majority of people who have entrusted their right to recourse to the Court. SA is 'different' on a continent that is struggling with bringing to bear the international norms and lay the legacy of colonialism to rest in the process of endearing the societies across Africa with just and esteemed characteristics of a society that is developing. The courts of SA give hope to the future and the test of this is what are the matters that the courts are interested in having in front of them, in order to establish the avowed promise of the letter of the law but also to test the reality of several sectors of society, the arts, sciences, business, sports etc, as having an avenue to interact with the law where infractions and legal impropriety amongst constituencies occur.

I never imagined that I would write a book in a country where art suffered and was stifled as a result of the history of SA, where the only books that emerged were of protest and embattlement. In a place where people who wrote books went against the grain of the authorities for so long and it was rare to find expressions of casual stories of love, comedy and social parody, as these did not resonate with the times. Twenty years later, SA is a free country where much development and growth are the order of the day and people are writing about ordinary experiences. I dare write about something so far from daily experience, a story inspired by the people of ancient times and modern researchers who have not forgotten how the past impacts and still has a bearing on modern times. I do however recognise that the topic of a world that is influenced by forces that lay beyond our everyday scope are not easily entertaining let alone make for eager readership, because we do not want to imagine that our world as we know it is prone to afflictions that may be due to forces that we only learnt about in geography and science lessons. We never thought that school lessons would come alive in such a manner and affect us directly. Also our generation may have to face up to the reality of uncertainty when it comes to cosmic influences on the planet earth. I have been one of those people that have been deeply affected by the broadly available knowledge that our planet is prone to cosmic forces that are good and sometimes bad. Our state of development and our hopes for a secure future do not lend us on a daily basis to even contemplate that our planet is part of a bigger environment of planets that are sometimes prone to unruly cosmic influences. These are scientific *forces* that often play out in space out of our sight and out of our daily experience and this has led us to keep this reality out of our everyday circulation of experiences, only limiting our knowledge of what is happening to our immediate planet and the natural events that occur within the limit of our *known* world. Any generation like that of the 21st century is however, whether we want to admit it or not part of the planetary system and for intents and purposes we have to face the truth and reality of what this might mean and accept that the only thing we may do is take precautionary measures to protect our species and civilization from the effects of cosmic forces that may be out of kilter and that might impact us negatively. We have not in our *knowledge* factored this reality into our outlook and as a result we sit on planet earth not knowing what to expect if anything at all. I intimate that we should by now be able to imagine and to think freely about the possibilities that the people who have written and researched this reality of cosmic forces beyond our scope have done, for the benefit of the people of the planet. These people are not lunatics who have nothing better to do with their time, either than to contemplate gross horrors. Just as we know in our lives that risk is a real factor and phenomenon and we insure everything we value against unforeseeable circumstances, we should think likewise about the planet, that it too is prone to risk of a cosmic nature. The problem is that risk is a remote but real possibility and so we only encounter it when it happens and we often react to the effects of risk rather than mitigate it. The reality and truth is that whether we like it or not researchers and scientists at leading space centres are looking at the possibility of cosmic risk on a daily basis and when something of that nature does occur we are told in the media about for example solar outbursts where the sun ejects huge amounts of plasma that if it were to head in the direction of our planet, would have severe impacts on our satellite technologies and everything that is operating or is dependent on these installations. Another factor is that most of these experiences have only been written about in ancient mythologies and stories that do not seem to have bearing on our reality and so we ignore the aspects of these stories that do not materialise on a daily basis. This cannot ensue and we have to take steps that filter this information into our knowledge of risk and accept that we have to think about the possibility of cosmic risk. This book is about how we should try our best to not ignore this information and to indeed do something that will make sure that should the reality of cosmic risk materialise we are not helpless. It is not an easy subject to broach and most people would not give themselves to being the authors of such information for fear of what people will think of them and what they might say of them. One-way or another, this is our reality on the planet and we have to treat it as part of our life where we are always prepared for anything. Please familiarise yourself with Graham Hancock's books, especially *"Fingerprints of the Gods"*, where he illustrates in a sober, non-philosophical way the realities that we ourselves in our generation have not internalised because of the disturbing nature of the reality and information, but as free as we are to speak, to think and to act, there will always be people like Graham who bring us a sober truth and reality through years of research and logical dissemination of information.

## PREFACE

SOUTH AFRICA (SA) has come a long way and the proof of it is when SA can allow people to take it to the brink of Hollywood style stories in the public domain when issues as a bizarre as the claims of the Meso-American people are being discussed and given a fair looking at. For long America has held the title as the land where the maverick and bizarre happen and it is *normal*. SA has its share of stories that stretch the imagination and show us that imagination is not only the preserve of Hollywood where the *strangest* things are allowed to burst onto the public scene without anyone flinching.

This book is about a past event that has not seen closure simply because many questions will recur every time a natural event occurs that seems to remind us of the claims of the Mayans. The 21st of December 2012 might have come and gone, the lingering question of the future having postponed itself and the event lingering somewhere in the future is large in our minds not because we are fatalistic but because we are realistic. We know that the earth is not controlled by a corporate or single government and that at any moment it reminds us that we are a part of a great system that has an independent whim on a scale that we are in awe of. It does not please a single one of us when we bear the brunt of natural disaster and we seem miniscule and finite in the face of it all. Why would business corporations spend a large part their revenue on risk and averting the effects of risk? Why does the insurance industry still loom so large in the affairs of economies even when we know that the chances of insurable risk are a small margin of our desired order of the day? Because we recognise that we are not in total control.

This book shows us how our society takes seriously any warning whether a false alarm or not and we take actions that seek to mitigate any threat to our order and regime of life as we know it.

This is an illustration of an action that we took as our conscience would not allow us to do otherwise to compel ourselves to be in the loop about things that we all do not control...nature!  This book also illustrates how SA has evolved, to a point of even letting the people speak to the court regarding any matter as long as the people prove that it is the interest of the public.

# PART 1 :        AFTER FEBRUARY 2013

### CHAPTER ONE

### THE JOHANNESBURG FORMULA

A letter to Graham Hancock, the illustrious Author of *Fingerprints of The Gods...*

Sir, Mr Graham Hancock

**H**aving read your book *"FINGERPRINTS OF THE GODS"*, I recognise the circumstances that you describe in your book in these terms... *"an eerie feeling that an ancient intelligence is compelling us to discover hidden codes and formulae that they themselves embedded in our culture and tradition long ago"*. I have felt it necessary to agree with you and to place this reckoning on record. I got hold of your book after a friend called me from hospital in March 2013 while being admitted for observation following an episode of what was diagnosed as mild stress. He bought the book *"Fingerprints of The Gods"* from the book-store at the hospital amongst other books. When I had gone to see him for the second time of two evenings, he showed me this book and he thought that I would be interested and offered me to read it. He knew that I would be interested because the topic to him sounded similar to an issue I was involved with at the South African Constitutional Court where I requested that the claims of the Mayans be reviewed officially. The only book of yours that I had a previous encounter with is *The Sign and the Seal*.

I started to read *Fingerprints of the Gods* on the 05th/04/2013 and I was captivated by the details and really got to learn a lot from the book. While I was trending through the middle of the book, I was visited by a realisation that something was absent that could only have been visible at this point in time, when the main claim of your book (that the Mayan calendar would come to a head in 2012) is supposed to have lapsed. By now everyone but a few have lost interest in the topic for 'obvious' reasons of the claims having registered a no-show.

While reading *Fingerprints of the Gods*, it became obvious that there were discrepancies with calculation and that the date of 21st December 2012 would be overshot and the world would think that the Mayans were spurious.

May I highlight a margin of error that is bound to be incurred when dealing with a big date number such as 5125, according to your own research in *"Fingerprints of the Gods"*, and the years 45 BC (when the Julian calendar was introduced), 1582 when the "Julian vs Gregorian calendars" was the topic of the day. It is possible that in the era, the issues of abridging the inconsistencies of the leap year phenomenon were difficult. The assumption would be that for us to reach the date figure of 5125 years as the duration of the 'final/last sun' or our epoch, we would have to apply the premise of the Gregorian calendar. It seems that before 1582, the Julian calendar seemed to present persistently, inconsistencies and the inability to accurately reconcile the '366th' anomalous day (known as the *leap year* day) that would come up on the calendar every four years. This is the reason that it was changed as you also state in your book.

It occurred to me that the plain reading and assumption of the dates being correct is obscure because we know that the calendar has been subject to changes through many attempts.

Also we know that in the present, not every nation and culture of any country use the same calendar. Some calendars are faith based with the observers asserting the accuracy of the said calendar with supporting evidence as to why the calendar is relevant. I have been aware and keenly followed the issues around several calendars from the discipline of anthropology and faith practice. The calendar that is found in many homes across the world has various faiths' observed calendar-holidays printed on it. So it is known that not everyone observes the same calendar, with various faiths practicing and observing respective holidays. This is more glaring in post 1994 South Africa, where the State does not proffer a particular faith but practices an inclusive constitutional mandate of faith observation.

The theory and formula that I inclined to while reading your book *The Fingerprints of the Gods* was the fact that the Mayan calendar would have to be looked at as a function of knowing that the Julian calendar was replaced by the Gregorian calendar, the calendar through which every assumption about dates is made. We have to somehow revert to the introduction of the Julian calendar. We have to ask the material question of what was happening before the Julian calendar was introduced.

My assumption is that this was the moment when the phenomenon of the leap year was addressed as a challenge of inconsistencies in observing the solar year.

I first assumed that the challenge of 'leap years' stopped at the Julian calendar and that we had to calibrate our reckoning to the change of calendars to the time when the Gregorian calendar was introduced. I had initially assumed that because of the acceptance of the Gregorian calendar as currency in 1582 that this was where the miscalculation resulted from. I assumed that the miscalculation of the Mayan date of 23rd December 2012 started at this point. My first attempt at rationalising this suspicion of a missing quantum of time from the direct translation of the Mayan calendar to the modern calendar was that we would have to take 5125 divide it by 4 (that represents the leap years' period of four years in the Gregorian calendar) and divide the answer by 365 (that represents the number of days in a year without a leap day). We would then get an answer of 3 (and some decimal odds) that represents the years that all our assumptions have been off by. It then means that in 3 years (from the auspicious 2012) it will be 5125 years of the epoch and therefore it is still 5122 of the epoch date in 2013 of our date (Gregorian calendar). So either in 5128 (of the Mayan epoch, having added the

14

margin of error) if we assume this 2013 to be aligned with the 5125 of the epoch, or 5122 if we subtract the 3 years from the 5125 and align 5122 to 2013 since the date of the Mayan epoch was at the end of 2012. This was the approach earlier in the year when I was still very animated about what seemed to me an important fact. This was to prove incorrect when I realised that the introduction of the Julian calendar was also initially a solution to calibrate the solar year. So I would have to move further back to the moment when the Julian calendar was introduced to plug in the numbers. The more correct estimation of the sum of the deficit is illustrated at the end of this chapter. I decided to leave this chapter as it was when I was calculating the deficit from the moment of 1582 instead of 45 BC.

The conclusion is that there has to be more than one approach of calculating the margin of error that should have been built into the calculation when reading the prediction of the Mayan calendar. We also hope that the Johannesburg Formula forms a basis for further points of view and more accurate calculations of how the margin of error may be read into the assumptions of our determinations and conclusions about the Mayan calendar.

Kind regards

Author.

*The initial view that started at the Gregorian calendar to assume that there was a deficit went like this:*

**The Johannesburg Formula:**

- 5125 = epoch
- 4 = amount of years/period when 'leap years' in a Gregorian Calendar era formula occur
- 5125 ÷ 4 = 1281.25
- 1281.25 (the number of years that would have been leap years according to the Gregorian calendar)
- 1281.25 ÷ 365(days in a year) = 3.51027
- 3.51027(years) = amount of time that the Gregorian Calendar-based assumption of 5125 years is off by.


*Another approach would be:*

- to minus 1582 (date of change from Julian calendar to Gregorian calendar) from 2013 (for example)...2013-1582=431 (years that incurred the leap year calculation since 1582) ÷ 4 (period of leap years since 1582) =107.75 (number of leap years since 1582).

- 107.75 (Days) = 3 and a half months

*This approach is inconsistent because of the shifting calculation that always depends on the year we are in (2013 for example). However, this calculation does show the number of leap years from ever since the Gregorian calendar was used.*

**The Johannesburg Formula** got its name because I was in this city when it dawned on me that Mr Graham Hancock (and others) could have overlooked an important factor when pegging his timing on the 5125 years. This for me is another avenue of bringing the facts and truth of your book to bear with the entire findings of *Fingerprints of* *the Gods*, which may not and indeed are not being dispelled by any authority any-where in the world, even from any quarter.

The specifics of calculating dates up to the minute impose an auspicious burden and would have the 'book' literally 'thrown at me' in case of an incorrect outcome. Also I do not want to move away from the specific mandate of scientific inquiry as you also have been strict about sticking narrowly to the duty of empirical inquiry.

Your findings Sir are compelling and guide us to an inevitable truth. It is obvious that your inspired bout in *"Fingerprints of the Gods"* has been lulled by the quite passing of December 2012, when you concluded that the claims of the lost civilization were expected to be proven correct. Reaching the conclusion of noticing the *calendar oversight* while I was reading your book in April of 2013 was not expected at all and I was loath to commit myself to something that could be 'refutable'. I concluded that theory is always transient and went ahead with my own assumption of formulating the theory cited in The Johannesburg Formula. So I would value your opinion on *The Johannesburg Formula* as someone who has been on the trail of these up to now, so called *speculative* findings for long.

The reference to co-author, Robert Bauval with whom you wrote *"Keepers of Genesis"* (I have not read it), at the end of *"Fingerprints of the Gods"*, shows that there are many scholars, researchers in your field of study and line of inquiry. As you will see later, I was compelled to go the route of instituting a hearing as a way of highlighting the importance of the findings of this field to elected officials and government. The option to go to court was the only resolve to make sure that the issue is reckoned with as a matter of official course.

The collation of your findings (including that of others) and the research that is being done *officially* (through agencies like NASA) should yield a mega-picture of the reality that is ensuing as life goes on. The idea to institute a hearing at court came from frustrated conclusions that we reached, that it would be impossible to get official commendation or officials to look at the matter, not when other more *"practical and realistic"* matters are pressing. So, far from being a book in the genre of research and travel as yours is, *The Johannesburg Formula* is about the resolve to act on the findings of the Mayan calendar inquiry in general.

The Johannesburg Formula: I noticed the possibility of this formula on the 03rd /04/2013 while reading *Fingerprints of The Gods* by Graham Hancock. Because Graham's book is littered with theories and formulae, it was a definite labyrinth, but one thing that is for sure is that I figured that I was one more *organic* theorist for observing the discrepancy in the dates mentioned. In this regard, it is a number of theorists that Graham employed to illustrate his claims in *Fingerprints of the Gods.* The Johannesburg Formula and theory is but one more thing that he may consider while he ponders his obviously '*unfinishable*' book that finds a sequel in other people's minds across the world, including myself. Your book showed me that as theorists, we do not have to be right or wrong, we just have to be theorists when the need arises, and leave others to do the same. This is so that the big questions may be answered when a big picture emerges out of a culmination of several small efforts.

Graham your book has left a gaping hole in our outlook about the world because nothing in it may be disputed casually, not even by the most knowledgeable theorists and other extended sources. No one so far has dared to say that you are wrong, even if the date postulated by the ancient societies that form part of your subjects of research has lapsed.

How the Johannesburg Formula fits in is that it assumes that there was a compelling need that caused the Julian calendar to be replaced by the Gregorian calendar all throughout the world. If the Julian calendar was used as the translating medium, the period we would be questioning is from the 13th August 3114 BC to 23rd December 2012.

To follow what the issue raised by The Johannesburg Formula is, here are dates that are important:

- The Mayan dots-and-bar is said to begin on the 13th August 3114 BC.
- The Gregorian calendar came into effect in 1582.
- 3114 BC to 1582 AD is the period we assume would be the calculated period that the translation of the dates from the Mayan dot-and-bar is effective by.
- 3114 BC to 45 BC is another period that has assumptions that overlook miniature details like the effect of the leap year phenomenon on any calculation that bears on the Mayan epoch of 5125 years.
- The Mayan dot-and-bar was decoded in around 1940.

What is the issue?

Well the issue is that in 1582 the Gregorian calendar came into effect, in 1940 or so the Mayan dot-and-bar was decoded and this leads us to an observable margin of error. If after 1940 we assume that we can use the Gregorian calendar to calculate the date that the Mayan Calendar states would be a day of cataclysm through most of the world, we would have committed a mistake. The question is this, for the period that the Gregorian calendar was not in effect, was there an anomaly with the calendar that there was a need to change it?

For the period from 3114 BC to 1582 AD, the Gregorian calendar does not account for the leap year anomaly and so the period of leap years from BC to AD is the amount that is missing from the date number that is deduced to be the translation to 23rd December 2012 in the Gregorian calendar.

As per the revised factors of the formula at the end of this chapter, 3114 BC to 45 BC is the period that compels us to assume that there is a deficit of time that is not calculated in the period that we assume to correlate with the translation of the Mayan dot-and-bar calendar.

It follows therefore that we should calculate the number of leap years from 3114 BC to 1582 AD, as this is the period that is supposed to be unspecified. If the assumption is that the decision to change the Julian calendar to the Gregorian calendar was valid, then there is still no problem in sight, right? This calls into question the reason for changing the Julian calendar. If the reason was for a more accurate reading of dates and the process of justifying leap-days, then there is no assumption that those who changed it were wrong to do so. What is questionable is the fact that the Julian calendar did not seem to be dysfunctional. It is still being used in some parts of the world. As a matter of fact, the Julian calendar still works just fine and is current in some countries today. The only peculiar thing is that there is a seven year period between the Gregorian calendar and the Julian calendar.

We know that *The Johannesburg Formula* gives us a period of roughly 3 years as the outcome of determining the number of years that we should focus on because it assumes that the seven year difference between the two calendars is a given. The reason that we assume that the total anomaly amounts to 7 years is because the Johannesburg Formula only highlights the obvious defect. It is obvious that the outcome of using the Julian calendar to translate the Mayan Calendars would have given us 2005 as the year of the Mayan prediction. The actual difference between the Julian and the Gregorian calendars is a complete scope that accounts for any shortfalls when *The Johannesburg Formula* is used. So does this mean that this is a red herring? No, the issue is that there has been a shortfall because the reading assumes that the calendar has always been the Gregorian module and does not pick up the shortfall of the period from when the Gregorian module started. In the 1940s when the Mayan dot-and-bar calendric system was decoded and read, the shortfall was not taken into account. The fact is that the Julian calendar would not have picked up any leap year discounts.

The conclusion is that the calculation, the reading and translation of the Mayan calendar was not done properly and therefore this means that the date of the 21st December 2012 was incorrectly calculated.

The reason that it is still important to determine the correct date is that the Mayan dot-and-bar is not being brought into question and neither is the message of the Mayans without credibility. The ball is in our court to translate it correctly using a consistent module. So one might assume that it does not matter whether the Gregorian or Julian data is plugged in. This is not the point, the point is that when the dot-and bar was decoded, the 1582 calendar change was not accounted for and therefore there is a clear shortfall.

The findings of *The Johannesburg Formula* are enough to raise a suspicion, but the actual difference in years between the Gregorian calendar and the Julian calendar is a sum that speaks for itself. In other words, it seems to be an arbitrary fact that there is a seven year difference between the two calendars.

The question is this: What was happening in the calculation before the Gregorian calendar was used? Was the decoding of the dot-and-bar calendric system affected by the period in which it was decoded, i.e. the Gregorian calendar in place of the Julian calendar? It is obvious that more research needs to be done here, because as the author of the book *The Johannesburg Formula* I do not assume to be qualified to effectively postulate on an error-free theory with any scholarly authority. What is indispensable is the *question* raised by *The Johannesburg Formula*. I hope to interest Graham Hancock in *The Johannesburg Formula* and have him look at it as a derivative of the information that he presents in *Fingerprints Of The Gods*. Also I hope that he will be able to intervene as someone who has been engrossed with the study of the topic that involves many fields and subjects. For this purpose he looks at calendar systems and how they affect our way of life. He investigates messages and codes that are embedded in ancient relics and formative calendar systems. Can Graham get the team that decoded the dot-and-bar and the team that calculated the date of 23rd December to use the Julian calendar to establish what the outcome will be? The date still has to be established and this is our verdict after looking closely at the events surrounding the Mayan predictions in 2012.

I wonder what Graham is figuring where he is after the 23rd December 2012 (or 21st December 2012 as some authorities have it) was a normal day. Through a casual Google search, I am astounded by the amount of people who have been involved in the process of investigating the Mayan claims. Graham spent years piecing together teams and people who are avid enthusiasts. I wonder what they are all figuring after everything they researched proved to be accurate safe for the calendar prediction coming true. I say that after all what has been found out, it is probable that there is something behind their findings. What is also astounding is the question of why Africa is the place from where the question is asked as to the inconsistencies of the Gregorian calendar assumption and the shortfall in relation to the Mayan calendar and predictions.

We do not want to say with authority what the date should be because of the formula. The actual instruments need the respective professionals to review them and make the calculations within strict and regular parameters. What we may do within our domain, is to raise the question to this fact and have the regular practitioners attend to the matter of determining the actual date. What we can say is that the decoding and translation of the 1940s was inaccurate as it overlooked the changes in the calendars and the implications of this.

Later at some point when I saw the definition of the Julian calendar in the dictionary, I realised that the Johannesburg Formula was inaccurate because according to the dictionary, the Julian calendar is "calendar introduced by Julius Caesar, with a year of 365 days, every fourth year having 366".

I realised that the Johannesburg Formula as I had thought of it previously was inaccurate because it assumed that the Julian calendar did not account for leap year deficits. I was wrong. I initially thought of rewriting the chapter of the Johannesburg Formula. But this was not appealing to me as it would rob me of even the artistic intuition to write a story. I later decided to settle for the option of leaving this formative version and amending the development based on this information that I discovered. I wanted the reader to see the imperfection...the mistake that I had made. How embarrassed I would be had I not realised the mistake and committed to publish the book without revising. After all I had worked tirelessly to reach this point and to erase it all so that the reader would never see was shallow. I decided to leave it all in so that the reader may witness the process of trial and error.

The Julian calendar did factor in the leap year because every fourth year in would be a 366 day long year. So we would have to shift our calculation to the year that Julius Caesar introduced the Julian calendar. This should be around the year 1 AD. The formula would have to change completely.

It would be interesting for the reader to see how the Johannesburg Formula developed through mistakes in calculations and all...this is what theories are about trial and error. I thought about what the research community would say about receiving inaccurate information and this was a difficult realisation. I was glad to reach a refined resolution of the Formula. All we want to show is that the calculation of the 21st December 2012 was incorrect because of the leap years that were not factored in and that over such a long span of time, the *"missing period"* would add up to a substantial amount that would affect modern day interpretation of the Mayan calendar.

The reason I decided to leave the incorrect version is so that I may illustrate the point poignantly, that in the 1940s when the Mayan calendar was interpreted and decoded, mistakes similar to this one could have been made.

The correct calculation has to assume that the leap year deficit applies to the period from when the Mayan calendar starts, to where the Julian calendar is put to use.

The Julian calendar was introduced in BC 45 and this means that we have to add 45 to 2012 (the years that the Julian calendar has been in use).

The Julian and Gregorian calendar did factor in the leap year. We have to look at the 3122 years that did not calculate the phenomenon of the leap year. Therefore:

- 5125=Mayan Epoch.
- 2057= years since leap year was inculcated into a calendar since BC 45, therefore we have to note that our initial assumption that the Gregorian calendar started in the year 0, is a factor when the proper calculation has to be made. We had left out 45 year (from 45 BC)!

Let's move on...

- 4= amount period of years that were leap years in the Julian and Gregorian calendars :
- 5125-2057 =3068
- 3068 (is the amount of years that did not factor the phenomenon of the leap year and therefore these years are not calculated into the assumed period of the epoch of 5125 years)
- 3068 ÷ 4= 767 (767 is the number of years that do not register the leap year phenomenon)
- 767= (the assumption of the numbers of days in a year without factoring in the phenomenon of a leap year)
- 767÷365= 2.10137
- 2.10137 = the number of year that the calculations of the end of the Mayan epoch is off by.

## As opposed to: a revised take...

The Johannesburg Formula:

- 5125 = epoch
- 4 = amount of years/period when 'leap years' in a Gregorian Calendar era formula occur
- 5125 ÷ 4 = 1281.25

- 1281.25 (the number of years that would have been leap years according to the Gregorian calendar)
- 1281.25 ÷ 365(days in a year) = 3.51027
- 3.51027(years) = amount of time that the Gregorian Calendar-based assumption of 5125 years is off by.

The seven year gap between the Julian and Gregorian calendars does not change but proves that over a long span of time there would be a deficit and this deficit is seven year ...(deduction). If the Julian and Gregorian calendars were both accurate in depicting the real circumstances of the annual orbit of the earth around the sun, then there would have never been a need to change the calendar.

(We deduce that): The mistake was to assume that the Julian calendar did not factor in the leap year. I suppose this came about because of thinking that the Gregorian calendar was in fact fixing this calculation of leap years that did not feature in the Julian calendar. This is a typical oversight that anyone could have had.

Proof that there is a disjuncture between the Gregorian calendar and the Mayan calendar is found in the fact that the Mayan calendar is more accurate than the both the Julian and Gregorian calendars in factoring in the real time fluctuation caused by the leap year, a feature of precession. We will never know the exact amount of time but for all intents and purposes, the difference of seven years between the Gregorian and Julian calendars is a (given) start. The Mayan calendar will prove to be correct in its reckoning that at the end of the 5125 cycle, there will be a cosmic change characterised by cosmic upheaval. The miscalculation is brought about by the fact that the Julian and Gregorian calendars were introduced more than three thousand years after the beginning of the fifth cycle of the Mayan calendar consisting of exactly 5125 years. We will have to wait it out to see what the discrepancy of the deficit amounts to.

Something also has to be said for all moments when it is decided that a calendar has to start or end. These are always important times. The Mayan calendar started 5125 years ago, when supposedly the 'fourth sun' ended. The Julian calendar started when the era of Christ was recognised and it is a well presumed supposition that the modern calendar is counting the years from when Christ was seen. The Gregorian calendar was to implement a momentous finding in science, where the closest account of the solar year was calculated. Calendars throughout the world mark specific moments in the history of mankind that can be said to be influential. For the most part, these moments when calendars are said to begin, all have something to do with either a beginning or end of an era that is marked by something significant. The advent of the Christ, cannot therefore be a small occasion if it took a beginning of a calendar to be calibrated as a tribute the moment.

So at this point we are open to the possibilities that authorised mathematicians may come up with an error-free calculation that may factor in even aspects that the Johannesburg Formula may overlook as any theory in time is wont to. We hope that the Johannesburg Formula is a debut to a review of the assumption that was made that could very-well be off the mark.

Here are dates that are glaringly important in any calculation whether be it accurate or as close to that as possible:

- 45 BC (introduction of the Julian calendar)
- 5125 (Mayan period of the specified epoch)
- 3114 BC (time of the beginning of the Mayan epoch to date)
- 1582 AD (date when the Gregorian calendar was adopted to replace the Julian calendar)
- 1946 AD (year when the dot-and-bar calendar was translated)
- 2012 AD (date when the Mayan epoch is thought to end)
- BC-0-AD (date of the beginning period leading to current year)
- 2057 (number of years that the Johannesburg formula assumes accurately depicts period wherein the challenge of leap years out of the 5125 year of the duration of the Mayan epoch is)

- 3068 (number of years that the Johannesburg Formula assumes DO NOT depict the phenomenon of the leap year and therefore present the possibility of the
  existence of an error in the calculation of the translation of the dot-and-bar calendar)
- 3068 is the number from the total of 5125 minus 2057

The main discovery that our modern generation is faced with is the fact that the Mayans, is a civilization that is thought to have been exceptional. Then there is the fact that planet earth is a home to us all and the truth is that we do not know everything there is to know about it in terms of its cycles as a planet that is millions and even billions of years old or in existence. The Mayans say that on a cyclical basis the earth goes through upheavals and erratic changes. There are numbers that are derived from measurements and we rely on this information to determine the state of affairs on earth. It is anyone's guess what the ultimate true nature of things is.

In hindsight, after all is said and done, the most important finding is that there is a discrepancy in dates and this may also be found in the discoveries we allude to in the chapter titled *"The earth was round"*. This chapter speaks of other influencing factors that may be deduced from the suggestion of the changing shape of the earth and therefore an almost inestimable amount of time of the orbit, *on which* dates and calendars are based.

# CHAPTER TWO

## "DON'T GET ME WRONG, GET THE MAYANS RIGHT"

**D**eciding to go ahead with having this book published was not easy for several reasons. Ever since the Mayan Constitutional Court story in the media in December, I had read some reviews by people and comments left online. Most of the comments left me unsure of whether people would like to still be in the loop about something that is as remote from a perception of reality as the Mayan calendar that *never pitched*. Just to digress a little, in March of 2013, I attended a media launch of a political platform that I thought I should witness because the lady who was launching the platform, a prominent business leader and historical activist, was from my alma-mater, the University Cape Town.

The political platform was being launched at Constitution Hill, Braamfontein, Johannesburg. There I met a well-known radio journalist whom I recognised and approached to introduce myself. I introduced myself as the person who was interviewed at their radio station, Khaya FM in Rosebank, Johannesburg in December regarding the Mayan predictions. She said to me that they (her and other colleagues) thought that I had gone off the railings because of the issue that we have since dubbed, 21/12. It seemed strange that she said that "they thought" rather than on her own, say that she thought that what I did was whacky. She was obviously referring to the Constitutional Court application in December 2012 regarding the Mayan calendar claims. When I considered the exchange with her later, it appeared to me that it is possible that as a journalist she had been aware of the February 2013 asteroid and meteorite events somehow. Because obviously reading from her statement that "they thought it was mad", this could have been a retraction of "their" thinking at the time of December 2012. I thought that maybe journalists as per their professional routine could have also seen a link between the 21/12 'no-show' and the February 2013 asteroid-cum-meteorite reports and they then decided based on that, that the 21/12 guy wasn't off the rails after all. Still to go on and publish a book out of something so morose and with as little appeal to the ordinary reader as a football game that is taking place at the bottom of the sea! This is to me a test of character as I entrenched myself deeper into the unknown world of perception, but to go ahead with it, I would rather close my eyes and do it.

Also as I had rationalised it further, the audience for this sort of book is largely not in (SA) South Africa my home country, because the issue is a bit out of the *ordinary*. South African appetite and bandwidth is not yet coupled for this sort of off-the-hinge foray into obscure accounts. The USA on the other hand is ripe because ever since the advent of Hollywood and the economic boom of the sixties, American society and perception has expanded to even the outer limits of what is possible and what is not. If I was in America, I told myself, I would not think twice about publishing the book let alone, boldly appearing at the door of the courts with the similar request that we had of the SA Constitutional Court. America, I figured, is ripe for the eccentric, the maverick and the bizarre. The nature of the society is that enough time has lapsed for the freedoms and rights to be a reality to an extent that nothing is left unexplored. As a result, it has been possible for Americans to lead the world in social freedoms and boldness of expressing even the timidly normal and the extra-ordinary.

Our perception of the USA is that it is indeed the land of the free, free to be off-the-hinge and free to be straight and narrow. The Americans have for long managed to unlock their public intellectual capital and have achieved feats such as moving fiction to non-fiction through the bold claims and expressions of *Americanism* that have even influenced global perception. Even the most conservative and anti-American sentimentalists dabble in something 'American' even while shunning the overt expression of Americanism. "Unto whom much is given, much is expected" and this is the expectation of the world of Americans. That is why in December 2012 when I filed the Court papers, the second respondent was the USA government because the information in question, has been interrogated by Americans for the longest while, even if it affects the whole world because of the cosmic nature and cosmic jurisdiction of effects such as solar flares, asteroids, meteors etc. Americans for as long as we have known have spent the most budgets on exploits such as the exploration of outer space and research into the relationship between outer space and our global environment. So somehow we expect the Americans to be the most answerable when it comes to issues such as the possibilities of cataclysmic incursions on a cosmic scale.

It comes as no surprise to open the newspaper on the 29th May 2013 to find an article titled: *'Space watchdog to scan for asteroids'*. This article speaks about the office set up by the European Space Agency called the (NEO) Near-Earth Object Coordinating Centre in a place called Frascati, near Rome in Italy. This article shows how seriously the world has taken the threat of space objects like asteroids to the earth, as being real. What is worth noting is that this public concern with asteroids is a new phenomenon that affects our generation. (see: The Times on www.timeslive.co.za for a full report).

NB! (The BLOG below was WRITTEN AFTER THE 15th FEBRUARY 2013 Asteroid appeared...)

*Blog Title*:

"DON'T GET ME WRONG, GET THE MAYANS RIGHT". ©2013.

Author: Robert Sefatsa (astro-anthropologist, scenario enthusiast and entrepreneur).

Ever since the 22nd December 2012, I have waded through experiences of misplaced celebrity, ridicule and bemusement as the public gawk, stare and pass comments about the guy who claimed that the world would end. I did not say the world would end, I was saying to the State through the Court that "hey!", we the unsuspecting and unknowing public deserve and need to know what is happening because we hear talk about the end of the world. Since then, I have not had the chance to visit my on-line Facebook profile (to see what people were saying) because the costs of going to the Constitutional Court in December left me financially flustered. I invested all what I had into something that I viewed as being of national importance, international importance as per the prerequisite of a Constitutional matter. The reason why I have been invisible in the front-line of the Pandora's box opened by the Mayan question, is because the costs prohibited me from taking the matter further, in other words, to regularise the application as the Court felt that it was irregular. I frankly did not care for due process because I viewed the matter as urgent and of an emergency nature.

When we do our own analysis of the environment, it seems as if the Mayans were correct, the only thing is that we were duped by the Gregorian calendar that came about because of indiscretions in the method of accounting for leap-years and days that were correctly recorded by the Julian calendar. The Julian calendar was done away with at the council of Nicaea roughly 500 years ago, when a worldwide council of churches decided to adopt the Gregorian calendar to fix the problem of calculating leap years. This could account for the discrepancy of about fifty days that have lapsed from the 21st December 2012 to 15th February 2013 when the first visible impact of cataclysmic solar induced activities hit not only our planet, but all the planets in our solar system.

Ever since the 21st/12/2012, I have met people who know me who have said, "nothing happened, so what were you talking about? Others say this is the guy who said the world is going to end and it didn't... well here is news...Today on the 15th/02/2013 an asteroid crackled above a suburb in Russia. As the world waits to see an asteroid that is reported to be moving from the southern hemisphere to the northern hemisphere, passing within the atmosphere of planet earth... is to my knowledge part of the Mayan prediction that around this time we would be going through some cataclysm. We cannot relax as it is not all over. The reason being that the asteroid was sighted a year ago (beginning of 2012) and the astronomy services around the world have kept an eye on it to see what would happen.

In December 2012, heads of states came out strongly refuting the claims of the Mayans and yet all what those official denouncements did was to only make it more difficult for the public to see the strong connection between the asteroid explosion on the 15th February 2013 and the events that were forecast for the 21st December 2012. NASA also refuted the claims of the Mayans because there was nothing conclusive and the asteroid dubbed 2012 DA14 was far-off in the solar circuit to concern us as part of the reality outlined by the Mayans. This is peculiar because we the public rely on our governments to be forthright with information about what is happening on earth and also in our solar system. We have to deduce the truth ourselves and fight tooth and nail to determine the true disposition of the planet in relation to our planetary-affinity with other space objects and electro-magnetic relativity in our solar system. According to a caller who phoned the South African radio station, Talk Radio 702 on 04th/January/ 2013, on host Ray White's show, the caller reported that an international broadcaster stated that other asteroids would follow 2012-DA14 in March of 2013. We do not know for sure what the destiny of these following asteroids that are headed in the direction of planet earth is. I gathered from a source who watches television religiously that the sun had ejected the biggest amount of plasma at the beginning of January 2013 and it was said that this was the biggest flare in recent times, thanks to sightings using modern telescopes.

To the avid astro-anthropologist and cataclysm watcher that CAB (Central African Bureau- a self-styled cataclysm watch organisation that has been facing challenges to formalise itself) is, ever since the launch of a Constitutional Court application and the story that was widely reported in December, there is a list of dots to be joined and a picture emerges. The solar flares, the sighting reported on 05th/ February 2012 on Saturn, the asteroid that struck Russia on the 15th/ February 2013, the lighting that struck pupils in Soweto (Protea) at the beginning of 2013, simultaneous lightning at King Edward School in Houghton Johannesburg, the asteroids that are known to be tailing asteroid 2012-DA14 (expected to make headline news on 22nd February), 25th March 2013, 28th March 2013  known to be 4km in diameter), the snow storm that hit North America in February 2013 and the storm known as Sandy in America all speak to one event. The reporting of the spectacular solar flare, where the sun is said to be doing a 'dance' that occurs once in several centuries is also thanks to developments in astronomy instrument in time to enable us to know the planet's destiny in terms of cyclical cataclysms.

I suspect that this is only the beginning and not the end ...of cataclysms that we may avoid a confrontation with, if we simply inquire into the Constitutional Court recommendation to the USA, SA and other governments who are concerned about the truth of our times. To the world, this was an odd period because this was the time around when Pope Benedict handed in his resignation. A month earlier the papacy came out in December 2012 saying that nothing would happen on 21st/ December/2012. Yet coming short of telling the faithful that all that stuff about the injunctions of the Mayan calendar was only delayed by 'fifty days' (to the day that the asteroid breached the atmosphere), because of differences in calendar systems used around the world. For instance the Julian calendar that is still being observed by the *orient* and some occident orthodox states is seven years behind the Gregorian calendar and the faithful swear by the accuracy of the Julian calendar in terms of keeping time as accurately as possible.

I am amazed by how these issues have been peripheral and only get a few seconds of media coverage. It seems that only consistent radio listeners and television watchers who are sensitive to the obscure topic of astronomical activity, calendars, and other so called esoteric realities, is all this going on. Where does this leave the public, even after we made attempts to tell government all over the world to act and to be in line with the injunction of the Universal Declaration of Human Rights, national constitutions and more importantly the Mayan Calendar (that is not the only one that talks of a change in temporal realities).

Don't get me wrong I am not a party pooper or end-of-world monger, get the Mayans right they did an astonishing job of leaving us crucial information about our cataclysmic future so that we would be prepared, and that we avoid careless loss. For instance we hear that six people lost their lives in the American snow storm and one thousand and five hundred people were injured in the Russian asteroid explosion and we have to ask ourselves if government may be held accountable for these losses, especially after being warned by the Mayans and others. We are also distraught by the casual way that business grinds on as usual in the light of colossal evidence that needs only to be viewed as a big picture of joined dots that seems to be grasping our solar system at large. I was taken aback by the media on the 5th February 2013 where I heard on radio 702 that NASA had reported sight of a super-storm on the feisty planet called Saturn, where the head of the dust-cloud storm was seen to be engulfing the planet and the head was seen overlapping its tail... the head appeared to be swallowing the tail. Come on, this is the sign that many esoteric religions including the theosophical movement are based on as: the Orobus known to be the snake that swallows its own tail and surely this is a sign of the times and they knew that a cataclysm would ensue by this sign alone.

The secular media pushed this report of the Saturn incident out as an isolated event and this is incorrect because we occupy one solar domain and events on other planets and especially the sun and moon influence all other objects (including planet earth) through electromagnetic affinity. That is why asteroids that have broken their orbital circuit are hurtling towards planet earth. This obviously means that there is a lot more we are not privy to and yet it is unfolding in our solar system. We may not claim ignorance. Especially after such an undermined culture as the Mayans (according to our own measure of reputable cultures), who were sure that they are linked to us in the future through genealogy warned us. We do not seem to take to mind the warnings of bygone civilizations. It does not tally and something is amiss because we have to rely on information that comes out in bits and drabs from the sources of established media, that is already entrenched in the issues of markets and daily affairs that even hoard the centre of media attention. It is business as usual. It is understandable why and how the established interest of life as we know it are averse to real information and news about astronomical cataclysm, that is by now visibly claiming a stake in our modern life, with seemingly *"inexplicable"* events…This is not right nor is it commendable. I question the vested interest of the principals of media and governments who appear to be behind the astronomical curve, when this leaves us in a position where we can only pretend to be victims in this time of reckoning.

I have been trying tirelessly to contact the media who interviewed us in December 2012, when the Constitutional Court acknowledged our application. I soon learnt that there are no favours or privileges in the business of daily media who make money from tantalizing stories that blow our minds with maverick stories and no more or less. I was told that the media was not prepared to talk about the Mayan calendar because according to the perception that the media held out "nothing had happened on the 21st December 2012"and nothing more could be written...Well then enter the asteroids and meteors that are opening 2013 with a suspicious follow up and I wonder how many people are suspecting that there may be a link between the Mayan calendar and recent events that may portend an uncomfortable ride into the future. According to mostly fringe media reports, we are already aware of pending asteroids that follow on the heels of asteroid-2012DA14, weighing 130 000 tons. As reported by the astronomical observatory in Cape Town, *this is not the end neither is it a spectacular event for keen astronomers to be entertained by, we are simply relieved to be out of the course of this asteroid and we do not have conclusive information about other asteroids that are hurtling towards our direction.*

No one may rely on reputable sources for news about the epoch period the planet is in anymore. There is no commitment nor are they keen to admit that the planet is in a difficult time of astronomical transition (as sighted in the submission to the Con-Court). Officials of the State and other reputable research institutions like the International Space Observatories Network (ISON), have not reached a timeous conclusion about the big picture, through linking the recent erratic events on planet earth to other similar cataclysmic events in our solar system. It does not mean that there is no-one out there who sees causality and a big picture of related events that may lead us to highlight the irrefutable reality that is prohibiting the state to listen to the public. Even when we intimate that the lightning that struck in Johannesburg and Soweto on the 11th and 12th of February 2013 in South Africa and the asteroid explosion in Russia are symptoms of an ejection of super-nova plasma from the sun that has tripped the solar system into a chain reaction of astronomical events that culminate as radical weather on planets specifically and in our solar system in general. The reluctance of the States of the world to admit that the story is important enough to be looked into, suggests that we the public have to tolerate commissions led by governments to investigate the causes of loss only after the events, even when we know that the writing is on the wall.

In relation to the function of CAB of being a cataclysm watch agency, the explosion of an asteroid over a Russian city is not an incident that we may shrug off, as the cost of the damages has been given in figures and the impact on the people is something even more obscure to calculate. Moreover, no-one had foreseen where on earth the asteroid explosion would be in the second month of 2013. To us as we had watched the seamless transition over the Capricorn to Aquarian epoch, we view these events with strong aversion.

Everything from the suggested course of action and the determinable future in view of the Mayan injunctions, is laid out in the 158 page application that we launched in the Constitutional Court of South Africa and let me add my thanks to the fairness of the administrators and case management system of the South African court. You simply have to Google to catch up with the story and how the Court application went, regardless of what the application was advocating or propagating. In the meantime, we still wonder what it will take for the rest of us to be brought back onto the Mayan bandwagon that was abandoned on the 22$^{nd}$ December when it seemed that "nothing had happened". We all jumped off and we reverted back to our hardy nationalism and hope, that we the people (as intimated by constitutions worldwide), ride through good and bad times and we have a triumphant outlook that enables us to win at any cost.

The success of the 21$^{st}$/12/2012 awareness measures that we took is visible. It was really to inform and to sensitize the people to cataclysmic and astronomical realities beyond our visible grasp. So that should anything happen as it did in February 2013, when our expectation was December 2012, we will not say that we did not know.

*This blog was penned after it became clear that 2013 was another year of surprises as we saw the incidents mentioned in the blog take place and no one could say anything because it was proof that there are many things out of our control and we have to humble ourselves and behold the majestic influence of things to come.*

As 2014 begins, enthusiasts are gripped by the phenomenon of end-times theories even tighter as information of asteroids litters the internet landscape in the purview of those who have been keeping an eye out for such information. What is becoming increasingly clear is that the 21st December 2012 was a symbolic moment that ushered in the *beginning of the end-times*. What this date signifies is the beginning of a period that is filled with uncertainty and definitely bearing the signs of a cataclysmic end to our civilization. For the asteroid that exploded above Russia on the 15th February 2013, to follow so closely, some 57 days later, means that we have to look at the significance of the message of the Mayans closely.  -end-

Today is the 14th January 2014 and I am perplexed as to how this book is going to make light of day but leave it to natural providence to find the answer and way for that to happen lest the manuscript perpetually linger in a hard-drive while its currency lapses...

What is becoming clear on this date of 14th January 2014 is that amidst the talk of the asteroid known as -2003QQ47 making its way to earth and bound to make its presence felt on the 21st March 2014 according to predictions all over the internet, the asteroid season is a show of strength and rallying banner for the Age of Aquarius. It seems to be a repetitive pattern that when the planets reach the position of the Aquarius constellation in the months influenced by the Aquarius constellation, February and March, the position of Jupiter and Mars where the asteroid-belt is orbiting seem to be opening a window for disruption and dislodging of an electromagnetic energy that propels any wayward asteroid in the direction of the earth as well the general circular direction where planets are orbiting the sun, and a line of collision could be established arbitrarily due to intercepting pathways. This could be an errant view because the cause could just coincide with the period of February and March as evidenced by the asteroid that belted towards Russia on the 15th February 2013. This feeds the nascent theory of seven stars that is embellished in chapter three of this book.

# CHAPTER THREE

## OF CANDLES, STARS AND TRUMPETS

A candle is a metaphor for the sun as they both illuminate the dark and bring into sight an environment that would be otherwise enshrouded.

It is safe to say that we never know anything and only by wanting to know do we know. Even when we know, it is never enough because the shifting sands of time always prove what we know to be transient. For the purpose of scenario determination, speculation is instrumental to the function of elucidating all possibilities. It is therefore proprietary to say it is highly possible that the conclusion reached by all the governments of the world regarding the 21st December 2012 was off the mark due the facts that are stated in this book. It is an error for our society to read any book of faith (or any faith) as a pure academic humanist science, including reading for the practice of faith alone. Books of faith and especially in focus here, the bible are also books about natural sciences, when looked at from an empirical vantage. We should or could read these books for other reasons either than faith practice and beliefs. It is highly recommended for these books to be read for natural science purposes also, as they also depict evidence about natural sciences.

For instance the book of Revelations speaks and depicts in allegoric terms places and events on the planet earth. It would be an interesting exercise to determine which places are spoken off in the chapters as they proceed. For one, when writing, or initially *receiving a vision* to write, the author of the book of Revelations is in Greece on the island Patmos. Further there are places that are spoken off and it would be interesting for the reader to determine these on your own without any one imposing their view or their determination.

Anthropology for instance is an academic humanist science that also explores the issues of culture, ethnicity and faith in relation to many diverse developments for study. Belief systems and faith practices are studied and analysed comparatively in anthropology to determine the impact and influence of several fields of natural and humanistic sciences on these anthropological determinations.

As a matter of comparative analysis of films, it is vital to point to the academic capacity of films as source material for real events. Many films have a documentary value as they often depict aspects of reality to a large extent. For instance the location of the film, the linguistics employed in the film and numerous other real factors make films a rich resource for the purpose of anthropology and determining the influence of film as an analytical source material. Both fiction and nonfiction collapse into an *unspecified* area of field of study in analytics for source material. A lot may be deduced academically from films as these have embedded in them real information about society regardless of the intended plot of the film. For example the study of literature and music at schools, colleges and universities could well lead to a vibrant area of study of films for the purposes of analytics rather than the production of film as it exists in film schools. Film study for analysis as source material could form a department on its own, similar to literature study. For this book, several films would be ideal analytic source materials and the reader is encouraged to locate and interrogate a few films (that you have or have viewed) that would be relevant comparative materials in the readers mind.

For example, in the movie the Da Vinci Code, the leading characters are cryptologists who decipher embedded clues and use the science of cryptology and cryptography to read obscure and abstract data to make it plain, so that they may find answers relevant to what the essence of the plot is. The *book of Revelations* is a cryptogram and it has to be read as such. Basic cryptology has to be employed to figure out what the author is letting off. The book by Graham Hancock is one of the books that illustrate how patience and forbearance are part of the science of cryptology and many clues and encrypted messages are followed through to release a complex network of knowledge so that we may relate to it in the modern context. *The Bible Code* by Michael Drosdin and Professor Eli Ripps is another illustration of how complex the old books are and these two scholars show us how the Bible in its Hebrew format is not just a straight forward text but a cryptogram embedded with numerology. For a specific purpose of making sense of the cataclysmic plot of the book of *Revelations*, it may be relevant to deduce the cryptology value of the *Bible* by also referring to *the Bible Code* and Graham Hancock's book.

...Today is the 15th of July 2013, and the 14th did not pass without me pondering what all this means, especially my encounter with the *book of Habakkuk* recently in a way that I would say is peculiarly coincidental. This year earlier I was lent a copy of Graham Hancock's book and this gave me an enriched insight into the Mayan civilisation. Recently in the media there are reports that the British education department is revising the curriculum and that classical topics are to be included so that children in Britain can have a better grasp of events that shaped the future and the Mayan civilisation is one of the subjects that would be included. Also the fact that I had the case in 2012 where I filed an unusual plea to court that left me simmered, because of my unease at the perception of the public being tentative at best. I was left in a situation that left people wondering about me, especially those who are familiar with me. Today I would not just doze off as usual. I lay awake and a flood of a personal revelation hit me. Earlier in the year I had rationalised *the Johannesburg Formula* and yet this was inconclusive because it is still only but a theory that is open to review. Today when it dawned on me that something else is missing was like being an active participant in the storyline of *The Da Vinci Code*. Somehow it occurred that the book was not complete...this is when this chapter was surreptitiously born.

 More interestingly, publishers in England phoned me a week or two ago to inquire about my preparedness to publish this book. Fortunately and ironic as it sounds, I was not ready due to the amount of money that is required and the fact that I did not have it in hand meant that I could not go ahead. This happened for the only good reason I know besides not having money, the fact that the 14ᵗʰ July 2013 would arrive where a new twist in the story unravels itself to me and the baseline has only but to change due to the clarity. I saw the movie *Da Vinci Code* twice last week and it left an impression on me and also sent my reckoning wildly, as this culminated in a conclusion on the 14ᵗʰ July 2013, that the year 2019 is actually the year that the whole world missed as the date of the Mayan calendar 2012. The Mayan calendar now in 2013 as we speak had not reached the point that all legend claims…that of 2012. The study of calendars is the key here and the third element in the plot is a third calendar, the Julian calendar. All the while we have been looking at the Mayan calendar in comparison with and through the modem of the Gregorian calendar. The missing piece of the puzzle is the Julian calendar. If we were to look at the puzzle of three calendars then something else would emerge. The climax arrived today and I don't know how many people know of the scenario of being an only audience to a story and the uncertainty of sharing a story that you alone give credibility to. It is a fazing feeling but what makes us human is the risk that we take to open up to others and let them peruse the depth of our private mental and emotional space.

Nobody can ever say that it is easy being them, I could not. But after today the brouhaha and fear of the opinion of others, of what they may say ebbed away. The Julian calendar is alive and well and being observed by a nation with a story like no other. In Ethiopia the thirteen month calendar is still preserved and the traditionalists of Ethiopia have kept this record in play for a reason only closely guarded and kept well by them. I do not know of any other country that still observes the Julian calendar as well as the nation of Ethiopia. To make the link between the Mayans, the Ethiopian calendar and the "secular" world that observes the Gregorian calendar is no mean, or "credible" feat. I can only attribute this to patience and avid interest in topics like calendars, ancient societies and how these impact on modern societies. I am only interested in stating the facts and letting you the reader reach your own conclusion without being desperately overbearing and wanting to influence you perception. Having reckoned that *the Johannesburg Formula* is a valid premise for a theory, I was left with time to reflect on this premise and the moment of today to arrive when I would make the link between these seemingly disparate topics.

Reading the *Bible* for the purpose of being informed about its content is not something that everyone does. Most of us take it as an obligation of practitioners of the faith and so do not or have not read it. I have not read the entire book also and for interest I have read some books out of it and the *book of Revelations* is one of those that I have read.

The *book of Revelations* is one of the most gripping reads for a while and this is why it is part of one of the most widely read books of all time, *the Bible*.

After having read Graham Hancock's book earlier in the year, I am more informed from an anthropological point of view and my interpretation of the furtive format of the allegories and metaphors of the old book is given a lease. As I made the dots connect it becomes apparent that I have to reread this book and state my case to the reader. This is how I see it... The candles and the stars spoken of in *Revelations* could refer to the circuits that the earth makes around the sun in its orbital journey. A candle according to this reckoning is a year that is marked by the circuit of the planet earth around the sun over a year, so seven candles refer to seven years. Seven years?... Yes the seven years between the Gregorian calendar and the Julian calendar. There is a seven year difference between the Gregorian calendar and the Julian calendar. The seven stars in the book of Revelations for this purpose refer to the sun. The sun is one of the stars amongst the millions that are visible to us in the night sky. Seven stars refer to the seven times in seven years that planet earth orbits at any given time, and this time in particular, especially after the Mayan calendar has referred to the end of a five thousand (plus) year period.

Many scholars have speculated about who some of the characters are spoken of in the *book of Revelations*. It is not easy to attribute some of the titles to any person, but for the purpose of scientific reckoning, it is our generation that unknowingly is a product of the change from the Gregorian calendar and the understanding of the people of that time in the decision to change from the Julian calendar. This generation has been influenced by the decision to adopt the Gregorian calendar as far as the interpretation and reading of time is concerned.

There is no use apportioning culpability in this instance, our resolve should be to find out what the books say is destined to happen and to act in accord with the directives of the prescriptions if any is relevant or proves to be a solid guideline. Especially in recent times when modern science has taken priority over lasting circumstances and questions from the past that are still unanswered.

It is not possible to attribute the process to change the calendar to one decision maker, so it is fair to say that the council in quorum took the decision and for reasons that were thought would advance the accuracy of reckoning with the amount of time is takes for a year to proceed in orbit around the sun. On the other hand the Julian calendar has remained in place and today it is being used by one amongst the oldest civilisations.

It was the council at which the Gregorian calendar was adopted and the decision made to install the calendar system that would in the future leave mankind in intellectual peril, not being able to use the resources of scientific findings and the design of the calendar system correctly. The Julian calendar as a persistent model is the reason why the Gregorian calendar fits one of the characters depicted in the bible. The current state of knowledge and the custom of attributing sophisticated rights to people, as practiced by modern nations means that we in our capacity as citizens cannot and probably should not cast culpability. The reason for this difficult proposition is that because of the acceptance of the Gregorian calendar, it was not possible to make sense of the claims of the Mayans and the

Mayan calendar as it was billed to illustrate a specific time generation. The Gregorian calendar makes it impossible to read the current circumstances in relation to the Mayan calendar and its injunctions.

Because we were looking at the Mayan calendar through the eyes or spectacle of the Gregorian calendar and interpreting it through the modem of the Gregorian calendar the world assumed that the 21st December 2012 (according to estimates of the Gregorian calendar) is the time that the Mayans and their calendar spoke of. It is not...when we factor in the fact that the Julian calendar is a prototype modem to reckon the times with, a different picture emerges. The risk of ignorance that the Gregorian calendar bestowed on this generation is what renders the characters spoken of in a verse of the book of Revelation highly likely as non-fiction. The people who installed the Gregorian calendar were real characters with capacity, capability and they knowingly or unknowingly inserted themselves in the roles of a character in the Bible by changing the times. What we experienced as the year 2012 in modern terms according to the Gregorian calendar looks more likely to fit with the year 2019. The Julian calendar is the calendar through which we are supposed to look at the Mayan calendar in order to deduce the immutable claims made in the Mayan teachings. There is a seven year difference between the Gregorian calendar and the Julian calendar and so the 2012 that the Mayans spoke of or still indeed speak of is in 2019. So it reckons that according to the Julian calendar 2012 is actually 2005 of the Mayan calendar's estimated translation.

The prognostic attributes of the *book of Revelations* and the Mayan calendar philosophy is indeed perplexing and we may only be humbled by the fact that these records are not erased from the hard-drive of the many civilisations that humans have traversed. We nearly missed the insight into the records because the 1582 council's decision held the world to ransom and the scholars that are illustrated in books such as Grahams would have worked to nought. The risk of misreading records for the purpose of use in modern scientific interpretation would have visited us had it not been for the overwhelming precedent of the Julian calendar. The Julian calendar brings the Mayan story back into vogue as the prospects of interpreting it are viable through the steady modem of the time record kept. In the allegoric language of the author of the *book of Revelations*, the cause of ignorance is literally to take common and ubiquitous knowledge from others through obfuscating reality. The 1582 council may not have been aware of the unintended consequences of this action but the author of the *book of Revelations* took time to write a missive to future generations about pending circumstances. So did the Mayans, and it seems that there is instruction in these records. These records are valid sources in case of modern scientific intrigue.

A possible mistake would in this instance of reckoning be to miss the parallels between the seven years that the book speaks of in the first instance. Surely the author of *Revelations* does not intend to generalise nor hide the meaning of the metaphors. This could have been done in the case that there was nothing of the sort or if this record was fiction. It is a known and accepted fact that the 1582 council changed the way time is reckoned with.

What does this mean?...It means that the seven stars or candles that are spoken of are metaphors for the seven years from 2012 to 2019. The highlights and events held to observe the 21st December 2012 date as speculated by the Mayans was a trumpet to awaken us to the most important seven years in our time. 2019 in the Gregorian calendar is the correct time that is heralded by the conclusion of the Mayan calendar and is the correct year 2012 that we should have been looking at. The Ethiopians' is a country that mostly is identifiable with the straightforward and scientific reading of the book of *Revelations*. Even for this purpose I would not like to impose my own view but would rather leave it to the reader to peruse and read the story of Ethiopia in relation to the *Book of Revelations* and see how much correlation one finds.

The Julian calendar may not have been *obvious,* but for all purposes it corresponds to the seven years alluded to as depictions and metaphors of seven candles and seven stars in the *book of Revelations.* This is the deduction... made with the assumption that the Mayan calendar did not end in 2012 of the Gregorian calendar but will do so in the 2012 of the Julian calendar. The *book of Revelations* is a prescription and guideline, with vital information rather than a dogma that compels us to act in any way. We should make up our mind as to the action we take and do so only after having reached a conclusion on a personal level after having seen all the facts on the table and being in accord as to what is best.

The seven years from the 2012 date to the 2019 date is a crucial moment to observe to see if we have not left anything unheeded or left a blind spot ajar. The momentum to the 21st December 2012 and analysis from all quarters need to be revived with a seriousness that only the avid scholars did, even when the ironic disappointment followed. Graham, I hope to meet you to thank you for your book that changed the way we view astronomical risk to the planet and the way of life at all.

Is it possible that some chapters in the allegoric *book of Revelations* unfold within a specific seven years? If so then we need to look to Africa as a stable tectonic plate and geographic safe zone. It is known that the African tectonic plate is the most solid landmass that would withstand a high level of disruptions to the lithosphere.

The public do not control the flow of information, so for this reason we the public are gullible to inconsistent reports. The public depends on media perceptions to form opinions and to make decisions. I do not prescribe a conclusion but rather invite you the reader to do your own research and to reach your own conclusion.

Having read Graham Hancock's book I can only say it is advisable for everyone to read this book, to go and look at it so that the dots may be arranged and that you may have insight into this meandering story and humanity's great challenge.

I reckon that without any imposed opinion, the reviewing of the book of Habakkuk, the book of Revelations, the book of Peter and Graham Hancock's book are pertinent at this point in time. Indeed if we are to make sense of why the December 21 2012 date came and went without any event, even when the Mayan world had thought that something in the order of cataclysms as sighted in Graham Hancock's book would take place. There are also many other references that other similarly astute scholars know of and would consult in order to enrich their perception of the claims in this book.

It should be reasonable to reckon that the sequel to the Hollywood blockbuster film of the *2012* is in the offing with an oriented perspective that takes into account the Julian calendar. The movie was made as a means and system to at least make viewers aware of the realities of the conditions of the Mayan calendar. When 21st December 2012 came and went the emotions of people around the world were relieved and observers of the phenomenon of the Mayan claims were unhinged and lulled at the same time. I figure that with the reassertion of the Julian calendar as a more authoritative reference and oriented modem we all need to revisit our sentiments and motives around the Mayan phenomenon.

It is amazing how the world watched the movie 2012 without questioning its credibility and the source of the information of the author of the film's script. It seems as though the public accepted it as some form of information and quietly went home to wait to see if the claims of the movie would eventually tally up with reality. So why is it so incredible to reckon with the author of the book *Revelations* and today's authors like Graham Hancock, with the same stern resolve that the world watched the movie 2012 with, without questioning the pervading effect of the information in the film on the senses of the viewers? The reaction of most people who were baffled by the December 2012 court application to the Constitutional Court in South Africa does not tally with the reaction of the same audience to the intrusive information from a film like 2012 and all others in the same genre that may be compared in effect to the knowledge of the viewers.

It looks like there is lot of homework that we all still have. For one, we should read authors that we would not have read for reasons of incredibility such as Graham Hancock. To read books that we would not have because we regard them as inflexible and specific to faith practitioners, just so that we may catch up with the fleeting effects of time and the things that cannot be undone. The movie 2012 might have to be rerun and we should all reckon with it again, after we thought that it was a hasty depiction of realism that stunned our senses only while the movie-reel was on at the cinema house. It would now seem that the author of the script of that movie had something else in mind rather than to take a profit based on the worldwide spree and a market-run for Mayan paraphernalia, when everyone was convinced and bewildered by their claims.

There is a possibility that on 21st December 2012, time collapsed and the metaphor of seven years depicted as seven stars and seven candles eclipsed the gap of seven years and the actual seven years from 2005 to 2012 thus began. The significance of the symbolism of seven candles and seven stars became visibly possible only after reading Grahams book that illustrates in detail the course and circuit of planet earth around the sun in an annual orbit. Time is "intangible" and it is possible that the Gregorian calendar modem has been breached by the Julian calendar modem of reckoning with real time. Rather than the device of perceiving time that the generation of the 1582 council bequeathed to the world, what was in place before the council may suffice as a reference in modern scientific circumstances.

Symbolically, any scientific realism that transpires like the asteroid incursion in February 2013, may be an indication of a specific seven year period. For example 2012 to 2019 in terms of the Gregorian calendar reckoning that correlates to 2005 to 2012 in the Julian reckoning of the time modem. The false alarm of the Gregorian 2012 could very well be a trumpet to alert us to the reality of the seven years that proceed to 2019 in the Gregorian calendar modem. The foresight of the author of the *book of Revelations* and the Mayan calendar is confounding enough for us to give due regard to and not just dismiss it capriciously. Modern society is progressive and astute enough to be risk averse and anything that threatens our way of life is considerably mitigated. The emphasis on the seven stars and seven candles could very well be a risk alarm that highlights a specific seven years rather than any seven years. It is also advised to the reader to look at various scenarios that are from a bygone era as told to the future by many civilisations, including the Mayans and those of the author of the *book of Revelations*. It is possible right now that the Gregorian calendar modem is ambiguous and as such the present generation is lulled into a a an erroneous sense of time and that the Julian modem is the correct perspective for determining past events in relation to present events.

If our theory of metaphoric stars and candles is close to true, then the theory of metaphoric trumpets may be feasible. (Refer to the *book of Revelations* to see is said about stars and trumpets). Our sum is that a candle and star are the same as a trumpet, and therefore a year represents a trumpet as depicted in this book of metaphors and allegories. The message of trumpets refers again to a specific seven years. The one that is denoted by the 21st December 2012 (of the Gregorian calendar) is a trumpet that was signified by the *false alarm* to awaken the consciousness of the world to the impending sounding of trumpets, the seven candles and seven stars. Why can't a *false alarm* be a trumpet?

*The Johannesburg Formula* indicates a difference of 3 years between the Mayan modem and the Gregorian modem. This is odd when other factors like the Julian modem is unaccounted for to fulfil the spectrum of possibilities and to peg the number at the seven years indicated by the deduction from the *Revelations* source. This is what theories are about, trial and error until confirmed and proven.

The government and society in the USA was the most active in efforts to allay fears and to research the credibility of the claims made by the Mayan dossier. The American public were the most active in the whole world regarding public debate and speculation about the 21st December 2012. The fanfare went without event as the 21st December went out of play and the bandwagon tilted everyone's attention away from the issue. Then ...wait for it...15th February 2013, an asteroid breached the atmosphere and resulted in an asteroid explosion that even hurt people in Russia? What bewildered and bowled me out of the park was that in December 2012 we spoke about asteroids in an interview that we had with the television news channel in South Africa, eNCA. When I reviewed footage that was captured on a cell phone while the interview was on, I realised that the people at eNCA missed that part because it should have dawned on them that in South Africa we factored possibilities of asteroids being part of the toxic mix attending to the planet while no other country made announcements or said anything about this. This should have made the people at the television network eNCA ask themselves the question, what was the possibility of this happening? They never focused on the entire interview which lasted for more than two hours and so they missed the part where asteroids were made mention of in December 2012 and it actually happened that there was an asteroid explosion in February 2013.

Some governments clearly and admittedly had no prior insight into the 15th February 2013 asteroid explosion. This means that according to the theory of the seven candles, seven stars and trumpets it is plausible to deduce that the *seven years theory* is a feasible proposition because something extraordinary happened on 15th February 2013. Without casting aspersions, we realised that the practice in the media industry of airing stories and issues that boost viewing rates is as real. The issue was shelved early by all the media, and as a result, by January 2013 there was no mention made of the Mayan calendar. The connection was not made between the 15th February 2013 asteroid explosion and the 21st December 2012 Mayan claim. *The Johannesburg Formula* does exactly this, it makes a clear connection between all these issues and aligns them in a logical sequence that was unintendedly unscrambled by the historical event of changing the modem of calendars.   This does not in anyway accord fault on the media business. We raised the issue at the Constitutional Court in South Africa as we view the court to be an official structures linked to government. We on the other hand recognised our limited capacity to bring the issue into the main stream or centre of public interest. Our expectation was for government to react, even from anywhere in the world at all.

Fine, the government did not react then maybe because it would have been a burden to review the matter as the 21st December 2012 was an ordinary day without a sign of the stark claims of the Mayans. This is an indication of the idiosyncrasy of events and the natural unfolding of what was to be. Today this book claims that everything that proceeded and the events of 2005 to 2012 (in the Gregorian calendar), were outlandish (moreover predated) and that the actual 2005 to watch is of the Julian date. So the false alarm was a trumpet to collapse the old time and synchronise temporal realism to the Julian calendar. 21st December 2012 was a herald to remind us that the actual 2005 is still proceeding. We implore government officials all over the world to look at Graham Hancock's book, the *book of Revelations* and other related books on the topic and see if they would not reach the same conclusion that we did, even the conclusion reached in *The Johannesburg Formula*.

We have no intention to campaign or mount a *road show* for a pesky reason. We are just as perplexed as anyone would be by the realism of the time we are in. We suggest that government should factor in the injunction of people (and civilizations) that have been here before. Why did they explicitly and systematically warn of the possibilities of *unknown cataclysm*. The main preoccupation of *The Johannesburg Formula*, the book, is not to advance a date or dates, but to advance a theory regarding dates. This is so that scholars may make assumptions, do calculations and reach their own original conclusion without a prescription from us. Debate and research is the main outcome that we aim to foster so that we do not rely on a narrow notion about the credibility of the claims made in this book. One thing that is not obvious is the eerie similarity between the story of the book of Revelations and the accounts of ancient civilizations like the Incas and the Mayans (as one may see illustrated by Hancock). What could this mean? For us it is the compelling exercise of rationalising the modern day story of calendars and the embedded issue that this unravels.

 It is a foregone conclusion that the film directors and story writers in Hollywood have the machinery to pass to the public the messages of timeless stories and important messages about the destiny of humanity. The persistent reinforcement that is seen from one movie to another in the same category is pleasantly surprising.

Another illustration is the film *'One night with the King'*. Here, one of the main characters, Esther regales Xerxes the Persian King with the biblical story of Jacob and how he meets Rachel the daughter of Laban at the well while she tends her father's flock. Jacob is taken with Rachel and offers her father Laban seven years of his labour in return for her hand at marriage. After a swift passing of seven years, he (Jacob) has to wait another seven years as Laban offers him Leah, his older daughter instead. This theme of seven year means that the message or code of seven years is strongly embedded in allegory for the people of the future to unravel. The motif of seven years is also told in the story of Joseph who has a vision of seven lean years and seven years of plenty and he is the one who successfully brings Egypt out of a famine. In the story of Esther, the allegory suggests that Rachel is a form of government that Jacob wants to court and marry. Jacob represents the nation of earth's humanity and Leah the erstwhile worldly government that is imposed on the world's people/(Jacob). The first seven years of Jacob represents in the context of the *Johannesburg Formula* the seven years according to the Gregorian calendar and the next seven years represent the seven years according to the Julian calendar. Using tools of symbology to view the meaning of this story, the presentation of Leah represents the date 2012 (according to the Gregorian calendar), that proved to be out of sync with the Mayan predictions. The Julian calendar is as Rachel to Jacob in the added seven years of labour, as the seven years he spent only to be presented with Leah is represented *symbolically* as the Gregorian calendar.

To see what this all means, we assume that Leah is the Gregorian calendar "presumption" and the Gregorian 2012, perhaps and supposedly spoken of by the Maya. After we plug in our assumptions and findings, we see more clearly that perhaps the Julian 2012 is the time spoken of by the Maya instead or indeed the true bride Rachel. Research into theological scholarship reveals that there is a cryptologic basis of allegory that the stories of the mould of Esther's are written in. This is made plain by the fact that some of the themes are persistent almost as if to emphasise that the theme is important or prevalent in the way things are designed.

Seven years has resurfaced as a real phenomenon in our generation as this is the number of years that the Gregorian and Julian calendars are spaced by. Seven years is a strong theme in biblical stories, the question is "should we ignore this coincidence or is it coincidence at all?". If the seven year theory of Joseph, Jacob and the Julian calendar are related through cryptographic allegory then should we not decipher what is intended to be communicated to the modern generation? Is it fair to presume that the bible and other books in their original form were written for future generations so that they would be a source of guidance, security and answer some of the perplexing questions of modern days?

The one thing that we established while looking at chapter 24 of *Fingerprints of the Gods* is that it resonates with the story of Esther written in the bible as depicted in the film *One night with the king*. In this film Esther is recognised as a learned contender for the Persian throne, where Xerxes was king. Esther regales the royal eunuch with her knowledge of the story of Gilgamesh the king of Sumer. Esther became the queen of Persia thanks to her indepth knowledge of the story of Gilgamesh, in her trials as a contestant to become queen. This supports Graham's contention in chapter 23 that humanity has a legacy of cataclysm events embedded in mythology. As we learn in Graham's book also, Gilgamesh was enraptured by the story of Utnapishtim, a king who survived *the great flood*. According to Utnapishtim, "*the flood raged over seven days until his vessel rested on the seventh day on a mountain top"*. The point here is that even the story of Esther reiterates Graham's theme…

 The materials in the form of old world books and records make for a rich analytical source in the modern era. There might arise time when the world is in a position of needing to go back to historical and old world content and context to figure out what is happening in the present. For example the movie *'One night with the king'* is a rich source of direct hints. For example, Esther hands over her priced heirloom in the form of a necklace that she has inherited from her grandmother and intimates to the king that: *"it is her past present and future"*. Surely when she talks about the future she is talking about generation's including the one in this time. King Xerxes refers to having *"seen the stars"* as a reason why he believes Esther over the *prince of the face*, Herman the Agagite in one of the closing scenes. The stars that are illuminated by flames when Esther's necklace is reflected on open-flames are not seen by the Agagite and this makes him an adversary to the realisation of the king that Esther's story of Jacob and Rachel the forbearers of the twelve tribes is a relevant story in that it affects the future. The message of *seeing stars* is one that we reinforce in this chapter as relevant to the stars of the *book of Revelations*. The stars of the *book of Revelations* are an allegory and not plainly illustrated as to their meaning. It is therefore important to find a link with other references to "stars' 'in the bible as the primary source document as is done in Esther's story, when Xerxes sees stars.

The practice of source analysis reveals many relevant messages that are apparently crucial for the present generation. This proves to reconcile the knowledge that humanity has stored up for all time as being crucial to determining the future. For the purpose of appropriating *The Johannesburg Formula*, the cache of illustrations from the American entertainment industry is hereby dubbed as the "Book of Hollywood". The movies all reinforce strong messages that are practical and applicable to modern life in the quest for answers to challenges and dilemmas facing present generations. For example the cryptex in the film *"Da Vinci Code"* and the stoneball in *"One night with the king"* are similar devices that hide important messages inside of them and it is a challenge for those on a quest to discover the hidden meaning of the message. Esther's story tells us how persistent the linear sequence of past, present and future events are. Esther's era is more than five hundred years to when events that are directly related in the film play themselves out again. For instance the story of the Agagites and the story of Jacob in this film, prove that it is impossible to walk away from events of the past as they signify events of the present and of the future.

Comparative analysis of movies reveals reinforced themes especially, *"The Da Vinci Code", "One night with the king" and "The day the earth stood still"*. I have watched these movies several times and links appear that make the reinforced story between these seemingly unrelated stories persistent. In other words if we were to watch these movies comparatively we would deduce a theme that is common, that seems to speak of a bigger picture. The subliminal outcome is to reinforce a central theme, in this case, of the challenges in modern times to the destiny of humanity and experiences of messages that have been communicated to the future in order to assist future generations to deal with generational challenges.

On the 5th August 2013 we reached a conclusive realisation, by pondering and asking the question *"since when does a year open with an asteroid exploding over a province in Russia?"*. This is an anomaly that even most people have forgotten about by now because not many people know first-hand of asteroids and neither did anyone expect an asteroid to actually blast through the atmosphere. But according to the *candles theory*, we figure that the asteroid is a star as spoken of in the *book of Revelations*. 2013 was marked by an asteroid in February as a star and as there are seven stars spoken of in the *book of Revelations*, is it possible that every year of the specific seven years will be marked by a similar incursion of an asteroid symbolising that these are a peculiar seven years. Will there be an explosion of asteroids every year of the seven years until an asteroid that resembles the wormwood star that fell into the sea described in the *book of Revelations*? 2013 of the Gregorian calendar was a peculiar year by all counts as the asteroid marked it as a year like no other.

Asteroids catapulting into the earth's atmosphere are unusual and for an asteroid to have marked 2013, hmm...that should have pricked up our ears. If another asteroid strikes anywhere on planet earth in 2014 or any other, we will know that this is a code or message, and one that has been foretold in the *book of Revelations*. It is outrageous to overlook the incursion of an asteroid as if it is a normal seasonal occurrence. If something resembling the asteroid of February 2013 should occur in 2014 or any other time later, maybe we should take notice and definitely look out for a repeat or consistency of signal in 2015 (or beyond) and then we should know for sure that we are in for a bumpy 2019. The seven year theory in the form of the candles theory might just be playing out and we will have to look at these Masoretic texts for more clues of how to unscramble the science of epochology. Those who are responsible for informing the public about substantive matters get away with not doing so because the public do not control the flow of information and the public's attention is always peddled away to focus on issues that sell viewer airtime and boost ratings.

We may have asked, is this an index of things to come?.... or is this a marker of a period when asteroids can just feature in daily reality and we just carry on as if this is normal? Sure specialised and government sanctioned units are looking at these matters, but for the public not to be as immersed in these issues, is still a deficit.

Can we easily refute without reservation that the postulation of "candles and stars" is not plausible as regards the year 2013 (Gregorian calendar) and the beginning of a specific seven year period that might have been known to the world long ago. We are persuaded that the message of this book is a relevant starting point for anyone who wants to gain a view of this issue in the event that the calendar theory is a reality. A film like *"The day the earth stood still"* resonates with the furnishings of the Court Application and this is proof that somehow people are even subconsciously aware of pending extra-ordinary environmental circumstances. We only got to see the film *"The day the earth stood still"* in 2013, long after the court application. In one of the scenes of the movie, at the beginning, a team of scientists assembled for an impending scenario discuss the possibilities of an object that is said to be hurtling towards the earth as being an asteroid but that is ruled out because of the movement of the object. The plot is surreal and is resonant with an end-times scenario described in the *book of Revelations*. This movie/film is presented as fiction but most of the plot is anchored on real life situations. In another scene, the projection at the NASA centre, of the earthbound object's movement could very well have been depicting a real scenario such as February 2013, when an asteroid invaded the earth over Russia. The message of urgency in the film to rectify human behaviour comes out powerfully. In the film, the storyteller does something captivating, instead of resorting to human agency to act in a global predicament, they exaggerate the issue by leaving the intervention to an extra-terrestrial race that comes to the earth to resolve the issue of environmental damage. The plot of the movie illustrates an action plan in a typical extraordinary scenario. The fact that the movie has really serious issues of environmental anomaly and environmental recession is indicative of the efforts by the film industry to take on the mettle of addressing issues that are not being mainstreamed for attention by either government or the news media because of the highly controversial and real impact of these issues. The film explores the reticent nature of government when dealing with similar scenarios. The flat-footedness of bureaucracy is brought into full expression. The film also illustrates the fact that the government of the USA is the most sensitised to the issues that the film explores even though the film parodies the US government. As a result, it means that the US government has been informed by its citizens of severe issues even if it is through the communicative medium of film, yes you guessed it...from the studios of Hollywood.

Objectively, the Bible is a non-disputable dossier in its entirety. In addition, it is established and known by the academic community that the *lost scrolls (or lost books)* were recovered from Egypt and Iraq in 1947, these books should also be part of our submissions to an inquiry if at all. *The Bible* is written in ancient allegory, metaphor and figurative language. Graham's book goes a long way to indirectly make some hidden messages of ancient books plain by exploring and explaining astrology for the benefit of the reader. The achievements of science in making the mysteries of the world plain should be seen as an unveiling of the language of the ancient scribes who had a peculiar language and code of writing and describing the world. Since the rediscovery of these texts, the world of science has leapt in bounds through grasping the philosophy and art of science as a whole. Graham's book is not the only one that delves into what we refer to as *"scientific anthropology"* to unravel the mysteries into a recognisable subject. This is the generation that is supposed to grapple with the meanings of these messages. For many people across the world, the message of the Bible is a treasure trove, source document and has an immutable meaning. No one aspect of relating to what the message means is absolute. The message is singular but we all receive the meaning in unique ways, as persons from our varying positions to the message. This should not be a divisive characteristic but should be a landscape of diversity so that the puzzle of the meaning is seen.

Could the Gregorian calendar have been a dry-run for the Julian calendar? Could everything forecasted in the mode of the Gregorian calendar be relevant to the realisation of the value of the Julian calendar? If this is a possibility then it might also figure that the abandoning of the Julian calendar for the Gregorian calendar is one of those enigmatic puzzles yet to be solved. This is because it is possible that the trumpet would not have been sounded by the false alarm of the Gregorian calendar and the world would have been lulled into accepting the non-efficacy of the messages of ancient societies. Apparently, nature has a way of correcting itself and this could have been just one of those quirks. This is of course the optimistic side of the Gregorian/Julian polarity viewed from a modern perspective keen on embellishing everything with the paradigm of rights and privileges.

Was the February 2013 asteroid incursion a small thing? Probably not...We think that the solar system has the propensity to tell us something through visual and graphic messages. The asteroid incursion is probably a message that should be heeded. After all, everything is about communicating right? Colour, shape and sound are components of any known thing to communicate something about the thing. Could the solar system, the earth and the cosmos have a language that we don't see or hear? Yes, if people that are subsisting on the substrate of the earth can develop acute and advanced tools of communicating such as a spoken and audible language, why would the earth or the solar system not be able to communicate at all? Communicating is not only limited to a linguistic dimension. Other algorithms are forms of languages and communication. So we should be aware, just in case the asteroid was a piece of information that we are supposed to decipher.

# CHAPTER FOUR

## A CLOSE LOOK AT FINGERPRINTS

Graham Hancock cannot be read alone. To read Graham's book for any reason on its own would be a way of missing a point. He is informing us, schooling us, preparing us and aiding us to be proficient in other exercises that we may encounter in the future. Graham's book should be read with the Bible as the main course. Graham's book is a starter and map to discovery. I experienced this phenomenon first-hand when I discovered the *Johannesburg Formula* as an unwritten part of the book's legacy. As with anything, everyone has interests and preferences. So everyone will find what suits them out of every situation. The same applies to Graham's book, in it there is something for everybody of various persuasions and interests. We discovered the extended premise for *The Johannesburg Formula…*

In every volatile situation the main focal areas are the various scenarios. The book *Fingerprints of The Gods* by Graham has enabled him to leverage off the in-depth research by the high calibre personalities that he shares the research platform with. We benefitted from the several scenarios and looked at every possible outcome in order to arrive at the theory about the Gregorian/Julian dichotomy and possible diversity. Graham's book delves into severe scenarios, from the part that furnishes evidence of the cyclical nature of the cosmos to ordinary conversations about the state of the planet.

*The Johannesburg Formula* is inspired by the findings of *Fingerprints of the Gods* to an extent that the decision to validate the formula was because of the book's mission to stake a claim on the 21st December 2012 deliberations as definitive.

I never thought a book would be as informative and as insightful until the encounter with Graham Hancock's book for the purposes of subject research. The origination of the *Johannesburg Formula* is embedded in a realisation as we trolled (*Fingerprints of The Gods*) from chapter to chapter discovering the details of the *Mayan end-times* theory. I have to take the reader through a headline description of *Fingerprint of the Gods. Fingerprints of the Gods* is too much of a scientific showstopper for it to be rudderless. The gems of data yielded in this account can only but have a consequence. Many of us have read books that we have never remembered for anything and soon forget the significance of, *Fingerprints of the Gods* is not one of those. In order to consolidate our own assumptions about calendars we followed the course of Graham's book to arrive at *The Johannesburg Formula*.

For anyone who has not read Graham's book, this chapter of *The Johannesburg Formula* presents some headline analysis, part synopsis and renders an interpretation and views on the subjects that Graham articulates in relation to the objectives of *The Johannesburg Formula*. After reading the book we came to a conclusion that there was more to the story and it did not end with the 21st December 2012, the date at the centre of the plot, as anyone would assume. This chapter does not however give the reader unfettered details and wholesale insight into Graham's book and neither is it meant to. The reader has to look at Graham's book as well in order to follow the developments and the unfolding direction of *The Johannesburg Formula*, even though in part. We recommend highly that the reader familiarise themselves with Graham's book, it is a gateway to a contextual placement of *The Johannesburg Formula* in some ways. Graham's book *Fingerprints of the Gods* is a travelogue and research journal published in 1995 in Britain. The book is a well-researched tribute to the legacy of the ancient world. Graham goes back in time to crack some of the questions of the modern era. The calibre of researchers and participants who contributed to the book is compelling.

The opening of the book explores ancient maps and questions traditional truths versus modern realities. The aim of these explorations is to bring about alignment with ancient secrets and knowledge to today's notions of scientific realism. The discovery that Hancock makes about the superior knowledge of the past is startling compared to the secular assumption that civilisation started with the scientific industrialisation era that lead to our modern world.

Initially, Hancock's book traces the development of maps and the knowledge of ancient societies around the world. He discovers that they possessed knowledge that confounds our own modern science, when it was thought impossible that they would have. The anomalous data found on the maps that he explores lead him to conclude that something is amiss with modern science and the assumptions about society before the industrial age. Graham proves that the ancient world that was supposed to have been uncivilized was more than highly civilized having reached a state-of-the-art higher than our own modern, post-industrial technology era.

In part two he explores the South American civilizations and proves that they achieved feats that modern history finds hard to account for and even harder to reconcile with. The belief systems of the South American nations are examined in depth. Graham shows a transitory link between historical societies across the globe where connections would not be obvious because of being geographically apart. Also, the traditional notions of historicity do not celebrate the global links that Graham comes up with. Graham shows us anthropological links between South America, the Middle East and North Africa (Egypt) etc. Furthermore, the Old Testament and the account of cyclical cataclysms, known the most around the world as the deluge of Noah's generation are at the centre of this part of Graham's book.

Graham's inquest into the high civilization that the pre-Inca societies founded for posterity reveals amazing data that is still 'inconclusive' according to the views deduced using modern scientific verification tools. The dazzling look into antiquity is breath-taking and edifying at once.

The book explores architecture in the period only reckoned as *antiquity* and safely establishes the fact that mind-bending achievements were realised. Similar reed boats were identified as having been used by the people of South America and those of the river Nile, in Africa's Egypt during periods recognisable as antiquity. He exposes the reader to discoveries of *ritual architecture* in such an advanced state-of-the-art, that it is impossible to explain the instrumentation that was used to fashion these ancient buildings found in South America. Hancock shows that these antiquated civilizations had rudimentary but sophisticated observatories and they were aware of solstices and equinoxes as they could record and predict variations in seasons. These observatories were in the form of hewn monoliths arranged to map celestial procession and he proves that they kept forms of calendars using the same devices. In chapter 10 called *The City at the Gate of the Sun,* we see how a rudimentary calendar of the past was recorded in glyphs carved in stone by what appears to be an advanced scientific community.

Graham's tour is centred around discovering the secrets of time, dates and calendars. The outcome of Graham's quest is to establish data that is related to time and calendar dates with the 21st December 2012 being a focus. It is no wonder that he goes to uncompromising lengths to prove that the South American civilization that he investigates, is more or less fifteen thousand years old, when what he refers to as the institution of *Orthodox History* is doubtful of this fact. For reasons that would be obscure to a person preoccupied with the modern day aspect of living, the spectacular adventure that Graham goes through to bring us illustrious and irrefutable data is bewildering. After the discoveries alluded to by Graham, it is with due regard that *The Johannesburg Formula* has to be premised on sound "speculation". It is safe to say that a theory is a form of speculation because it is an entry into a stream that may lead to further findings and discoveries by those exposed to its rigours. A special focus of Graham's book and the issue at hand in *The Johannesburg Formula* is calendars and dates, Graham spares nothing to visit the origination of calendars and the methods used to arrive at calendars ever since.

Other keys in the development trail of calendric systems and data are the symbols that Graham explores in-depth. He also discovers that symbols thought to be recent inventions, had been used thousands of years before. The development of calendars started as a complex preoccupation derived from the observation of the skies and the solar system. The reasonable suspicion that Graham's sources confirm, is that our modern secular perspective of where the earliest civilization might be found are challenged by findings in South America, some of which the Mayan civilization belong to. Graham's time travel is enchanting, taking us through periods of time that we never learnt of ever. The methods that he employs are similar to an investigating officer who solves a cold-case, frozen by lack of substantial tools of analysis. He uses a historical dating method similar to the *'dustbin exercise'*, where the remains of a location are analysed to determine the behaviour and the social context of those who *deposited* the remains. He uses archaeological, astrological, anthropology and other scenario disciplines to bring us a view into a period that we never suspected that we could peer into. Graham studies languages, methods of agriculture that were all practised by the societies of antiquity to prove that these are still relevant to the information of modern society.

Part three of Graham's book explores the enigmatic and cryptic subject of symbols used in coded architecture. The opening paragraph shows us a ziggurat located to the north of Yucatan, Mexico that is built as a symbolic calendar with ninety one stairs on each side and the platform making up 365 steps, the number of *days in a solar year*. The point that is being reinforced by the outcomes based search into antiquity is related to the messages that have been transmitted to the future, our present, by the enigmatic societies that were previously ignored or also deliberately obfuscated.

There are unhappy accounts in the book that Graham goes into, not for fascination with the morbid but to show the reader the truth about some of the beliefs, rituals and cultures of the societies in antiquity. The book shows the level of fear driven rituals that found justification in behaviour that would be abhorred by today's measure. Almost all societies on the earth went through chilling episodes of social adaptation fuelled by ignorance of the true reality of the world. Humans have behaved according to their psychological position in relation to the world and peculiar environments that are distributed across the globe. The reader is warned that some of the depictions in Graham's book of antiquated society are not for sensitive readers on account of the rituals described. For the purpose of this book, we focus on the influences of the events on the practice of observing time.

The book further digs into several accounts of *the creation of the world* from comparative studies and records crossing the planet. All along we hear of the destructive impact of colonial conquest on posterity and records that were bequeathed to the future. The reason why the world is in such an incomplete state is because information from the past was destroyed by zealous marauders who sought to impose their legacy on the undermined societies. It is perplexing how the account of the South American societies of antiquity is similar to those of the Bible and other comparative accounts across the world.

The rationale behind some of chapters of *The Johannesburg Formula* begins in Chapter 13, Part 3 of Graham's book. Here he talks about the Mayan calendar, and describes it as being: ..."*Expressed in terms of the modern dating system*"...This excerpt from a subheading titled: *Lightbringer*, caught my attention because this is where the challenge of the account in *The Johannesburg Formula* begins. The fact that the Mayan calendar is being read through the perspective *of the modern dating system* is the questionable issue at the centre of advancing *The Johannesburg Formula*. It is not easy to transpose a modern system on an antiquated system to extract accurate readings or results. As the reader has seen in chapter 1, The

Johannesburg Formula illustrates the data deficit suspected of being an unfortunate "veil".

As I reached a passage in Graham's book titled *Tres Zapotes* in Part three... there! *there* was a second key to the "enigma". Graham categorically states that *the Mayan dot-and-bar calendric system* was decoded around the 1940s. This locked the puzzle in place as it became apparent that no-one in the 1940s could have imagined that the Gregorian calendar could or would be anomalous (or inconsistent) for the purpose of reading the Mayan calendar to correspond to a modern interpretation. Graham further deals a blow to popular theory by revealing that it is possible that the Mayans could have inherited what is known as the Mayan calendar, from the Olmecs whom are said to have been *Africoid* and were revered by South American societies of the past. Could this be relevant at all for any purpose? Well yes, because the place where the Olmecs are said to have come from more than roughly 15 000 years ago is unmistakable and central to the topic of *the prediction* related to the Mayan calendar. Graham focuses on specific aspects of research as sighted in his book.

For the purpose of leading evidence towards what culminates as the *Johannesburg Formula*, what we had to ask Graham is...*Could the Olmec's statues that were unearthed in Mexico be an "anatomical map" that is to be read in conjunction with the Mayan calendar?* Could these monolithic heads be "talking heads?". Why was there emphasis on exaggerating the size of the head? These people must have figured out that posterity would be sensitized to their logic of symbology and what we refer to as 'anatomic symbology' for that matter. I wonder how Graham would react to this line of inquiry into points that he introduced by his book. If I was not looking for it, it was there starring me in the eye, the Olmecs intended to say, follow the heads! Follow the heads to where?, well to where they came from. The Olmecs came from Africa and this is symbolic to the end-times predictions of the dot-and-bar calendar because of the geodetic and tectonic nature of the continent Africa. As the reader will see in Chapter 9 and Chapter 11 of *The Johannesburg Formula*, this is what we are saying, that global evacuations should be destined for the land of origin of the Olmecs. What this also means is that the reader will have to look at Graham's book to follow the story of the Olmecs and how it links to *The Johannesburg Formula*. ...Graham, in the passage titled *Tres Zapotes* you mention that Matthew Stirling *"unearthed a giant head"*, *"lying close to the calendar stela"*. So Graham could this not be a clue to show that the heads and stela are components of a rock hewn puzzle that we were meant to find and piece together so that a picture should emerge?

(The reader is advised to excuse the one side of the apparent dialogue between myself and Graham as I ask him some pertinent questions stemming from my reading of his book. Please be advised to look at this book, it is a rich source of the debate that ensues into the future without waning.)

...Graham, yet again, in the passage titled *San Lorenzo* in Part 3, could the systematic and "deliberate" interment of the statues discovered by Michael Coe not be another direct message? To me it appears as if the "mutilation" of the sculptures fits into a theory of deliberate *triggers* being prepared from the past by the people of the past. Could they have been warning us to evacuate the area where the relics were found to a place where the Olmecs had come from? This is a theory that has developed throughout the theme of *The Johannesburg Formula*. Could the Olmec enigma be as plain as what is suggested by the theory of *anatomic symbology*? Could the mutilation and the exaggeration of scale of the Olmec heads mean that they were saying: "we the Olmecs are passing a big message, and the message is written in the dots-and-bar system, that if you do not evacuate to the direction that the Viracocha and Quetlcoatl disappeared to on their vessels, then you risk being mutilated and interred, like this mock interment of five sculptures and statuettes?" Graham, with all due respect, is it possible that *The Olmec Enigma* is partly answered by the leads (in the form of questions) posed by *The Johannesburg Formula?*

For the benefit of the reader, I do not intend to have a dialogue to your exclusion with Graham in this book. I am making a point about the reader having to look at Graham's book in order to follow *The Johannesburg Formula* without giving away the details of the plot in *Fingerprints of the Gods.* Mind you, it is possible to read *The Johannesburg Formula* before reading *Fingerprints of the Gods*. The constant referral to Graham's book in some chapters is a reflection of how interactive *Fingerprints of the Gods* is, by posing questions for others to ponder and perhaps respond to after reading Graham's tome.

Graham relates to us how the Mayan civilization was obsessed with time. This could very well be informative to our modern culture that is the opposite and in fact extremely averse to the reality of the effects of passing time on our reality. Not to be crass about our modern day society and generation, it is clear however to see why we are not sensitized to the grand scale of time. No one walks around with a clock that measures thousands of years. This was the case with the societies of antiquity, they were aware of grand amounts of time and were watching thousands of years as we would perhaps periods of years. Their consciousness included time as a real and ritualistic phenomenon, just as we would be aware of modern day preoccupations like sports, economics etc. Modern society is intricately different to those hardy civilizations of the past. To deal with or face the subject of the reality of cyclical cataclysm and datable epoch is not a daily preoccupation for modern society.

 Apart from the delicate and instant modern life where almost every act of human life is accomplished through a push of a button or switch, it is understandable why our generation is completely averse to the knowledge and inquiry into cataclysm. I would think that it is better to face reality and act to avert unreasonable collisions with the grand clock of time. It is also probably a question of the period that any generation occupies along the time scale of cyclical cosmic procession.

An epoch is defined as an apportionment of time. For our discussion this would be several thousands and more years. A generation living at the early phase of an epoch would not be as preoccupied with cataclysmic inevitability, as would a generation that occupies a later period of a cyclic epoch. The fact that we view time on a watch with a two centimetre screen on our wrist has probably impacted our view of "the time-scale" and we are not inclined to the epochological clock or grand scale of time. It is not easy to accept as part of our daily life the reality of the grand scale of time. Our preoccupation with the push button life of our generation has led us into a 'blind alley'. We do not perceive the cyclical nature of the forces of the cosmic environment. Our preoccupation with the demands of modern life means that we are very well aware of the period of orbit around the sun, a year. Also, we are in tune with the details of the year in the form of seasons. We do not look at an issue like *precession* as a factor of our daily realm and this is our reality.

It is suspiciously clear from the evidence presented by Graham that the people of these antiquated societies were more than obsessed with leaving an early warning system for posterity. The practices that are described in *Fingerprints of the Gods* show a sentiment for the future and fascinating state-of-the-art that sought to communicate with future generations. Could these societies have been so aware of the vast expanse of time, that it was possible for them to clearly visualise our generation's time of tenure? Maybe their 'beliefs' were so soundly refined that they felt an intuitive attachment to the future as a primal instinct. The rituals practiced by these societies reveal the fact that they had a shrewd affinity with the future and referred to the future in their preoccupation. Everything they did was centred on communicating to posterity. Could they have had residual psychological trauma that compelled them to be so obsessed with the well-being of future generations whom they knew would be their descendants? They probably had a sense of the cyclical nature of time and events, and so they could visualise a future.

A likely answer to the questions posed in the passage titled: *Conspicuous Strangers and Hypothetical third party*, is that the trauma of the last real cataclysm compelled the survivors to get onto the business of informing future generations of the cyclical nature of cataclysm and that they spared nothing as well as employed their genius to do so. Moreover it is possible that they had survived a cataclysm that evaporated a fully formed scientific civilization so the initial post cataclysmic generation escaped with a record of a matured scientific civilization. The record of the earth's true age tells us something about the possibility of societies in a forgotten time. It is widely accepted that the earth is as old as the longest time, so speculation around how long civilizations have been around follows on closely.

Could societies of antiquity have been masters of the grand cycle of the grand scale of time? Could they have mastered a science that we may rudimentarily refer to as epochology? The biblical saying... "nothing is new under the sun" is extremely poignant for the purpose of answering questions about these societies. For instance in the sub-heading *Children of the Fifth Sun,* Part III, it is proven that these people could see or even map events that straddle epochs. So is it possible that they could map the behaviour of society over the duration of an epoch as they had measured four epochs. The South American civilization stated that this present generation's is the fifth epoch. According to Graham, the Aztec priesthood show *that the universe operated in great cycles* or epochs that last roughly four to five millennia each. They revealed that we are in the fifth cycle or epoch as referred to in modern language. In chapter 18 of *Fingerprints of the Gods*, Graham points to stele that had hewn on them the likeness of a caucasian man. Graham I don't know if the question that you pose *'Who were these conspicuous strangers?'* in chapter 18 has been answered, but according to our view of the points that you make about emphasis on racial characteristics in the rock hewn artefacts, it is clear that a message is being passed. Could these societies have foreseen unintended behaviour such as racial bigotry that would be practised by societies towards the end of an epoch...? this epoch? Maybe a form of the science of epochology enabled them to foresee trends such as racial bigotry amongst the people of the world. In our epoch the practice of racial bigotry gripped humanity for thousands of years, only beginning to thaw in recent times.

May I point to an assertion in chapter 19 with a subheading titled- *Monte Alban: the downfall of masterful men-* where it says... *"If a great civilization had indeed been lost to history, and if these sculptures told part of its story, the message conveyed was one of racial equality".*

So although they were from a racially unambiguous society, they could have highlighted racial characteristics to warn us of racial bigotry. They were probably aware that racial bigotry would undo future generations. Anatomical 'race' has been one of the most astounding questions of this generation, for reasons that are lost by now.

The question then becomes: why would such a message stand out amongst others as being so important that these societies should spend energy and resources to make sure that it was transmitted successfully? Answer: they were aware of a period along an epoch where the behaviour of humans declines and racial bigotry becomes a way of life. They were aware that racial inequality would be a risk that put the people of the future in any succeeding epoch in danger of being separated while in reality they face a challenge that cuts across race, in this case the cyclical cataclysm of cosmic events. They were probably saying to the people of our epoch "beware of racial bigotry, it will consume you until you are blind to cosmic risks in your generations". This generation has been eclipsed by the uncanny challenge of unleashing racial inequality on each other. This could well mean that we have lost time, knowledge and capacity to deal with the cosmic realities that challenge or are faced by any generation that happens to live at the end of an epoch. It is possible that the whole of the empire in South America was a canvass on which a grand message to the future was written.

To reiterate the sentiments at the end of chapter 20, with the sub-heading *A science of prophecy*, Graham you refer to *"knowledge that we have only reacquired very recently..."*. For the purpose of *The Johannesburg Formula*, we are inclined to simulate this science as "epochology", a science of measuring, studying and observing an entire epoch. This would entail the varying peculiarities of the opening, the middle and end of an epoch as being distinct. Also an epoch would have attributes, generations, variable social outcomes, social norms, behaviour and pre-occupations. If ancient societies could visualise and plot an epoch, then they would have been able to predict general sciences required to cope with each segment of an epoch.

However, Graham's book is seminal and is essentially a map for our generation to find other clues embedded in "other" locations. In chapter 21 he says:"...*Geography is about maps and astronomy is about stars.*" ...Not far from the topic, for instance in the *Book of Revelations* there is a reference to stars at the opening of the book. Stars are an astronomic phenomenon and in formative instances were mostly used to find bearing and location. Could the stars in the *Book of Revelations* be a map? A date map?

If the Olmecs bequeathed the long-count system to the Mayans, did they take it across to them from whence the Olmecs themselves had come? Chapter 21 of *Fingerprints Of The Gods* may be letting off more than what meets the eye. If the long-count was brought across, then the message of the tradition was brought across. This means that the Olmecs actually and symbolically went to 'fetch' the people from across the Atlantic and showed them what to do at a specific era of the epoch using a rock hewn technology. Were they trying to tell them to follow the dot-and-bar to where it came from at a specific and indicated time? This is what I make out of the hidden clues 'embedded' in the passage with the subheading title *"Knowledge out of place"*.

Accordingly, the number of 0.0003 is significant to *The Johannesburg Formula* because it is the number that the shortfall is based on. The amount of 0.0003 is the fraction of a day's length that the reform by Pope Gregory XIII corrected the Julian calendar by. The findings of the *Johannesburg Formula* purport that the deficit is a number of years that were not factored in when the dot-and-bar was decoded and a translation value made. The Johannesburg Formula is a claim that the process overlooked the entire "leap-year value" of the period before 1582 AD to 3114 BC.

The deficit sighted by the Johannesburg Formula explodes in chapter 21 of Graham's book. He reveals that the Mayan calendar is even more accurate than the Gregorian calendar because it calculates 0.0002 as the default value. Graham, should we all be using the Mayan calendar instead of the Gregorian calendar instead? The whole purpose of the change from the Julian calendar to the Gregorian calendar was accuracy and the Mayan calendar is found to be more accurate than the Gregorian calendar. Another concern is this...why is there a need to calibrate the Mayan calendar to conform to a translated value of another calendar. Can the Mayan calendar not be read directly without calibrating another calendar? Maybe the snag is right there, the need to use the modern calendar to read the Mayan calendar. Maybe the Mayan calendar is saying something else on its own when read directly. Surely the Mayans read the calendar in a singular medium without decoding or translating it. We know that meaning usually gets lost when one language is translated to another, this could be the challenge posed to the interpretation of the Mayan calendar using the Gregorian calendar.

Could the time thief have struck or would this have been the price to pay? This is a question we have to ask in the face of a conundrum that does not tally-up. This is the situation here... was it ultimately a good thing for the future that the Gregorian calendar was introduced or not? Did this event in history turn the tide or not? Could we have missed the obvious false-alarm of 21st December 2012 or not? We might not be able to answer these questions here and now but it is useful to be aware of the possibilities of the answers.

Is it possible that the Gregorian calendar has overshot the calculations of translating calendar values? Could future interpretation of correlating Mayan calendar values be short-changed by even referring to the modern calendar? Our outlook employs a fixed calendar module without looking at the relevance of other calendars even though these exist independently. The modern system teaches us not to question conventions, acceptable standards, customs, protocols and norms. We take it that our knowledge of *"the world as we know it"* is sufficient for all the challenges that the world throws at us. We don't imagine that our calendar that we know for so long could be a curiosity. We write the date on everything, we are taught to date everything for legal requirements and official effect as a matter of formalities. It is easily likely that our view of our calendar is that of an unquestionable invention that someone bequeathed to us. So we would not imagine the calendar to be out of kilter. No-one would ever think of something as intrinsic as the calendar being deficient, right? This is possibly the risk factor of this millennium. The one thing that we value much, that it is past our noticing as the thing that could lull us into a mistaken sense of reality, for any purpose.

While reading *Fingerprints of the Gods* for the second time, I decided to search for the author on Facebook. On September 10th 2013, Graham updated his status with information about a site in Tepe, Turkey where they discovered a neo-lithic record from more than 15 000 years ago. One of the updates made by a lady responding on Graham's Facebook profile said that she had learnt that the occupants of the site in Turkey were living in the previous epoch and were highly tactile, being able to communicate telepathically. This made me realise that the questions that Graham posts regarding these neo-lithic finds were being answered by people who are familiar with his work and who interact with him on his profile page. The theory that *The Johannesburg Formula* advances is that of the possibility of the neo-lithic societies discussed in *Fingerprints of the Gods*, having known a lot about the "psychology of epochs" advanced in *The Psychology of Epochology*. Is it then possible, following on the lady's assertion and the light that this sheds on the *epoch psychology theory* that these societies could predict human behaviour at specific moments in an epoch? The lady's input gave credibility to the theory proposed in *The Johannesburg Formula* that these people could map the psychological make-up of the inhabitants of the world through specific times of an epoch. This means that we may also assume that human behaviour is specific to the time-frame of an epoch. Behaviour at the beginning could requires that the inhabitants are at the highest state-of-the-art, if the inference is made from *Fingerprints of the Gods* that intact blue-prints of civilizations survive the end of an epoch to be implemented wholesale at the beginning of another, giving the succeeding epoch the reserve of proficiency based on relics from the previous epoch. If for instance as suggested in Graham's book, that knowledge or science compounded over an epoch is kept alive by an 'esoteric' formation of *scientific gnostics*, then it follows that at the end of an epoch, it is possible to assume that behaviour will display trends of *nihilism* and frequent *apocalyptic inclination,* where the extreme end of human civilization is overturned from civil to destructive psychological traits (especially by people who perceive themselves to be outside any formation/s of a *scientific gnostic* community). This is possible if cosmic changes are a reality and the whole biosphere is subverted by chemical and physical variation. The scientific gnostic ideology assumes that preparation for a post-apocalyptic scenario ensues while having means and ways of surviving a cataclysm. This is to enable the re-establishment of a high level of civilization almost immediately after recovering from an end of epoch cataclysm. So it is possible that a generation that lives at the middle of an epoch are generally non-affected by the beginning and end of epoch social scenario, state-of-the-art and psychology. Have we not seen this trend in our generation of heightened awareness and consciousness mingled with suspicion of an apocalypse? Everyone in this generation has inherited a social genre of a so-called millennial consciousness where society's trends in industrialization, technology and psychology are changing at a rapid speed coupled with a general awareness of some latent apocalypse. Everyone knows about the possibility of the end-times scenario being the preoccupation of this generation albeit without commitment to realisation of preparedness or readiness for several peculiar reasons. These include a psychological make-up that says that by acting, then this would be admittance...or by admitting, the political system would face an unprecedented challenge. Why is it that the suggestion that an epoch's last generation seems to tumble into social degeneration seems so fatalistically palpable? This is almost the trend with this generation having recently fought two world-wars over the past few decades. Before that, the world was immersed in the colonial episode where one nation was merciless to another. The sudden resurgence of consciousness and humanitarian empathy proved to be a patch on an already overwhelmingly recalcitrant generation. Then there is environmental damage indicated by the efforts at industrialization. One of the topics of research that this book would like to enable, is the possibility of an *epoch psychology* (a subject of epochology*)* that might not have been transmitted to our generation as a singular subject of focus. This is due to an episode when colonial enthusiasts were rummaging the face of the earth destroying data from the past in some zealous process of *proselytisation*. All this is in the recent past and it could be overwhelming proof of the psychological challenges that the world has to overcome before facing off with a cosmic realism.

In chapter 23 Graham does not mince words when he reinforces the fact that the civilizations of antiquity had a grasp of high esoteric mathematics and that they employed the number *pi* when building the Pyramid of the Sun in Mexico as well as the Pyramid of Giza in Egypt respectively. The reason for this illustration of the sciences of these societies is to show us that they were astute and scientifically accurate so their predictions about calendar dates likewise were.

We defer to Graham's assignment, that of telling us about an imminent and predicted cosmic event. He spares no dime or sweat bead to bring us this compelling message and so *The Johannesburg Formula* is a fitting tribute to his courage. We do not claim to have the practical experience and insight that Graham and Santha do, but the texture that the book conveys in words is provisionally invasive and sufficiently instructing. Graham literally transports the reader to the location that he himself is physically immersed in.

In chapter 31 Graham describes myths that are written as a *precessional code*. For example in a passage with a subheading: *Times of decay*, he describes a temple complex in Angkor, in the jungles of Kampuchea. The temple with five gates, is said to be "purpose-built as a precessional metaphor". This struck me as being similar to the *book of Revelations* where a city with four gates is described that is built on a foundation of mineral stones. It seems that the book of Revelations is a *precessional code* similar to that described in Part 5 of *Fingerprints of the Gods*.

In chapter 34 titled *Mansion of Eternity*, Graham takes the reader on a breath-taking and gasping tour of the neolithic architectural mind. The admission that the builders of these neolithic super-structures were of splendid genius ties in with the science of epoch psychology to the effect that generations that live through the beginning of an epoch are untainted by the attritions of time. Is this proof that the theory of epoch psychology is valid as we see that these generations are said to have trumped subsequent generations in intellectual ability? Maybe as the theory espouses, the generations that live at the beginning of any epoch are endowed with a serenity that enables the highest expression of human capability. Is it possible that the cosmic energies at the beginning of an epoch enable humans to use more brain power and have a wider span of emotional tolerance.

 Maybe the IQ and EQ at the beginning of any epoch are above known averages and the abilities of earth's inhabitants wane as the millennia cascade in a cyclical rhythm.  Look I am simply taking advantage of the open book test that *Fingerprints of the Gods* gives the reader through the questions asked by Graham. I do not presume to answer the questions but as a way of being enthused to ponder the answers, *The Johannesburg Formula* is an opportunity for me to explore the privilege. This is without burdening anyone to reach the same conclusion. Also the point is to speculate around the question of whether these neolithic generations should have had such foresight as to calibrate monumental scientific works like the long-count calendar while also being an attempt to answer the question of whether they also had a sort of long view of human behaviour that spans through the entire scope of the long-count period. Wait a minute, in chapter 35, subheading :*Not like other tombs,* Graham compares Fourth dynasty and Fifth dynasty pyramids, he finds that in the Fourth dynasty there was apparently no fascination with the journey of the souls as compared with the Fifth dynasty where ritual objects were found with incantations to lead the Pharaoh on the journey in the afterlife. Could this further prove the decline in psychological outlook as the generations pace towards *a middle* of an epoch? This suggests to me that the Fourth dynasty were not psychologically perturbed and were not occupied with securing a state of mind of ritualistic reassurance. This for me speaks to the difference of behaviour in different periods of an epoch.

Further, Graham shows that the difference in quality of architecture from dynasty to dynasty bears marks of a decline as years advance. This plays well into the epoch psychology theory as proof that earlier works of architecture were of a higher quality and scientific resonance.

Coming back to the point of the direction of the book journey, chapter 36 asserts the inimitable purpose of the pyramids as time machines that are part of the precessional science legacy bequeathed to future generations, perhaps our generation. To reinforce the epoch psychology assumption and to concretise it into a viable proposition, it is worth noting the fact that the pyramids are still here. These monuments of architecture from the possible beginning moments of an epoch, illustrate the high calibre and state-of-the-art at the period that opens an epoch. Compared with architecture at the end of an epoch there is no doubt what the indication is. This coupled with the visible marker of decline in Fourth to Fifth dynasty prowess provides a basis for arguing.

The *epoch psychology theory* finds footing in several ways. That being the case, what room do we have to doubt the message of the Mayans totally, a message that seems to be written in stone so that even time could not brush it away or aside? We agree with Graham that the purpose for which pyramids were built is yet more than what has passed off. The purpose of communicating with future generations is without ready dismissal, as well as the more complex precessional key as clarified by *Fingerprints of the Gods*. The subheading: *A singular oppression* (out of chapter 36), *takes place at the location of* the pyramid of Menkaure/Mycerinus. He literarily takes us into the pyramid to show us the workmanship inside the structure and surely the theory of epoch psychology is once again retorted. We have been taught that our modern generation's state-of-the-art has improved from that of preceding generations. This does not seem to be the case, it seems that our generation's state-of-the-art is subordinate to that of the preceding civilizations within the same epoch. It is clear that the workmanship of these ancient monuments is outstanding and durable, lasting over several thousands of years. What this should also mean is that the preceding generations knew more than we do about epochs and that we should learn from their messages.

The 'modern day' perspective is that people from the past were less civilized and knew less, therefore anything that they might have said should be dismissed with disdain for harbouring crude and uncivilized notions. This teaching has become the risk-bed of modern society. Did these neolithics leave behind architectural enigmas that baffle modern science, so that we would be convinced of the infallibility of their message to the future? To quantify the parameters of an epoch, we can say that if an epoch lasts for 4000 years, for instance, then the first 1000 would be the opening and the last 1000 the closing. Behaviour would be mapped along the spans of such proportions. Remember that this epoch map is theoretical and is meant for the purpose of the questions we want to answer, of whether the epoch psychology theory is correct or not. Could these neolithic societies have had insight into every possible "academic discipline" that they mapped onto a time-scale as long as an epoch? Moreover there are longer periods that we may classify as super-epochs, for instance a time of 100 000 years. So the probability of variations in behaviour and social psychology are more likely over such a longer time.

Chapter 37, subheading: *Mind games of the pyramid builders*, convinced me once and for all that the theory of *epoch psychology* was and is a reality. Graham says here that: *"...the builders had used* pi *to demonstrate their mastery of the secrets of transcendental numbers"*. Graham shows us that the Egyptian neolithic society knew of transcendental numbers before the accepted version that these were discovered more recently by the Greeks. *Fingerprints of the Gods* is indeed testament to an inspiration for many throughout the world, electrified by the compelling massage and almost tangible interaction of generations across time using the residual energy field of the artefacts from the neolithic generation.

Chapter 38 depicts the mathematical genius displayed by the Giza monuments' surveyors, architects and stone-masons. The intricate way that enigmatic mathematics was employed to build the monuments as well as refurbish them with cryptic chambers, stun the mind of modern generations, only because it is *presumed* that the technology used could not have existed then. The point here is that their use of irrational numbers in cryptic architecture could be a device to communicate to the future. They were proving that such a period would yet arise in the cyclical journey of planet earth. Could these stone-masons have been instructed by the architects of Giza to tell us that an 'irrational time' would swing back? The Mayan calendar indeed speaks of irrational times where everything that was held in place by logic would defy sensibility. The enigma of cryptic architecture could be a message to alert us that we would also encounter an irrational passage of time. The builders of Giza could have deliberately left a cryptic architectural mystery in order to tune our minds to irrational times. They could have been saying, "no logic will decipher the time period at the end of this epoch". All what we have to do is to follow their prescription and do as they suggest for our times. This then sheds more light on the possibility that the Meso-American culture and the Egyptian culture were disbursed by a singular *scientific-gnostic* society who were trying to tie up the destiny of the whole planet to one eventuality. The Egyptian and Mayan legacy both speak the language of the possibility that they are two sides of the same 'message coin'. Graham is doing well by showing us the relationship between these two cultures that are unsuspectingly linked. So it figures that if the Mayans are talking of end-times, then so are the Egyptians in their cryptic architecture and anthropological relics.

The picture alluded to in chapter 39 (subheading titled: *Lord of Rostau*), where a diorite statute of Khafre (a fourth dynasty Pharaoh) is found 'ritually buried', is reminiscent of the Olmecs' statues also being ritually interred earlier in *Fingerprints of the Gods.* Could this be another signal of the end-times, showing us that even the most eternal of our works would be turned upside-down at an appointed time?

The process that began with research before and including *Fingerprints of the Gods* is just such a place where questions are asked. So anyone with the requisite accreditation may also attempt to answer as best as possible. The challenge is that this branch of research is on the margins because main stream is averse to some of the truisms of this branch. Could the 'abnormal' cyclical floods or deluge be some process to cool the earth's surface after the core is recharged and the dynamo is at full capacity? We should ask these questions so that experts and specialists may render return analysis on them. That is just what a theory is, right? This could mean that the earth, its inhabitants, flora and fauna have a corresponding frequency and that as the 'charge' wears-off, the decline is indicated in the calibre and quality of architecture, engineering capabilities and other state-of-the-art developments. Could a field of *techno-anthropology* be a reasonable academic subject from where to ask and answer these questions? As seen in *Fingerprints of the Gods,* there seems to be an ancient scientific-gnostic culture that has since ebbed away, that enabled top calibre civilizations to perplex the future with unsolved enigmas like the neolith megalithic architecture that goes against the grain of the accepted developmental and civilization trajectory. It is said that most of the answers to these scientific riddles are still shrouded in mythology and these myths have been hard to interpret for the most part.

Earlier in the book Graham discusses the Teotihuacan water pools found in Mexico. It is thought that they were a form of *advance warning system* for seismic activity. As it has already been expressed, the cryptic architecture from the past is still inconclusively baffling and it is the prerogative of the future to attempt to decipher what all these enigmatic structures could have been built for. Regarding the story in chapter 46, could the Osireion be a *'long-range seismic monitor'* similar to the one described in the subheading titled: *Hints of forgotten wisdom* (chapter 22)? Anyone who has heard Graham relate the story about Alfred E. Schlemmer's description of Teotihuacan in Mexico, would be convinced that the Osireion was a similar device. The account of the Osireion in Abydos

(Egypt) sounds like what was described earlier when talking about the Teotihuacan water pools. To me chapter 46 sounds like a comparative narrative of chapter 22 in as far as the Osireion and the Teotihuacan pools are concerned. I did not begin this process trying to answer all the questions posed in *Fingerprints of the Gods*, it just occurred that it is not forbidden to do so. Afterall this book is a research compilation that if looked at closely, is still carrying on as Graham goes on to post more stuff that is related to this topic on his Facebook page. The findings in Turkey where he was in September 2013 for example, are linked to the discoveries that are illustrated in his book *Fingerprints of the Gods*. (See Facebook). He even says on his Twitter account that he is doing a sequel. Is it possible that the structures that were built in the past were built to be used in the future? The Osireion, the Pyramids at Giza, the seismic monitor at Teotihuacan and others could have been designed to be used today. For instance, in modern times there is still no technology to forecast earthquakes or map the geographic sequence of locations where quakes occur. Earthquakes are the most random incursions on modern civilization, they occur at unforeseeable locations without any foreknowledge on the part of modern technologies and observatories. Geologists are still finding ways of broaching earthquakes in order to be able to pre-empt them and probably act on them. This is a disturbing reality about modern life and to the establishment of science. It is possible that we will be able to map earthquakes, predict where they occur through knowing the primary causes of earthquakes and predicting the behaviour of the lithosphere. If it is possible to map the direction that the earth-crust is displacing in, then it should be possible to make models and simulations of the locations that are prone to the next earthquake with reasonable precision.

Chapter 48 is another puzzle that beckons for questions and answers. As a mechanical reaction to the subheading titled: *The Pyramid/Earth ratio*, it appears that another factor could be imagined within the parameters of what has been professed in *Fingerprints of the Gods.* At the risk of appearing to be inserting myself between the lines and ideas of *Fingerprints of the Gods,* here we go again...It is possible that chapter 48 bears clues about the answer to why the earth is not a perfectly round sphere and it is oblong as observed successfully by modern science. Could it be that there is a point in the precessional cycle where the earth is more or less a perfectly round sphere? It seems plausible that the earth could change its shape and become oblate with the passage of time. In other words when the Great Pyramid was built, the earth was closer to a perfectly round sphere and that following the precessional cycle it became oblate. The reason for this opinion is founded on chapter 48, where Graham illustrates that the earth's true circumference is not equidistant from the equator to the poles. *Here the book reveals that a startling feat was accomplished. The Giza Pyramid was built to be a scale to ratio representation of the measurements of the earth's circumference.* He intimates this after a calculation reveals that an error of 20 feet discovered at the perimeter of the base of the Great Pyramid when looking at the expressed ratio of the pyramid to the earth's equatorial circumference, is a margin that is due to it being strategically located rather than not being an accurate ratio to scale representation. It could be that the pyramid was once exact to ratio of the earth's circumference and the difference is based on modern calculations that use the measurements of an *oblate spheroid.*

The earth could be subject to a rotational and spinning pressure at the axis that cause it to bulge at the equator over millennia, after achieving a near perfect spheroid shape every cyclical period. It is clear that there is some pressure bearing on the polar axis that is causing it to be 'flattened' from both ends. Yes, it is acceptable as it has been said that the bulge at the equator is a result of displacement of mass caused by the earth's spin. This could be one factor alone. The fact that the Giza complex represents the celestial picture from more than 12 000 years ago when it was originally built, could also reflect on the earth having been a near perfect spheroid at some point in the far past. The *physical effects* of precession on the earth could be the loss of the near perfect rounded shape, to cause the *oblate* shape. This would in turn affect any attempt at plotting calendar estimations perfectly over lengthy periods like millennia. This in turn would affect the accurate interpretation of dates in the current period that assume that the earth is always bulged at the equator. This appetite is also based on the fact that the theory of cyclical recharge of the earth's core seems to be on track. Then it would add up that when the earth's core is recharged anew, the distribution of pressure from the core is equal and this then remoulds the shape of the earth to once again become a near rounded sphere. If all this is correct, then won't it follow that the oblate shape that we are observing from this end of a definitive *precessional epoch* is an indicator of some *precessional state of the earth.* This is an opinion based on the propositions that leave the reader with a lot of questions. The offer is this, that if *'the sands have shifted'* and the appearance of the celestial map on the Giza Plateau is different from when it was originally located to outline the *Belt of Orion*, then it is possible that the shape of the earth has changed due to the physical effects of precession.

Again we suggest that the earth's shape correlates with the precessional model that is illustrated in *Fingerprints of the Gods* to the extent that the bulge might follow the trend of 'changes' in celestial positions. Again the science of precession is still a developing subject that may be founded on more questions than answers. It is up to enthusiasts to offer claims that may be rebuffed or endorsed depending on their validity. I don't claiming to have grasped the precessional model from cover to cover in *Fingerprints of the Gods*, it is an elaborate illustration that needs one to stay with it in order to go away with something. I will however not be shy to intimate that the subheading titled: *The Orion Mystery*, makes me suspect that the *'near perfect round shape'* theory is a huge possibility. Why would something as possible as this be ruled out when we all don't know much about what actually happens due to precessional reality from beginning to end of an epoch? There is a lot to consider, the speed that the earth is said to be hurtling at across the orbital path, the weight or mass of the globe if it has been worked out at all and a lot more that the global sphere is exposed to in real space as opposed to what we perceive in relation to our earth terrestrial perspective. It is impossible to rule out the 'near perfect rounded sphere' theory for anything because we have not observed an entire duration of precession or that of an epoch. That would be like saying the solar system is the only solar environment because there are no telescopes to observe the fact that space is littered with an infinite amount is solar systems.

It is also noteworthy that there are billions of people on earth who would like to be informed about the precessional model in very simple terms. From a South African perspective, we restate the fact that there have been lapses in the education system, this is still indicated by the *digital divide* across the world. A country like South Africa is unique in revealing the statistics of this point, the digital divide is also an indicator of the economic divide that means that on one side, people are excluded from almost everything including the luxury of educational topics like precessional science. The view of precessional science as being esoteric is inadequate because Graham proves that it exists in mythologies and metaphors from many cultures across the world. So it means that people know of this information albeit not in the precessional terminology and scientific jargon. For example in South Africa, the name for the country in one of the languages is *"Ningizimu"* to indicate direction. This word to me sounds like one of the precessional metaphors because it means 'a place of a many giants'. Could this be part of the technical metaphors to transmit information about an era when there were many giants in this part of the world? There are other similar metaphors and stories that have such embedded information that may very well be a form of transmitting and storing accounts of eras bygone. Similarly it has been said that the people in a place like South Africa had more advanced knowledge of metallurgy than was thought of by the orthodox account.

Already before the encounter of the people in South Africa with people from Europe, there were metallic implements fashioned for many settlement usages. The finding at *Mapungubwe* as anyone who has visited South Africa will know, proves the existence of a more advanced metallurgy culture and industrial application than was previously thought and assumed. Therefore if the findings of Graham's book speak of an intercontinental correlation of highly advanced civilizations like the Mayan, Olmecs, Egyptians and others, then this phenomenon of precessional science may be found to be more pervasive than previously thought of. It may be found in the future when the records are synchronised and a detailed appraisal is done, that the precessional model straddles areas that were not previously accounted for. So it would not be a wonder then if people from all over the world are discovered to be tributaries to an even vaster repository of knowledge about the past, especially a pragmatic application like precessional science modelling. The turning point will be when more research is enabled in places like South Africa where as much space is granted to enthusiasts, other coincidental discoveries and theories, as it has been for long in places currently known as developed countries. This ties in to the sentiments that colonial periods were not good for the repositories and stored artefacts that were supposed to inform future generations, as it was proven that in South America the colonial mission destroyed the records for posterity never to know of again. Could colonialism have interfered with the precessional model in terms of depriving the entire research enterprise of information that was supposed to remain in situ for future generations to find and to interpret? This is highly possible. One has to look at the arguments advanced in Graham's book to see that this is possible.

Our own attempt at ensconcing our opinion in the topic is just that, a lay perspective. Who says that the digital divide cannot be broken as far as matters like these are concerned. Also as we can see, this branch of science is restricted to practitioners and other casual enthusiasts and does not mean that people in general would be inclined to the specific science at all. *The Johannesburg Formula* is a theoretic bid that may be deposed by more incisive tenders. With all due respect the learning opportunity that found in *Fingerprints of the Gods* makes it impossible for one to walk away without questions. *Fingerprints of the Gods* neatly achieves an objective of knowledge transfer, something that is taken seriously in South Africa. For instance being able to ask the question of whether precession can have an effect on the reading of calendar dates is something that we never imagined would come from the Mayan question. In other words the fact of precession could also be responsible for calendars being out of tally and some being reliable. For instance a long-count calendar could calculate days when the sphere was near perfectly round. This could happen without distinguishing the effects of an oblate planetary sphere on accurate and corresponding calendar values. This also raises the question of the science of calendars at all for the purpose of predicting dates. Firstly, the fact that calendars are such a contentious issue that it was necessary for the Julian calendar to be replaced with the Gregorian calendar is a case in point. Also the fact that there exists through-out the world many calendars that are relevant to the practices of these several cultures is a moot point.

The accuracy of calendars could be something that is influenced by the physical change in the shape and structure of the earth and we would not know. We are looking at tangible physical evidence to deduce theories about the past and in the mean-time a lot of changes that we cannot see with eyes may be taking place. The Mayan calendar can especially be difficult to read relevantly because of such a long-period of time that it traverses. That is why *prophecies* insist on warning us that the end-times will come like a *thief in the night*. This is because in as much as we know the earth from our perspective, we are not sure how it comes about that the issue of the length of the solar year has been so complex as to attribute a specific measurement to, even after the Gregorian calendar proved to be more accurate than the Julian calendar in this regard. This did not completely make the Julian calendar redundant as many cultures and practitioners still observe it till today. This does not mean that we should stop research into the exact meaning of messages from the past as closely as it is possible.

What all this shows is that it might not even come down to calendar dates but visible environmental signs to determine a moment when things might come undone. We might not even have to forecast a determinable date in order to reckon with the precessional period when our planet shows non-returnable signs of cataclysm. Already people will be sceptical because the 21st December 2012 date was an ordinary day. What we have to look at more than dates might be physical signs. We have to ask questions about the asteroid that showed up above the Russian skies in February 2013. Throughout all this speculation we know that we don't know enough about the planetary environment and the machinations to be complacent. Maybe the Mayans are pointing us in a direction to look for signs of cataclysm. We also cannot have a situation where there is no controlled scientific research into this matter. The work started by Graham's research report is a good start and we have to be inquisitive about what is going on around us. We can't say that just because the 21st December 2012 was another day in the planets routine, we should abandon all concern. We are dealing with a planetary eventuality and we must invest time and resources into discovering its internal message about how it behaves in total.

 It is only fair to admit to the readers that it is impossible to know what day a full-blown cataclysm level incursion might happen because we are dealing with calculations that are based on shifting posts. It is however enough to say being alert and aware is also important. The Johannesburg Formula should be about acknowledging that it is impossible even for a sophisticated ancient civilization like the Mayans to say… "here is the date". It is more about saying the issue is not negligible as we know that most of the data from the scientific community is visible. *The Johannesburg Formula* rightfully proves that calculating a specific date is impossible and the reasons are such and such. The reader remembers that *Fingerprints of the Gods* was first published in 1995, so this tells us that Graham is experienced and we cannot imagine what has gone on in between up to now in his research. He could have discovered other facts to support his initial thesis. This makes Graham an authority on the subject when most people only heard about this information recently.  This also shows how long it took before his work could explode to a critical mass where in South Africa millions were exposed to the topic in December 2012 via the media. He is not alone and many others lurk in the shadows of undiscovered hallways of knowledge littered with people who have been aware of some changes in our environment and times.

From what we hear, the 1960s were about mass consciousness and enlightenment where the public and the young people of then, especially, were exposed *en masse* to a resurgence of ideas and information about liberty and freedom. This was the beginning of the state that the world is in today where there are more people than ever recorded who are privy to information that would have stayed on the shelves of unknown museums and libraries. The period from 1995 to 2012 shows the critical turning point in access to information. In 1995 it was probably a handful of people who could talk about the Mayan calendar in the open without being labelled as peripheral. It has taken roughly 20 years for the information to be broad-based and who knows how long it will take for it to be interpreted and reacted on. Anyone who reads *The Johannesburg Formula* would be exempted if they exclaimed that we sounded like the typical arm-chair tourist and that we cannot compare ourselves to real Mayan technicians like Graham Hancock. I have never been anywhere near South America, Egypt or outside of South Africa for that matter... but that has never stopped me from ensconcing myself into the topic, even into *Fingerprints of the Gods*. Why not, I have been interested in similar topics for as long as enough. There is no definite point beyond 1992 that I can say I wasn't exposed to even the bare minimum of this kind of literary environment even picking it up by ear or sight. I have developed through the years to be passionate about this genre and I will not be jeered off as another armchair experiential. Graham's book is picturesque and no matter how unwilling I could have been, I was 'transported' to the locations that he describes. He writes excellently with the ability to teleport even an armchair experientialist to his destinies.

In all fairness there are prophecies or books from the past that speak about the end-times in allegories and not so much in scientific terminology such as referring to the period as the end of an epoch. These records are just as valid even if veiled in mythology and metaphors. They might prove to trounce the scientific approach in highlighting the predicament of the end-times. The issue is that these texts are part of faith practices that not everyone may subscribe to and so they are relegated for the sake of expressing preferential faith practice. We may even find that these metaphors and allegories have a lot more than scientific accounts do, to describe what is meant to happen. Naturally these sources from faith books are generally not looked to as empirical knowledge and we may find that they are called for only after the fact, when their message has been ignored. Anyone can pick a faith-book of their liking that tells of the past and encourages the reader to be modest in life. These books also speak of end-times. Today's generation is even more advantaged than the one of the 1960s. There is an almost infinite amount of information on the internet that is easily searched as a topic.

Even the most untraveled and countrified of us have heard something about the end-times story. Reading a book like *Fingerprints of the Gods* does not make one less like Graham who brings the sights and sounds from the actual locations through being well travelled. It is also a matter of other un-prescribed circumstances that have given others the fortune to be applied experientialist.

The point is that we quickly dismiss credibility or authenticity from a heedless vantage and this will not help the efforts of dissemination. For instance what will anyone say who has to consider that Graham had to travel to South America and Egypt in order to come about and verify the resourcefulness and account of the precessional model. The locations and the people he encountered may not have travelled, but he found it worth a while to go to them. It figures that being untraveled does not mean one is un-resourceful. This illustrates a point about credibility and authenticity that we have to look at all angles and role-players to arrive at conclusions. This talks to the entire enterprise and psychology of the end-times story. I am making this point against the backdrop of how incredible this story of end-times comes across as.

Here's looking at chapter 49, the subheading titled: *The cult.* The conversation highlights something that sounds as if it is possible that there could have been a society of stonemasons that dedicated all their lives to warning future generations about the effects of precession. If what you and Robert Bauval talk about is true for instance, then it means that although the edifices prove that they may have been built over thousands of years by two similar scientific-gnostic traditions, then their whole culture was premised on communicating the precession message to the future and that this is what they lived for. There is a strong possibility that the learning culture in the ancient world was based on determining precessional events rather than developing a local science for mere day to day survival. Civilization would then be premised on precession as the main concern, a basis for scientific development and the building up of civilization.

Maybe their ultimate vision was to build a civilization that would be cataclysm proof, in other words they aspired to building a civilization that could enable any generation to survive any cataclysm.

We would have to ask then if our generation is ready for such an eventuality or indeed if we were able to receive this scientific precession conscious knowledge into the present. This knowledge seems to be cyclical and our own generation is probably supposed to have been able to pass this information into our own future. What if we are supposed to have been able to transmit precessional science into a future, let us say 10 000 years from now and code this science in such a way that in that time that generation should also do likewise. We have to be able to put ourselves in the position of those communities of 10 000 years ago. We would then have to see what they did for our benefit and should be able to do the same for a generation 10 000 years from now. This means that precessional science should be taught at places of learning. There is no denying that the world is a complex environment and that we would not have survived without the thoughtfulness of past generations who were apparently fascinated with warning and educating ours about epoch reality.

So I agree that the world-wide myths and technical allegory could have been designed to transcend across time. Your interaction and assertions with Robert Bauval open a new line of inquiry. How does this assertion that the orthodox developmental and civilization trajectory is reversed, tally up with the findings at Mapungubwe and Monomotapa in Zimbabwe? Could the *Fingerprints of the Gods* be giving our generation a credible license to intimate that these sites could be residuals of a high civilization? We have been taught that these initial civilizations are precedents that ushered in modern times. Is it possible that our modern civilization that learned everything from the past is the one that shows to have declined from a high calibre? Chapter 49 is indeed a turning point in cracking the cryptex of how history was told, as a forerunner to modern times rather than a declined stage from a highly scientific antiquated civilization. Your book Sir, takes no prisoners and leaves no stones unturned. If the world was asked to bring out their own peculiar precessional evidence out to your house, all the rooms would be stacked up from floor to ceiling and your hard-drive would be crashed by the submissions. I am convinced that what Robert Bauval says in chapter 49 is true: he says…"… *everybody who can bring a fresh eye and fresh skills to bear on these very important problems should be encouraged to do so"*. When it comes to the subject of precession, I notice that it is not an exclusive terrain for highly educated people only, even a country-side grown individual could tell you a story from a cultural perspective that you would realise to be linked to this model. Enough has still to be done to realise the intrinsically universal nature of the source of this story. It is like these antiquated scientific-gnostics knew to conceal the message in the meanest of places so that it does not desiccate due to tendencies of decline.

The story and knowledge of end-times or epochs is probably well preserved as an heirloom amongst the unsuspected peoples of developing countries. Graham's book is an entrée. Out of this entire book, chapter 49 is a showstopper, it is the substance of the psychology of epochology, the long-count behavioural monitor and the long-count psychometric monitor that we believe the ancients had. Robert Bauval and Graham Hancock reveal something intrinsic about life, that it is a series of self-generating questions and answers. They validate the theory of a long-count psychometric monitor that could not be overtly transmitted to the future. It is something that comes out of venturing into the discipline. So this means that all of human civilization is triggered by precessional awareness and knowledge. All developments in any civilization are intrinsically an episode of 'epoch-watch'.

As if by synchronicity, chapter 50 is a picture of the initial round of all the work I would have to do to further lavish the *near round shape theory*. I have no such structure to support the necessary field work required to mount formative research, that could one day prove this theory to be correct. As if I was not impressed enough by chapter 49, chapter 50 is a beginner's marvel because there it is, just what I needed to give credulity to the theory that once in every cyclical period, the earth is a near perfect rounded orb that 'changes' shape into an *oblate spheroid*. The second read of *Fingerprints of the Gods* has proven to be phenomenal as I see more clearly what this whole book is about. Chapter 50 is music to my ears because Graham supplies the theory of a near perfect rounded earth with perspective. This now inevitably makes *The Johannesburg Formula* a gateway issue to *Fingerprints of the Gods*. In chapter 50 Graham is looking for a lost continent that disappeared with a process of earth crust displacement, a process where continents are propelled vice versa from the equator to the poles and the other way round in a cyclical time period. Information is not always useful to everyone all the time. There is functional information and there is information that is reserved for purposes when the need arises. Stating that the earth has a period when it is near perfect round is useful in this regard to support the theory of precession.

Along chapter 51, the penny dropped, it became clear to me that the reason that the theory of *earth-crust displacement* seems or seemed incredible is because we were looking at an *oblate* shaped earth. It does seem to me that the *earth-crust displacement theory* is viable only and if only the *near round earth theory* is viable. *Earth-crust displacement* is not an erratic process, it follows on the earth's core being charged by microwave energy to full capacity, the earth regaining its near perfect rounded shape and the process starting over again either in correlation with every 15 000 years, 26 000 years, 100 000 thousand years or longer. We also have to accept the real notion about epochology, that we won't know a lot, about some of the stuff that takes place because no-one has lived over the entirety of an epoch to witness and know without doubt what corresponds with what. At the moment we are working with pieces of disparate puzzles that come from all over the world and it will take time to see a whole picture which is only visible over an entire duration of an epoch, however long that is...

Chapter 51 of *Fingerprints of the Gods* is the most surreal, it speaks of unimaginable realities and antiquated allure. Graham reveals that his research proves with no doubt that the Antarctic was at some point ice-free. The implications of this fact on the *round earth theory* are overwhelming because it throws our known academic assumptions into another zone of the unknown. Scientific knowledge is thrown into a zone of *believe it or not* as everything proves to be transitory and not permanent data. In other words the laws of physical science could be contrary to the reality of the period when the poles were ice-free. Everything becomes transitory because reality could just be a product of shape, the shape of the earth! If *Fingerprints of the Gods* was a swimming pool, then chapter 51 would be the deepest end. Any unsolvable question arises from interacting with chapter 51. Does glaciation need a landmass above sea–level to occur? Could glaciation occur below sea-level? Answers to these questions will inform the thesis of a round-earth theory as far as reinforcing the fact that friction or the increased amount thereof has some great deal to do with glaciation at the poles, even at specified periods.

A point that quickly becomes clear is that the ancient civilizations knew more than we do about planet earth. They knew everything that modern man knows and more. They could have witnessed another state-of-the-planet, either through records or had a glimpse of a totally variant physical reality than what prevails in our records and known reality. This could have implications on everything. For instance the age of space travel could very well be dependent on the speed of the planet's orbit and therefore its absolute shape. If I was a judicial officer to whom evidence was being submitted as it is in *Fingerprints of the Gods*, I would have passed a unanimous verdict by chapter 51, to the effect that we need a moratorium to review our state-of-reality, period.

Everything known about the earth's planetary behaviour including; *obliquity, orbital eccentricity, the earth's centrifugal motion and the effect of the sun's gravitational tug, that of the moon and planets*...is totally reinvented by the round-earth theory and the derivative approach to the laws of physics. Thanks to the book *Fingerprint Of The Gods*, it could be common cause that science is advancing in ways still not allowed through the classroom at a cost and risk to global tenure.

In subheading: *The icy executioner*, Graham illustrates that a colleague, Hugh Auchinloss Brown wrote about concerns for the ever increasing mass of the South Pole ice-cap. We have forever presumed that the increase is due to the pole becoming colder, which is also true. Have we ever imagined that this could be because of increasing friction due to increasing speed of rotation at the axis? We have all heard of how people often comment about how time seems to be moving faster...could the increasing ice-cap be a result of the earth increasing its speed of rotation at the axis, due to a constant change of the shape of the planet resulting from mass and momentum? The trick is that we will never deduce the mixed effect of differentiation in rotation at the axis and orbit around the sun, this double-bogey needs a considered approach to even calculate. Yes with due regard we acknowledge that this is a veteran's game. We may not be qualified to answer these questions but we are definitely not disqualified from asking questions. Imagine a Ferris wheel with swivelling passenger cars, totally nauseating and disorienting right? No wonder we don't think about what is happening when the planet orbits and rotates at the axis everyday, we would have a headache everyday! The thought of it alone is enough of a headache. This is exactly what is happening. Have we ever thought or imagined that all planets are habitable and that this is only determined by speed of axial-rotation and orbit that may vary from time to time of periods of thousands of years. What if the planets in our solar system that we observe as inhospitable are just transiting from some oblate shaped planet to a round planet and vice-versa. This means that sentient microbes are absent because of extreme conditions resulting from the determination of shape and speed. Could life forms resume once a period of shape distortion passes through in time? What if the earth itself is susceptible to periods when it is totally sterile while transiting through some unimaginable state of near-perfect round planet to a *distorted or warped* oblate shape that is conducive for elements to thrive because of variations of heat retention and thermodynamics that initiate habitability for microbes? What is the use of even arguing because this could be some unobservable but imaginable realm of reality. So is perception limited only to observation or can imagination form a part of reality? This is important to ask especially in view of the strict discipline of academic science and the reality of the unknown.

The question of whether *continental drift and earth-crust displacement* are not one and the same thing is also subject to change. The pendulum of continental drift and the hammer of earth-crust displacement are one instrument, a pendulum mounted on a hammer. Earth-crust displacement and continental drift are various sequential features of the same process that happens to take time over vast periods of time, longer than we can observe and record, so it is something out of the scope of knowledge but some logical deduction in the realm of the unknown.

What we may also come to find about precession is that it is a systematic process that is multi-factored and sequential. Any one of the "known" cosmic or geodesic cataclysmic events are not random. For instance the round-oblate dichotomy insinuates this fact strongly. The earth in the initial period when fully charged and round, is susceptible to geodesic cataclysm triggered by specific cosmic influence. This is when earth-crust displacement is frequent. Once the oblate shape has set in probably over a 100 000 years, then the nature of the cataclysm might change being characterised by earthquakes, that indicate lithospheric resistance due to the tugging and snagging effects of an oblate shaped earth.

The eight edition of the Pocket Oxford Dictionary identifies *volcanic action and convulsion of the earth's surface as a result of faults in the strata* as the only causes of earthquakes. We would venture to throw the oblate-round dichotomy thesis that stipulates the snagging of the lithosphere on the oblate shape of the earth as the primary cause, into the causality mix. The dictionary definition is in our view a secondary attribute of the causes. Shape is the primary cause and this leads to short term causes that include what is defined in the dictionary. The dictionary definition mentions faults in the strata as the cause of an earthquake without specifying whether these are vertical faults or not, and this is probably the case. When we look at this assertion, it seems that faults in the strata and volcanoes are secondary causes of earthquakes. We leave this at the door of the *oblate snag of the lithosphere* theory as a primary cause.

For the subject of epochology, earthquakes and other similar environmental occurrences, are indicators. Earthquakes indicate the primary geological reality of an oblate planet offering resistance to the lithosphere when it moves in a process described as *displacement.* Whenever there is an earthquake we know the area of the lithosphere that is snagging and we should be able to identify the direction of displacement. With modelling of the previous two or three earthquakes, we should be able to ascertain a pattern and map the probabilities of the next, in terms of time and area of occurrence.

On the other hand, polar shifts are more probable with a rounded earth, because a full-blown earth-crust displacement is possible. We can then see from the numeration of the cataclysm category events, cataclysm tributaries, and short-term geodetic eruptions that there is a sequence and map of what is likely to happen given the time in the period of the super-epoch (a time-frame of 100 000 years), the earth is in. For example a global deluge is a feature of the early times of a round-earth because centrifugal heat energy is equally distributed along the entire surface of the globe. A microwave influx resulting in a combustible atmosphere is likely in an oblate-earth period because the lithosphere is offering resistance as it grapples the earth's shape and this is a possible scenario characterised by a frequency of earthquakes. Polar glaciation begins to occur at a time between the late periods of a round-earth and the second half of a super-epoch because this indicates resistance at the axis and the need for the earth to cool the high temperatures at the poles due to an increase in friction offered by an oblate earth-shape.

It is obvious that geology as a science has also not isolated the logic of causality of the observable geodetic events that may be classified as cataclysmic. What the round-oblate dichotomy does is to draw a rational picture of typical characteristics. It illustrates the sequence and predictability of the characteristics of the cataclysmic events at a moment of the precessional cycle. The round-earth has its own features, characteristic and events, and so does the oblate-earth. Of course the cataclysmic incursion is not isolated from the cause of the attendant cosmic and geodetic triggers. According to the dictionary, the study of the shape of the earth is known as *geodesy*. What the round-oblate dichotomy is thus the study of the effect of *geodesy* at any time. *Geodesy* is central to the effects that we observe. For instance, why would a cataclysm at a certain period be of a nature of a deluge and at another be a microwave influx characterised by a combustible atmosphere?

In chapter 52, to answer Graham's question in subheading: *An urgent mission*, about *recondite influences of gravity, the precessional wobble, the effects of axial rotation and the growing mass of the Antarctic icecap*, I would say that the oblate-round dichotomy is a clue. We can see from the round-oblate dichotomy that *earth-crust displacement* is dependent on shape. So at this point when the planet is already heavily oblate as shown by the difference in the polar and equatorial radiuses, a full-scale crustal displacement can be ruled out, unless the snag breaks due to mounting force. Heavy earthquakes however can be factored in. What we are looking at is a combustible atmosphere caused by the periodical charging of the earth's core after the long super-season of a lithosphere displacement resistant oblate earth shape that we are currently on. The argument also shows that a number of characteristic cataclysmic category outbreaks may occur simultaneously given the transitional position over the super-epoch period. This could also account for why there are planets that exist in the solar system that seem to be totally uninhabitable.

The subheading: *Walking in the last days*, when Graham recounts chapter 24 and reminds the reader of the assertions of the Hopi (from Arizona, America) and their account of how the first, second, third and fourth worlds had ended, is a sure precedent for the round-oblate dichotomy and theory. This science of the Hopi proves The Johannesburg Formula's round-earth theory without doubt by showing the different types of categories of global cataclysms. In fact the Hopi's assertions show us that there exists a 'super-super-cycle' where this sequence rolls out and restarts again. We can intimate from how the first world ended that it was oblate when the cataclysm took place. The second world was extremely oblate when the cataclysm took place and the third world was round when the cataclysm took place. We see from the Hopi account that in sequence, a combustible atmosphere is followed by ice, that is then followed by a deluge. This is a super-epoch cataclysm cycle that is defined by characteristic geodesy. So it is safe to say that a super-epoch is characterised by this sequence of cataclysm categories that take place over a cyclical period of 100 000 years or so, with an intermittent smaller category of earth interruptions.

What we can also see from the February 2013 asteroid is that there are numerous characteristics of cataclysm that are time specific, because the earth is moving along a path of orbit. So the asteroid could have been limited to a time of the year because the earth is in orbit. It is possible also that the direction from where the asteroid came is a factor as well as the proximity of the course that intercepts the orbital path of the earth.

The date was 15th February 2013 when the asteroid struck over Russia. Coincidentally this was a marker of a truly big cosmic event, according to astronomers, the Age of Pisces was giving way to the Age of Aquarius. Is it a coincidence that the asteroid breached the atmosphere within the solar month of Aquarius, at the beginning of the Age of Aquarius? This tells us one thing that the asteroid was coming from the direction in the celestial sphere of the position of the solar Aquarian constellation. Could this mean that the next February of 2014 another asteroid is coming from the same direction that the February 2013 came from? We have to watch this space carefully.

Finally as a matter of statement we see that it is possible to intimate that precession is caused by speed and momentum, both functions of the shape and mass of a planet. The conditions that we observe on other planets, of near or complete sterility could very well be a result of precession. One inference that we can make without being shy of scientific credulity, is that whatever happens to planet earth on a cosmic scale also happens to the other planets in the same solar system. The big question is that outside of the effects of precession, what causes precession? As a matter of balance, we do not know everything, this the opportunity cost for the way our modern civilization is forged. Science still has many rivers to cross and a long way to traverse as an expression of accomplishment.

Many proverbs, idioms, mythologies etc, all "hide" essential messages to the future, for the purpose of transmitting keys to any extra-ordinary future challenges or circumstances, this generation ordinarily would never have been prepared to encounter. According to information online, other sources elsewhere, art, mythology and astrology, all coincide as cryptic transmission devices of data that should be useful to encounter unusual circumstances.

# CHAPTER SIX

## THE EARTH WAS ROUND

**N**obody will know until it is irrefutable, it is possible that there are moments when the poles are completely ice-free due to an equal distribution of heat energy from the core. This gets disrupted once a cycle matures and the shape warps into an oblate spheroid. Also, because *precessional science* is marginalised, it is easier for pundits to dabble, as in our case...

It seems to be an appealing reality that the equator is bulging and the climate is temperate only because of the dynamics of distributed heat energy from the core. There are two possibilities of what happens due to the oblate shape of the earth. Because the poles are spinning, the heat tends away and the poles generate additional heat from rotational friction. Ironically even though the poles are closer to the core of the earth than the equator, there is less microwave energy from the core that reaches the poles. This bias is attributable to the function of the poles as the axis. It is also possible that once the axis over-heat from frictional energy, the natural mechanism is for ice to build-up through high evaporation and condensation to counter the prospects of mechanical over-heating. The other possibility is that heat will reach the poles because of the shorter radius at the poles to the radius at the equator only after the earth has bulged at the equator through internal displacement. It is possible to conclude that the earth-crust does displace every so often in epochs, after a beginning of some (or one of the) multi-millennial cycles. Our contention is that only a *near perfect round earth* is susceptible to *earth-crust displacement*.

Another factor to consider is that when the *earth-crust displacement* theory is applied or is indeed taking place, we cannot rely on cardinal points and bearing that result from observing longitude and latitude. Longitude and latitude become displaced as points of reference. The rationale of perfect latitude and longitude cannot apply because displacement of the lithosphere may occur or take place diagonally instead of perfectly horizontally or vertically. Bearing based on longitude and latitude is completely thrown out of kilter. Displacement cannot be a neatly organised model that we conceptualise vertically or horizontally because this would rule out the possibility of the real situation, that of the shape of the earth being oblate. An oblate structure would not allow the mechanism of crust-displacement. A comparative example would be of a rugby ball as opposed to a soccer ball. A tight fitting sock on a rugby ball is almost impossible to slide over the surface whereas a soccer-ball is easier for a fitting sock to slide over the surface of. The long ends of an oblate-shaped earth would simply tug at the lithosphere and prevent displacement. Displacement is a cyclical mechanism that follows the condition of the earth being in a newly formed rounded shape. We know that we are not in one of those periods because the earth is *oblate* at the moment and displacement would happen after a rounded shape has formed.

The rounded shape can only be a result of the pressure of microwaves being equally distributed as if almost like in an fully inflated soccer-ball, that then gets left in the sun for days and weeks until it losses the round shape and warps into an oblate shape. Could the shape of the earth determine the nature of psychology of the inhabitants? Could a rounded earth be the making of a *"forgotten"* Eden? Could the warping over time impact on the psychology of inhabitants? Prophecy speaks of a time when wild animals and domesticated animals are congenial. Mythology speaks of *flying cows,* and this 'impossible' scene has filtered into language. These idioms could be lingering residuals of real aspects of the length and entire period of an epoch. It could be that the gravitational pull at the core is different when the earth is near perfect round and that it is in fact mechanically possible for this scenario, for a cow to appear to 'fly *over the moon'.* Could a near rounded earth expel so much force from the core that it is possible for mass to be lifted from the ground defying gravitational forces characteristic of an oblate shaped earth?

A near-perfectly rounded shaped earth would behave differently to an oblate shaped earth in relation to other planets in the solar system. What about speed? A rounded shaped earth would move slower than a warped oblate shaped earth orb. This informs us that the shape of the earth determines its speed at all times. The speed of the earth influences the perceived length of days. Could this mean that when the earth is moving slower around its orbit it is essentially a recipe for longer days and therefore exposure to more sunlight? Could this account for the period when the earth's surface was an impenetrable subtropical and tropical cluster? As for the oblate earth at present, the shape impacts on the speed. The earth could be moving fast around its orbit because an oblate shape is a dream of aerodynamic mechanics. There is a basis for a comparative analysis of the oblate earth shape and the near perfectly rounded earth shape, in terms of behaviour, and outcomes in view of the precessional theory. It is clear that the conditions on the planet are never uniform and that this is influenced by different parts of an epoch. Maybe the long-count calendar was influenced by this reality of different conditions along a length of an entire epoch. It does not rule out the possibility that the long-count was designed after a drastic change in the conditions of the surface of the earth and that these cultures wanted to record conditions at two ends of an epoch. The *oblate earth period* and the *round shaped earth period*.

Another time span made of epochs exists where at one time the earth is near perfectly rounded and then it warps into an oblate only to become reformed into a near perfectly rounded orb again after the passage of this elaborate cycle. All these periods would account for the several characteristics described by the several myths around cataclysmic occurrences. Why were the ancient civilizations able to count hundreds of thousands of years on their calendars? We have to tabulate the oblate and the rounded periods and look into these features and this could very well explain some of the unknown anomalies experienced at different ends of the super-epoch (maybe a period of 100 000 years). What is known at the moment is made of relics that survived long periods of human civilizations that were known to have been built against all odds. If we knew enough about the planet, then we would not be sitting-ducks for any cataclysm. We would have known of the Mayan calendar and developed a cataclysm ready civilization to beat the odds. At the moment we are still in the shallow end of the epochology pool. The trail to follow in order to figure out what is happening is to look at existing architecture that is 10 000 years and older, that is stronger and more resilient than our modern state-of-the-art that is big on aesthetics. This tells us that we have not reached a state in functional design that speaks to consciousness of the attending effects of precession. The people at the beginning of this epoch however seem to have been thoroughly aware of the attendant effects of precession and were more astute at epochology than we are presently. Our generation still needs to unravel a long view picture of the times we are in. We need also to know how we got to be where we are and forge ahead with questions and answers. It is time for questions and answers, big time. Question: Since when in recent times does a year start-off with an asteroid pelting down on a town in the northern hemisphere, on this planet? For now, epochology is essentially a festival of questions because these are the founding inquiries into what might be an interdependent science.

Could the oblate/round dichotomy hold keys to answers about the chemical composition of the elements of the earth?

For instance it is entirely possible that the salt in the sea is absolutely not present in a round earth. Evolution could be as a result of the interchange between the round and oblate periods of the earth.

Evolution may only be explained through the oblate-round-oblate-round earth reality. Why did countless species go extinct and others reappear having a totally different genome and DNA type? The microwaves during a round and an oblate earth differ radically leading to extreme changes in DNA configuration.

It could be possible that the mind being induced to remember conditions of the round earth period is what led to the miracles that the Christ performed. It is an accepted fact that he walked on water, maybe he could lucidly remember the conditions of the last time the earth was perfectly round and his life is a reminder of this potential fact. Maybe the Edenic memory is a memory of a time period when the earth was perfectly round. Could perfection as a state of mind be achievable during a round earth? Could space travel be easier due to the magnetism of a round earth? Maybe the so called myths are real accounts of a round earth period when space faring is a way of life, also because the earth's magnetism is reversed. An oblate earth is probably the only cause of the centrifugal force of gravity. A round earth would not have a centrifugal force of gravity but instead would enable anti-gravity flight. Maybe habitability is influenced by either of the shapes.

The chemistry in any sentient organism is also an issue of round or oblate shape conditions. Has anyone heard of people living for several hundreds of years? In the bible there are accounts of people having lived for a few hundred years.

Maybe this is a result of a DNA switch that enables a psychological reversion or propulsion to a memory of a round earth. If there was a round earth about to unfold with an initial process of a so called cataclysm, there would be some lingering anticipation in microwave susceptible DNA memory that anticipates this. Would we actually see so called anomalous behavioural characteristics like most of the scenes depicted in the book of Revelations? DNA research has been one of the biggest breakthroughs in the 21st century to prove and solve cases in the justice and enforcement sector, that were impossible before this discovery.

The question is whether DNA testing will be the technology that enables us to solve the mysteries of evolution. We may find out why species disappear and go extinct, why species suddenly appear that were allegedly not there before. We will know why some species are earth environment specific, in other words why some fly through the air and why some swim in water, why some are terrestrial bound and why some do neither. We might find causes in the bandwidth of the DNA induced spectrum of behaviour and characteristics that we see along the various species. DNA testing could reveal isotopes that bear microwave markers that show us that the environment that an element evolved through is from a period of this atmospheric pressure or that atmospheric pressure. Since DNA may conduct microwave EMF, it could be possible to determine some of the claims of the round-oblate dichotomy theory. We reckon that any flying species may have a latent DNA memory from a round earth period and that the earth bound species are susceptible to the *oblate earth period's* atmospheric pressure and DNA condition.

Our quest is to ultimately find out if there is any anomalous disjuncture between the logical DNA map over a 100 000 year period that does not make sense. To find out if there are breaks between periods that have been characterised by cataclysm and see if the DNA logic has remained the same.

What we are looking to find is the possibility of there being a difference between DNA that is exposed to conditions of a near perfect round earth and the DNA map of a generation of an oblate shaped earth, in microbes. This is in line with finding out whether atmospheric pressure, thermodynamics and planet rotational speed have an impact on the biological map of a species. Maybe comparative analysis between birds, fish and mammals would be a key into finding out any exotic differentials that may be a result of exposure to either round-oblate earth conditions. DNA is probably the vehicle for the later assimilation and adaptation to earth's transient conditions. The creation story in faith books and accounts is indisputable, it is the key to discovery of inalienable truth. I would not easily dispute the creation story of how the earth was formed. The creation story tells us that the Creator commanded the elements to form fish, birds, land animals and humans. There is a lot of enlightenment right there. On the other hand there is the story of evolution, where fossils from millions of years ago have been found and are displayed all over the world.

The theory of evolution and the story of creation, of how it was formed are complementary accounts that reveal a clear picture. Birds fly, fish swim, this is astounding, because these sentient beings have a lot in common. They do one thing very well, that is to live and adopt to the environment. It is worth it to discover what picture of the adaptation process would reveal if we slowed the reel down and looked at everything in slow motion. Would we see clear proof of the precession theory that resonates with the oblate-round dichotomy theory? Did birds fly as a form of adopting to an earth that was going through a cataclysm and stayed in the air to survive? Did fish go into the water to escape a land surface that was erupting with fiery chasms? The same book that speaks and describes how the earth was formed also describes cataclysm, as in the story of Noah who built the ark to keep all life in there until the flood subsided. The precessional story makes these questions feasible not as a simplicity but a matter of tracing how things mostly happened. It is an interest to find out what evolution theorists may say about the questions posed here.

At this rate we have to ask ourselves what else is influenced by the round-oblate dichotomy. Is everything and reality influenced by this dichotomy. Everything that we know to be impossible according the laws of nature could only be applicable specifically to an oblate earth. It is possible that a totally new union of immutable laws of nature turn out to be a whole new kettle of fish on a round earth, for the duration of that period. What certifies this reality is the fact that there seems to be a concealed realism that could be based on the time period for operation. For instance according to astrophysics, there are dimensions that we are not privy to in our ordinary course of reality. Like what? Take anti-matter for instance! All matter is influenced by microwaves of several kinds of energy that seem to be diversified by an oblate earth. When the several areas of the spectral band act in unison, a lot of the laws of nature could present another picture. This is the substance of a round earth. Many cultures and their mythologies speak of an "enchanted" reality as being a distant memory that was successfully bequeathed to the future as a story from a distant and forgotten past.

This is when the well hidden truths about the fact that we know little about this planet come jumping out of the closet. We are products of our environment and this should reflect in the way that we think. Had we known effectively about precession and been taught to think in these terms, our solutions, technologies and built up environment would have reflected this. Like the builders of ancient Egypt, Mexico and other similar places, we should have developed a way of life that is ingrained into precessional thinking. Not the thinking that an asteroid can be shot out of the sky with a nuclear missile that was originally conceived as a weapon to be deployed in fights amongst inhabitants of the planet. The strange retort that is at the back of our subconscious is that there does seem to be a latent consciousness about defending the planet against anomalous planetary behaviour. I once saw a film called *The Core* with a plot that seemed far-fetched but entertaining, only to discover later when learning of the *earth-crust displacement* theory, that this is in-fact a reflection on a latent reality that is explored as a fiction film genre. Maybe all of Hollywood film-makers should be questioned to find out whether they know something that we all don't know about the anomalous nature of planetary life. An adult film called *Supernova* (again last seen a while ago, so I recall faintly what struck me the most), opens up with a narrative that settles grown-ups into being comfortable about cartoons as expressions of anthropological phenomenon, that expose a latent reality about the planetary environment.

I agree with what Graham Hancock says in *Fingerprints of the Gods* when he talks about Robert Bauval's assertion that a polymath approach is needed to decipher what is going on in the planetary environment. Is it not strange that the cartoon and fiction genres do a vastly great job at informing the public about anomalous realities than do other premises for the mostly adult audience? Again many mythologies ride this under-current of urban mythology that is excellently depicted in cartoons and science-fiction... this is bizarre. My only comfort when I get a strange gawk while watching some cartoons is the knowledge that these are written and produced by adults, so I am not fazed. I have watched cartoons that made me wonder who the real audience is, for these high-voltage content adventures. Just explore one of the current science-fiction based cartoons and tell me if the language in there is meant for primary learners. Or is it a case of some unspoken agenda to prepare children for an inevitable moment that will require them to recall the super-hero plots of their childhood fascination and jump into action with a space age mentality? Besides most people know that what was relegated to the zone of fiction decades and even centuries ago, is today in the realm of well-practiced science that has led to astonishing technological developments. Is this how the human mind is programmed to work? Are we first supposed to imagine the impossible until sometime later, when time has gone and the brain has by some quirk internalised well-stored fictitious ideas, then churn it all out as a scientific possibility and an eventual reality?

This would be a psychological probe that would have to be given a platform in order to verify the workings of the unknown features of the human thinking process. If this were to be discovered as true, then it would follow that exposure to the pyramids would lead our generation to trump the civilization of the ancient Egyptians in the way the state-of-the-art is conceptualised. This could even mean that the ancients left us psychological triggers that would eventually lead to the way we think and design our own modern world to be cataclysm-proof. Also that would make us realise that we are in line and have to bequeath a cataclysm monitoring technology to the future.

The challenge is that this technology, what-ever its form would have to survive cataclysm in order to be recovered and deciphered by a generation of cataclysm survivors. This is how the mind and psychology of pyramid building societies was formatted on and thanks to them we know today that cataclysm is part of planetary tenure. Are we to believe that there is such a thing as a cataclysm monitoring technology? Well, this is what all this *strange* anthropological evidence is revealing. Could the *book of Revelations*

116

be one of these literary and oral devices, a cataclysm warning device? Could psychology hold the key into the survival of cataclysmic periods?

Well, the not so strange psychological environment, the human mind could be the place where all the knowledge about cataclysm is stored. In the same way that DNA stores linear data about the chemical characteristics of organs and the body at large, so the mind could be a residual programme and data hub about the far-off past. Could *"thinking"* also be a process of extricating and harnessing a latent mind of the past. People as a species are able to externalise the *"thinking"* process and express thought onto the environment in data various formats.

We often *"think"* of technology as electronic devices, and we all know the materials that technology is often made of is challenged in terms of durability. Also, how do you transmit technology that you know would be destroyed by the vagaries of environmental conditions, to a remote future successfully? Graham has already shown us in his book, through an *intelligent design of mythology* that can be passed on through word of mouth and some degree of rites. This we figured to be the imperishable treasure in books from *the Bible* and similar older texts. Knowledge is more enduring than devices made from any electronic equipment as a medium of passing-on an incorporeal technology. So was knowledge one of the greatest inventions from the past, that could be used as a medium to transmit reality to the future, even about cataclysm as a focus? Knowledge is not only what it is made to be, it is also an ubiquitous currency that is found in the most strangest and unthinkable of places and not an elitist instrument as modern era secularists *believe*. *Knowledge* was in and of its nature designed to be found everywhere even when *elitists* design it to be an exclusive currency by which to create a society of class and separation by degrees of wealth and access to perceived echelons and bastions.

In a time when a cataclysm is irrefutably proven to be looming, the class structure and exclusive elitism dissolve into a situation of want and needs that can be supplied by anyone. The simplest solutions usually triumph over elaborate equations about complex multi-compound contraptions that even reinforce a digital divide. So the notion that knowledge of a cataclysmic realism is the preserve of a few is outdated and dysfunctional. Why does the Bible state that the earth will be inherited by the *poor*? We should ask ourselves these questions. If we accept one aspect of the Bible as truth and applicable to our modern life, the fact of having to mend our ways, then why should we not accept also the part that says categorically that the earth shall be inherited by the *poor*. What does this really mean? It could mean that the elaborate schemes of the *richest* in the world may flounder and basic ideas and realities about survival kick–in in the face of cataclysm. This tells us that the *poor* also have solutions about circumventing an arduous time of cataclysm.

What does the often thrown about truism: *'truth is sometimes stranger than fiction'* really mean? Are there times when this statement is applicable? The academic discipline of anthropology is a really liberated zone because it allows scientist to think out of the proverbial box and to tackle the impossible, in ways that often embellish scientific realism. Traditional anthropology has come of age to enter and interact with formerly unrelated fields, venturing into natural science. Anthropology has potential to liberate secular perceptions through making linkages with natural sciences. Anthropology questions belief systems and often as we now know there are embedded technical truths that linger undiscovered in *humanities* type fields of academic endeavour. Belief systems are also about the scientific reality that has been uncovered to date. For instance natural science could be viewed as a belief system that borders on expressions of faith...

What remains intriguing, is the realisation that societies of ancient times, were so advanced and thoughtful as to bequeath the future with a *cataclysm monitoring artefacts, paraphernalia and knowledge.* We, out of our own arrogance have destroyed ancient knowledge, believing falsely that these treasures were unsophisticated and banal.

We are persuaded that on a round earth, the state of isotopic decay is reversed and that nothing decays due to any dysfunctional or obsolete radioactive microbes. Organic decay is characteristic of an oblate earth. Electromagnetic streaming and flow of microwave currents causes radioactive decay of elements, and we suspect that this is a feature that is reversed on a round earth. The isotope resonance and alignment on a round earth (or any other planet) possibly enables anti-matter and anti-gravity as a phenomenon.

The fact that the conditions do not exist right now to test this theory does not make it impossible, that is exactly the point.

What gives this DNA round-oblate earth dichotomy a chance in eternity is the very cryptic clue in the Bible, that of the how the earth and all that is in it was formed by the Creator. The seven day theory explained in the creation story could be a cryptic clue to other dimensions of this statement. The possibility or impossibility of this statement depends on the reader's perception or interpretation of the process of creation, especially of an impenetrable duration like nature. Nature is unquestionable and absolute in many regards and to question how, when or why it was created has been the most forbidding and ponderous question. Yes that being what it is, we would also not to question something that is infallible and impenetrable as the basis for creation. For the purpose of determining the validity of the claims of precessional science and the realism of epochology, it is imperative to determine what is possible to. It is impossible to discredit the theory of the Creator as the benevolent prime mover of creation. Our main interest is to realise that all science has been following this question. Science has unravelled the unknown characteristics of creation with science being limited by the reality of physical laws. The story of creation is leading and the biggest account about where we are.

Faith and science are not separate doctrines and we view science as an unravelling of the Creators mind complex. Science and faith may not be oppositional academic or practical subjects, they both account for nature from varying vantage points. There should not be incongruence about that. To be honest, in addition to what we know about the past from the artefacts and sites that survived the attritions of passing time, there is still a lot to learn. It is possible that the atmosphere and other environmental dynamics are forever changing. DNA testing and analysis will enable us to have a firm grip on the ideas that we have about the past. Could the current DNA mapping or sequencing technology hold answer to the developmental trajectory within a round-oblate earth dichotomy? Yes, it is probably a map that does not have the two ends of the original point and the terminal point, but somewhere in the middle we should be able to follow how development took place and make comparisons for the astrophysical implications of these pointers. We will need a multi-disciplinary approach to follow the DNA trail in order to deduce the possibilities of a *round earth* characteristic scenario. A round-earth simulation may be isolated as a standalone environment that is looked at in comparison to the possibility of a theoretical condition. The oblate earth could have inherited a lot of environmental markers and influences from a round earth.

It is a hard case to prove scientifically, but that is just the point of a period that we are far from because of occupying the other end of. The oblate spheroid period in isolation will show us anomalous traits that could belong to a round earth. It's like trying to prove that a liquid exists just because a cup exists. Even though we have never seen a liquid before nor know what it looks like, smells like or any of its properties.

The answer is implied in the question, the anomalies that exist, are an example. We can prove that a bird can fly but we don't know why it flies. The reason why these questions come about is still central to the answer of precessional science and epochology.

This is a case of reverse engineering in order to deduce the truth about the round earth-oblate earth dichotomy. It is sort of like saying that just because there is cheese, there has to be milk, even though we have never seen milk before. How do we then make the association between the milk and the cheese, it is almost impossible.

This is where DNA testing and analyses of the genome sequence comes in. For instance we presume that acidity in a micro-organ is a prerequisite for organic perpetuation (through preservation). What if acidity is a result of atmospheric deviation of the electromagnetic or microwave pressure distributed to chemicals and elements in general at an isotopic level, on an oblate earth? From the point of view of the earth it can be seen that anti-matter is a real condition in outer-space. We figure that if there wasn't this 'super seasonal' interchange between the round earth and the oblate earth spheres, then there would not be diversity of species and functions. It is possible that atomic biomass behaves differently on differently shaped planetary environments.

If there was no interchange between the shapes of the earth in various time periods, everything would have remained the same. It is this super-seasonal change in the shape (a primary characteristic) of the earth that induced variation of species. It probably boils down to the spectral level of atomic characteristics influenced by atmospheric pressures, thermodynamics, astrophysics and other factors. For this case we need several approaches, primarily looking at outcomes to determine the cause. A relative but logical deduction at the moment is that a round earth does not last as long as an oblate earth sphere does. The earth is round for a brief period of let us say 25 000 years and the oblate may last for as long as 75 000 year in a super-epoch cycle. Alternatively we should peg a more realistically at 250 000 and 750 000 years respectively (in relation to longer periods). These theories need a chance to mount this research as evidence of the reality of precessional science and the inevitability of cyclical cataclysm. *Entropy,* according to the dictionary is the study of the degradation of the universe, resulting in the decrease of available energy. This is an accurate description of the round-oblate period interchange. If we could direct this inquiry, it would start with etymology to deduce the embedded development of clues in linguistic insinuations and derivation of meaning related to precessional science and epochology. Chemical tests and physical science behavioural attributes would follow on.

Scale models may need to be replicated in order to carry on a test of the round-oblate dichotomy hypothesis. Already a visualisation of these attendant effects is within the reach of imagination. Empirical data is however more credible and assertive in order to reach practical conclusions about the state of the earth. Surely distribution angles affect a lot of the mechanical operations of the earth. So the angle of distribution of sunlight and radiation would be affected by the shape of the earth.

The polar axes are areas to watch to figure out exactly why they display the features that they do. Why are they ice-capped while they are the regular and perpetual spinning points. Should not these polar-regions that accentuate the respective axis be ice free from the friction caused by this concentrated spin? Is the ice-cap a result of this over-heating and relative condensation that forms and concentrates at the pole a direct result of overheating nonetheless? Is this overheating directly related to the shape of the earth and would the polar-regions be ice-free if the axis(es) were not strained to the extent of overheating temperatures by the oblate shaped induced aspect of the axial spin? This may only be illustrated on a computer model because a physical model would be cumbersome and wouldn't illustrate the internal view. What we would look for are angles of sun rays, distribution of internal energy etc. If the radius from the pole is shorter than the radius from the equator, then the pole should receive more internal heat. The theory of why the ice-caps endure is innate, over and above the friction theory. It is easy to think that the ice-caps are caused by lack of solar radiation. The ice-caps could be caused by friction and internal heat that creates condensation that is compensated for by lack of solar radiation and thus, result in the formation of ice-caps.

It seems that these questions on their own, are a new field that requires geophysics and other subjects that will become apparent as the answers unfold.

What may upset us when dealing with inquiries into the true nature of our environment, is that only a few are allowed to by the deliberate design of the education system. Empirical data is only reliable if it is from a reputable source and this leaves out vast sources of perspective. The digital divide indication also reveals the limit of the pool of submissions in the form of answers to the questions about our true nature. There are well over 7 billion people and this should tell us that there are 7 billion questions and answers to the nature of true realism.

It is possible that the prospects of space travel are based on the round-oblate dichotomy. What if we discover that the round earth period is suitable to tractable space communion and realism. It is possible that *thinking* about space travel is directly correspondent to the actuality of an oblate shaped earth that interdicts ubiquitous communal space travel or space activity. What if we discovered that an oblate spheroid planet affects all chemical processes including organic material that is at the centre of material composition for a space age state-of-the-art?

Talking about shape(s) is essential to the round-oblate dichotomy. For instance we may infer that the ancient civilizations were aware of cyclical cataclysm and this is what informed their scientific outcomes. They knew that more than building an architectural complex as a cataclysm monitor, the architecture had to be cataclysm proof. Pyramids in the most part across the world have survived untold eras of cataclysm induced wipe-outs. Surely the design of these buildings inculcates the fact of inevitable incursion by some class of cataclysm. This is exactly what is missing in the modern day concept of civilization. Aesthetics and maximization of resources has taken centre-fold above environmental outcome. We know the story of the modern civilization, of how often development always degrades the environment and leaves it in a state of disrepair as an outcome.

How many stories do we hear in recent times of buildings in city blocks collapsing due to several factors that come down to our notions of environmental development? This tells us that modern design is far from being informed about cataclysm and often it is more a cost aspect that determines architectural outcomes. High rise buildings are a function of maximising benefit and minimising cost rather than inculcating longer-term environmental risk. Something is chilling, we have to ask ourselves the question: why is it that 10 000 year old buildings from the past can outlast our modern buildings that usually exist for less than a 100 years? The pyramid's shapes tell us that this is a cryptic clue to scientific consciousness. The shape alone when one looks at it, induces a sense of introduction into some scientific consciousness. So the pyramids have many functions as cryptic clues to a cataclysm conscious society. These structures have built into them a message to the future, possibly as an indication of the direction that even architecture should take in order to be cataclysm proof. The pyramid is a cryptic clue to a *perfect* shape and the power of a *perfect* shape. Could they have been aware that the earth goes through a period when it is near perfectly round and that they tried to depict this in the pyramid? This seems to be a central theme in *Fingerprints of the Gods*. Could circular mounds be the extreme shape that our consciousness should have been awakened to when designing architecture? In other words pyramids are transcendental shapes between our modern age square and rectangles and circular mounds. It seems as if we are supposed to have been aware of pyramids and circular mound shapes in our architectural and built environment consciousness. In most of Africa, the circular shape has persistently been the most advocated architectural form that is probably supposed to inform the future state-of-the-art.

In the greater scheme of things, electromagnetic force, energy and microwave currents could have more utility value as a component of mass. The mass of the planet, (any planet) is supposed to be the most perplexing number to configure, to calculate and to know. I do not know if the mass of planet earth has ever been figured out but this is a point of discussion.

When the earth is 'charged', gasses and masses of component elements could face something that we may hardly imagine as inhabitants of an oblate earth.

The earth could be *elated* into a 'flying orb' at variable speeds that even the course of orbit around the sun decreased or increased by a margin. Could the Egyptians have known something about variation in speed of the orbital distance around the sun? Why did they make it a point to indelibly leave a monument that is a different shape while expressing a scale model of the earth to ratio on the surface of the earth at Giza? Could the shape of the pyramids be an indicator of a constantly changing shape of the earth?

The effect of warping and forming an oblate earth could increase the speed at a constant rate, we don't know. Maybe 24 hours is a variable quantum, depending either on a round earth or otherwise, that may even do more *hours* of rotation. The variation is unknown because of lack of empirical data and experiential data but is not unimaginable as a scientific reality rather than known truth. To prove that there are more than a million things that we do not know about the earth, it is accepted that the only way to deduce mass is through the actual weighing of the source of the mass. When would the earth been weighed? Using what? We are allowed to ask why there is variation in the speed of orbit between various planets. Is it mass, size, distance from the orbited object (in this case the sun) or does shape also have something to do with it all?

There are many attributes that square up to the mysteries and wonders of the earth that we do not know about. The earth is more intelligent than all the species that live on it. Everything that humans can ever think of doing, the earth is already doing it. If it is flying, living long, going to outer space...the earth has already done it all. The earth has more EQ and IQ than any being that lives on it. It takes three days for a human to dehydrate without water or any liquid, the earth provides water or any liquid that the human needs to survive. All species that live on the earth depend more than 100% on the earth for sustenance. The earth speak its own language, it speaks to species that can hear it. At the moment, the first language of the earth is spoken and heard by animals. In the year 2004, when the tsunami struck in Phuket, Indonesia, the animals evacuated to high ground. They heard the earth speak. The earth speaks to any sentient beings that live on it and who can hear it. It is possible that humans lost the ability to hear the earth speak when the earth turned into an object of trade. Geologists even say that they can hear sounds on an ultrasonic recorder of the earth making sounds from the depths.

It took 18 year for the central issue in *Fingerprints of the Gods* to come into the larger public domain. One of the predictions of Graham's book about asteroids found in chapter 52 has taken place. It took place in 2013 February. For all intents and purposes we need not mince words, Graham Hancock knows what he is talking about. He speaks of an asteroid incursion as a scenario and the first in our time was witnessed over Russia in 2013. This is phenomenal insight because not even elected officials and formal channels knew that this would actually happen until late. He spoke of this even before publishing this book in 1995. Either that or the information about the asteroid era was deliberately withheld from the public because of government being unprepared. A real fear of a public administration meltdown all over the world is a possibility if this information was put in the public domain as fact. What this is saying to the people who have been watching this screen is that maybe government is not prepared for this scenario because entrenched vested interest. Maybe government cannot tear away from the fast diminishing prospects of the unnavigable tenure due to cataclysmic realism. A neutral jury, privy to this information about cataclysm, would find the evidence too much to ignore. This indicates that government should have divested from business as usual and opted for a face-off with an encounter of another kind. *But then again the irony is that this scenario has only really played out in the movies...*

*Fingerprints of the Gods* is a real and dependable source for a formal inquiry. *The Johannesburg Formula* is an endorsement of such an inquiry, ever since ensconcing into the Mayan topic, from the internet and other sources, including applying to the Court in South Africa. We hope that this is not inelegant to the reader and especially to Mr Graham Hancock, the author of *Fingerprints of the Gods*.

What we would want to gauge is how others would react after reading *Fingerprints of the Gods*, even after only first having known about this book long after the December 2012 Mayan prediction. We suspect that there is too much information in the public domain that would extract the same reaction as what this book does. Then again the book is littered with questions, some rhetorical and some a genuine test of the readers interaction. Go on, engage the open book test sit-in with answers, Fingerprints is a formidable lecture, this is allowed. Answering or attempting to answer the questions that Graham poses is a privilege not to be taken lightly.

Without Graham's book we would not have the questioning determination of *The Johannesburg Formula.* After the attitudes that transpired from comments to news about the Court application, it felt like maybe we should have just kept the issue internalised, so as not to impose our own views. The February 2013 asteroid in Russia and *Fingerprints of the Gods* made us realise that there was no way that we would remain without an opinion. After the opportunity of reading the book, it seemed okay that we had approached the Constitutional Court of South Africa in December 2012. We realised that it is sometimes fine to be 'relegated' by divergent opinions. We experienced the reception of the mainstream first-hand in all its forms. The media is mainly interested in any story only if it is part of the *ratings* objective. In 2013 after the asteroid incident in February, we attempted to make contact with the media, to highlight the connectivity of the anomalous cosmic event, to no avail. As we read some of the post and comments left on Graham Hancock's profile it is clear that the issue is far from being panned-out. It seems that in September 2013 the issue is still trending, amongst the group who are reflected on Graham's profile as people who "Like" (Facebook lingo) the page.

What we are all going to learn is that Graham Hancock and his likes deserve accolades. We are grateful to have him as a writer and researcher. The most astounding thing we will discover after reading his book is that his other book *The Sign and the Seal* is tied to the story of *Fingerprints of the Gods* in a way that is not so obvious. This is a topic for another time though and when the correct moment avails we'll learn how these two books are connected. This also seems to be a puzzle made of a story codes in the form of several sources. The link between these two books will become clearly visible once the facts of the situation are tabled. To the author of these two books it was a matter of an innate journey to bring these books into the public space. When people ask questions about the outcome of the events of this time period it will become clear that the books are but parts of a *greater book* that the author renders along a journey. His work over the two books resembles that of the subject of his inquiry, enigmas that at first seem unrelated but for functional purposes reveal to be parts of a whole. *The Sign and the Seal* and *Fingerprints of the Gods* form a big picture that answers most questions about how all this may culminate. These two books are symbols that represent *the known and the unknown*, especially about the times that we are in. We implore keen researchers into the topic of Mayan predictions to look at these books. They open up a new world that speaks of the shape of things to come. Chapter 42 of *Fingerprints of the Gods* is a clue to the link of this book and *The Sign and the Seal,* both Graham's books. One thing that is for sure is that this is not the only issue that is discoverable. There are countless other breath-taking issues that we the public, have not known about for many reasons. Many more issues have just not been concealed, but remain unknown because they were simply undiscovered or realised up till now. This topic is worth research at relevant institutions to allow the public access to the theory of precession using empirical methodologies and state sanctioned research to compile data.

# CHAPTER SEVEN

## THE PSYCHOLOGY OF EPOCHOLOGY

It took a persistent toss and turn to finally commit this chapter as a stand-alone instalment. We doubted whether it was sustainable to venture into this topic definitively. The title of this chapter started off as *Epochology* and then we hit on the idea to explore the psychology of epochology as an enterprise on its own. It became clear that every circumstance that presents, is a play out of the topic of this chapter. Everything and every situation we looked at from now would be a practical illustration of the circumstances of the topic of this chapter. A close look at the reality of psychology as a basis for exploring the Mayan calendar and the predictions that they speak of became appealing. We realised that if a practitioner of psychology were presented with the task of appraising the Mayan issue, there would be a case. Initially we thought that it would be enough to just look at the scientific implication of introducing a study or subject of epochology, looking at the requirements and definition of what that would entail. When the opportunity to plunge into a holistic *psychology of epochology* arose, it seemed practical to embrace this approach. The whole field opened up as soon as it appeared to be an almost limitless challenge to define.

Much later in the year, just when we thought that the Mayan calendar issue was done and dusted...it came up again. On the 12th September 2013, the TBN bouquet on DSTV (the television network offered in South Africa), Sid Roth the host of *The Supernatural*, a faith television programme, pried open the possibility of a full-sprung chapter on the *psychology of epochology*. Sid Roth interviewed his guest Tom Horn on the channel and the topic was presented as a matter that the public should orientate themselves on. Tom Horn showed expert knowledge of the topic integrating issues about the founding of America and the supposed *conspiracy* to usher in an era of an uncharacteristic nature. Tom Horn also spoke about the Mayans and other things related to this topic. To find out the details, follow this episode on *Twitter* or *Google* by typing: Sid Roth and go to the September interview with Tom Horn.

Nine months after the December 2012 atmosphere around the world, the topic came around again. This is in line with the caveat issued to the South African media that if anything on the proportion of the known Mayan prediction scenario should not unfold, there should be an eight month moratorium to observe the environment. In February 2013, an asteroid hurtled over Russia and this was definitive. The screening of Sid Roth's show on the 12th September 2013, stealthily opened the field, when they were discussing the Mayan prediction as a current topic. We realised that the South African media was unintendedly letting go a responsibility to take on the issue because in the USA it is being tackled head-on, as shown by the 12th September 2013 screening on DSTV of Sid Roth's show episode.

Although not enough, South Africa did not avoid exposure to Sid Roth's show as it beamed via television and the internet. The subscription television channels noticeably are part of the opportunity to bring stories from the United States of America to South African. DSTV did it and the few subscribers with access this channel in South Africa saw the broadcast. It soon became clear that the field of psychology related to the epoch-end was going ahead full steam and we have no choice but to keep up and let the public into the loop as *The Johannesburg Formula* was in manuscript mode. The risk of contacting the media to revisit the issue was already foreclosed by the reaction of February 2013 when there was aversion in the media because of the perception that this was a non-event and automatically non-news worthy.

The establishment of the academic perspective and aspect was already trending as an idea and we began to outline the prospectus for the chapter. We came back a few chapters to include the *psychology of ephocology* commentary at the start of this chapter as we viewed it as correct to do so and to follow with the theoretic aspect as a subject unit. The next thing is that it dawned that exposure to information is indeed disturbing and highly volatile because no one is cold to hard facts as the whole scenario plays out. Being engrossed in this topic has prospects of being anti-social, as the topic can be relegated to a fatalistic fiction. How do other people cope when it dawns that this may be a way to proceed and face the topic head-on. Well, Hollywood has found a way of broaching the burden through screenplay. Psychologically, there is no doubt that whether the scenario is imagined or real, exposure to this sort of information can be disturbing. After the episode where Sid Roth interviewed Tom Horn on the Mayan prophecy was screened, we saw that even the manuscript for *The Johannesburg Formula* could have enough information to sustain a publication. Being an author is the furthest thing from what we thought possible. At this juncture, it is no longer a matter of a commercial pipeline to get a book out. It is a matter of embracing rights and responsibilities to embellish public interest regarding this matter.

It seems as if the development of the story in this chapter has been out there even before we could collate it. No-one is liable or responsible for the unfolding circumstances, this seems to be out of anyone's boundaries of control. Our decision to log on to the Mayan story is as a result of being initially exposed to this information and since applying to the South African Court. We knew something of a similar philosophy from anecdotal encounters and this is why we were attached to the story. Surely it would put anyone in a quandary of irrational sensibilities to be persistent with the Mayan prediction. After everything was said and done by December 2012, we had taken a break from the manuscript because there wasn't really much more to be said by us. The screening of Sid Roth left us without choice but to see that the issue is continuing with more people out there. So this is not a loner's game of fascination with this scenario as it has presented up to now. There are people out there who know more than we do about this general topic and it is now a matter of time before something in the order of a response from government as this information reaches and affects more people in different ways. The USA is the biggest case study of all. Yes sure South

America also has a big exposure because the story is anthropologically located there, but the USA has a bigger multimedia grasp of the story.

To avoid the story because of the unpredictable public responses, seemed less sensible or even possible. It became a matter of time before more people would square up with the topic as a realism. We ask the question of how the American government is receiving the information that was screened, even in South Africa on 12th September 2013, because this was presented on a documentary type show! The episode was obviously screened in the USA earlier than it was in South Africa on DSTV. The Sid Roth show is a reliable source of information because it has a legitimately placed following. We question what went in to the decision to screen this episode and what the producers foresee as a reaction to this information going forward from all sectors of society.

Rationally it would seem obvious that it is unfair for anyone to be exposed to this information because it is very emotive and invasive. Anyone with information like this should be vetted before it goes public because the effects are gross. We are challenged now because we do not know how the time ahead is going to pen out.

A sensible question to ask is whether this message of the Mayan prophecies is safe for us or not. Ironically, it dawns on us that any citizen who is publishing the reality of this issue should be in the controlled custody of the State. State custody is a reasonable solution for the safety of all citizens and the persons wielding this information. Society should not be exposed to an *uncontrolled* eventuality where the issue is being presented to the public nor addressed by civilians because it is unsettling. To encountering the implications of this information making way into the public domain in an irregular manner, from all the sources that it comes from is something else. We say that this information is volatile because the trauma associated with exposure to the realism of this information is palpable. We feel that it is the responsibility of government to make a call on this matter.

While assuming that all this is impossible, momentarily, as extravagant as it sounds, we feel that practitioners who are aware of the Mayan calendar as an impending reality should be monitored by the State and government. The department that we identify is the Department of Health. We cannot diagnose the situation and commit to the notion that these practitioners' condition is bizarre. Neither can we say that it is against the law since there is no commission of a classified crime by talking in public on this matter ahead of an official government pronouncement. However it is clear that there is a danger of uncontrolled and random exposure to anyone that the practitioners reach because of the nature of the information.

What is also curious, is the state of mind of anyone who stands up outside of official/government platforms to purport this information. For one, the unkempt way that one has to forego the indemnity of reputation or peer approval is astounding. By nature people are addicted to approval and we all thrive on being told how well we are doing. People constantly need to be reminded and reinforced of worthiness and embellished with acknowledgement. To forego and to risk all the approval and to square up to the risk of being labelled as some quirk, is a psychological phenomenon that has only to be experienced, to be felt. What kind of obscureness would compel anyone to shout at the top of their lungs that something like this is real? Surely this must be some sort of latent behaviour that is instigated by the external environment. A survey around the world of the various opinions of people from across the spectrum would reveal exactly what the situation is on the ground. For example what are the courses of resistance and what does it take for someone to be convinced that this is in fact reality. Social standing, level of access to information, faith persuasion and outlook are some of the initial points to be aware of.

For example Graham's book reveals that the genre of technical mythology that has precession as an embedded feature is broad-based and that it cuts across cultural, racial and geographic specifics.

It seems reasonable to appeal to the State to look at the information about the Mayan predictions, in the public domain and assess how this affects the public at large. We have looked at ourselves as a case in point because of having experienced acute exposure to this information. There is also no way to conceal this state of affairs and for the public to pretend that it is not affecting individuals in all types of manner depending on how the citizen interprets and processes the information. From here we would foresee an amount of danger in the form popular reactions that are not in line with structured process of State and private sector initiatives. Up to so far there has not been an obvious danger as the USA government has already seen how the public has reacted to several mediums that purport information about the Mayan predictions. The story as was revisited by the Sid Roth show is now stored on the internet, for anyone who has access to freely peruse and ponder. A scenario that cannot be allowed to unfold is that of citizens interpreting the information outside of a *guided and controlled* environment. People all over the world are in varying circumstances and this has to be taken into account. The critical mass has to be determinable and various actions taken to contain outbreaks of random and unspecified reactions. The government has the responsibility to map the way forward and to prescribe a reception and reaction module.

As much as the situation is undefined and everyone may intimate that this is a speculative issue that warrants dismissal, there is enough information in the public domain that points towards a turning point. People who have always been secure, will rely on their comfort-zone to set the tone of their reaction. People in already dire circumstances due to known factors of extreme and dire poverty, might also assume that they have no recourse and interpret the situation as it fits. What is noteworthy is also the digital divide and information divide. People in *poor* circumstances do not have the luxuries of being highly informed. The people in rich countries and neighbourhoods, currently have a lead on access to information. This is going to be a crucial run-up to the race for interpretation and reaction. How government reacts will determine the integrity of the reaction of the public. Already, this book and this chapter is an illustration of the typical public domain environment with diverse dispositions of citizens with several means and capacity. The immediate environment and knowledge of the details of what is unfolding will determine what happens next.

People with high levels of investment in the built-up environment, commercial and industrial interest and the likes will be challenged. As wild as this sounds, it is a possibility that people who can 'up and go' and leave everything behind are in a more viable psychological format. We do not believe for a minute that this is a made up and imagined situation, the evidence in overwhelming. Even if we had to go-away on holiday and imagine that this is all a dream, we cannot erase the information that is already live on the internet. We cannot imagine that an officially elected public servant does not see what we in the citizenry see. This is the psychological lay-out of the moments that are culminating.

Just looking at the academic implications of epochology, we decided that we would firstly define the several and diverse areas that may arise and be incorporated into the main body of knowledge. As a way to embark on this chapter, it became necessary to state that the world was now substantively affected by the psychology of epochology, because everyone can see that there is a change in the information scenario. The position now is that we have to keep our eyes on the developments going forth and look out for any accessible information outlet that touches the issue. That DSTV's TBN was already involved is a strong indicator that the information is trending even beyond the circles of the relegated sector that has been tackling this issue for even the longest time as the reader will note that *Fingerprints of the Gods* was first published in 1995. A search on Twitter for Sid Roth and Tom Horn reveals an online presence of a recent publicly broadcast account of the Mayan issue, as recent as September 2013.

The aspect of *epochology psychology* is playing out across the world as several forms of alternative media revisit the issue. We count a network show as media because it is a public broadcast by a regular authorised medium. It is clear that all the countries that view the format that is offered in South Africa by DSTV, saw the Sid Roth screening that became available to our part of the world on 12th September 2013. Sid Roth's television show *The Supernatural* on TBN (in South Africa), is a faith show and this makes sense because the broad interpretation, generally is that this is a faith issue. Our view is that to ease into this realism, we have to dispense with dogma and aversion to traditional myth. This may be a block to the psychological circumstance that we find ourselves in as people, whether we find this acceptable or not. We cannot imagine what is playing out in countries like the United States of America where the issue is being unpacked as evidenced by the 12th September 2013 screening of the Sid Roth television show. The citizens of the USA are first out of the block when it comes to being informed and this is a fact that we only observe as much. The situation has changed and it is a matter of urgency to find ways of communicating a message, to curb *fear* as a distraction from the best way of going forward.

The first broad-based reaction that should follow is denial of the realism of epoch psychology. This is institutionalised denial that filters through to the *public*, because the information pipeline is structured for profitability. If any issue is tangent to this objective, it becomes true that a blank-out ensues. As the author of this book, I am not specialised in psychology but I can imagine the paralysis that fear would unleash. This is what the December 2012 Constitutional Court application in South Africa also addressed. It is a fact that logical and sequential care should be given to how the issue is dealt with, because the state/government anywhere in the world, cannot afford to drop the ball on this one. What the South Africa media has not realised so far is that South Africa is the first country in the world where the matter of end-times has reached the level of being presented to a Court of law. This should tell us something about the position of South Africa in the future as it unfolds with the end-times story having clung to the public psyche. This only tells us one thing, that South Africa registered the issue as formally as possible, even having given serious media attention to the issue, and the citizenry showing the will to take the matter up to the courts. This puts South Africa in a position, where the issue can be formally led by authorities and direction given to the citizens as to what, where and how to react, should anything extraordinary happen. The South African government can be given a tip for not obscuring the issue that made way into the public domain against all odds after, a civilian plea to a court to recognise the issue. At the moment we have to cut to the chase and say, that we may not tolerate a situation where a government agency (in this case NASA in the USA) is the one that bears the responsibility of giving leadership on the issue of end-times, when the state itself has not committed to overt statements and an officially sanctioned position that is even given airtime in the chambers of the executive arm of government. Also, it seems as though we have to establish for ourselves as the citizenry the reason why no government on earth has committed to officially putting the issue of end-times on the agenda of the cabinet or parliament. The reason is that the officials know as well as do ordinary citizens about this issue, but officially government treats the issue as peripheral. The reason for this is that government views the end-times realism as a threat to its own sovereignty. Talk of end-times is a direct affront to the position that any government is in, because this talks of the end of government authority. This should not have to be the case, governments should be advised to take leadership on these matters, even in partnership with society to establish the best way forward in the face of this reality. This is not another campaigning issue that may be employed to gain good-standing with the electorate, this is a matter of survival for all of humanity regardless of colour, creed and nationality. The amount of information that is out there from NASA about solar storms and geomagnetic fluctuations issued by NASA researchers does not tally up with the silence from the executive arm of government on these issues and the matter on the whole.

Moving on, now in November 2013, if anyone should look into an internet search of the end-times issue, one will find that a Ukrainian space observatory has spotted an asteroid that they dubbed *2013TV135*. NASA has put a date on it, of when it might enter the orbit of planet earth, to 2032. The 1,300 foot wide asteroid is said by NASA to have a 1 in 10 chance of hitting the earth. The issue here is that this asteroid was spotted by the Crimean Astrophysical Observatory in October 2013. NASA learnt of the asteroid from Ukrainian scientists. The article on asteroid 2013TV135 appears on an online news site called 'MAIL Online' and it is written by Michael Zennie (published on 17th October 2013). NASA has since gone on to commit to monitor the asteroid from the Massachusetts Observatory in the USA. But we should be wary of following directives that are not formally ushered into the public domain as important. The last time when an asteroid hit over Russia in February 2013, no agency had committed itself to any direct authorship and reports of how that asteroid might behave were scant. We also have to be taken aback by the mild reaction of government after the Russian asteroid came so close on the heels of the date of 21st December 2012, that the Mayans spoke of. Government should not afford to have a civilian approach to this matter. Government is the most specialised entity that is supposed to be ahead of the curve of any development. It should have raised interest from government when the 15th February 2013 followed the 21st December 2012 so closely. According to a source who saw a programme on DSTV, there is consensus amongst specialists that the 15th February 2013 asteroid episode over Russia correlates to the Mayan 21st December 2012 date. Government should heed this research and look into it as a matter of wanting and needing to be ahead of civilian research on this matter. One gets the view that there is no commitment from the state to bring the issue into mainstream focus, the issue of asteroids are being treated as peripheral issues until after the event and even then, we see that there is no real authoritative claim by any agency to take control of the issue. So we wouldn't rely on any agency no matter how senior if the state has not pronounced to the public, a sanction and an official position on the issue in general. The internet has information of what is out there and we have to make our own deductions in the absence of official intervention and sanction. The challenge for many people is that they do not yet see the internet as a credible news source. If anything does not appear in the traditional print tabloid then it is still not viewed as officially being in the public domain. From where we are sitting, it seems as though this issue will not go out like a candle in the rain, there is still more to this issue than meets the eye. Just because the 21st/12 did not translate into the scenario depicted by the Mayans, does not foreclose forever on when the scenario might play out. Also another thing to note is that there is too much support for the scenario depicted by the Mayans in faiths that are not mainstream. What is in fact more glaring is that the scenario that was forecasted for the 21st/12 may play out at any other odd time when it is least expected to. It would be advisable to be cautious all the same about the possibility of the scenario as *pending*. What basis is there for the total denial of the scenario playing out?

More eerie, is the position of government…it is non-committal. This is shocking because one would think that government would take seriously the damage that such information being proliferated could have on society. Even in the face of the right to free speech, government should reasonably be concerned about the negative impact of such speculative claims on ordinary citizens. Is it a case where government does not want to say anything, whether positive or negative because of a fear of being wrong.

It is also worth it for government to intervene so that this does not turn out to be a jamboree of incorrect information and misleading interpretation. We should have a purely scientific and gnostic account that does not give room for any spurious tales. Already one can see that the overbearing freehand that has been created by the absence of the State and government is leading to uncontrolled information being doled to the public. We have found that having one source of the cataclysm story is biased and emotive because of the reasons that they may give for the cataclysm taking place. We have to be careful when we assume the position of bringing information to the public not to commit literary errors, even excluding our own assumed biases but rather making it possible that impassionate information is put simply and succinctly. We do not want to mention any specific examples, but would rather leave this to the correct authorities on the subject.

One thing that we can say though is that Graham's book does not have any interpretations that may cause discomfort or mislead the reader. He tells us objectively what he also got from sited sources without inventing a perspective. There is going to be a thin line between theory, an opinion and speculation regarding this matter. The reason why there is a discipline of academic inquiry is that not everything is known about the universe, and the planet earth. So it may sometimes be misleading to make traditional assumptions that may prove to be unsubstantiated and inadequate at another turn.

Clarity needs to be found as to what is allowed and what is not. We need to determine what the limits are of how information about the Mayans, that ends up with the public should be regulated so that fallacies stay out of it. It is hard enough as it is.

Expectedly, the first reaction is doubt mixed with denial of the gross implication of the possibility of the information being credible. The next leg of the reaction is to take a step back and possibly to insulate one's self or naturally protect one's self from being immersed in the issue as would be the case in with other issues in the public domain. This is normal right? Then let us move our objectives and process to a more organised and more capacitated institution, the State. The State has the impersonal resolution to absorb any impact of any factor that is hurtling towards the consciousness of the public. The State is our ultimate custodian and should avert anything that infringes on privileges and rights of citizens. But, can the State also plug our ears so that we hear nothing, cover our eyes so that we see nothing? The State is essentially doing and acting on behalf of and in the interest of the public, this should be the case with any situation. We asked the State through an application to Court to open the debate in this regard when it became clear that the information out there was suspiciously indisputable. Also, the information mostly became available in the media at the time that the described

140

scenario was said to be playing out. I wonder what conclusion anyone else would independently reach presented with the information even as it is out there. This is a clear case that illustrates that the public does not have enough information or is not accessing it at all. The bewildering thing is that like anything out there this information is available but only probably "concealed" by its obscure nature. No one can possibly know everything, there is something out there that we all do not know that may be known to others, we are in the same boat.

No one has to feel inadequate about not knowing anything, because no one is supposed to know everything. Even a medical doctor probably would not know what a 'bob rivet' is, but a carpenter would, so we are fine. Back to the information that this book purports to highlight, it is out there and the law strictly provides, having as a fundamental maxim the saying that *'ignorance of the law is not an excuse'*. So we see here that the law places the onus on people to know, this is not different. The law *presumes* that people should all know something about the Mayan calendar, should a legal circumstance related to it arise. If for instance anyone was to breach a legal right of a Mayan culture practitioner, by insulting one of the provisions of the Bill of Rights in relation to, the Mayan tenets or Mayan philosophy, a plaintiff could find recourse in a court of law that protects the *right of association*, the *right of consciousness* or holding a view, *the right to culture* etc. In other words the *Bill of Rights* as in South Africa expects that *everyone* knows not to discount or divert a practitioner of Mayan culture, because *everyone* is presumed by the law to know that such a right is not scalable. So the presumption by the State that citizens are up to speed is a rigid feature of the machinery of Statehood in relation to citizens. This is interesting because for any valid or relevant reason, the State should be the first to realise the rights of the Mayans, their philosophy and way of life, even if this is presumed to be expired...

Could *denial* be the steep precipice from where we tumble? Ironically we doubt that anyone in a correct frame of mind would just accept a situation like the one being illustrated as the end-times scenario. There are nations, families and individuals who have built up incredible amounts of wealth over long periods of time. The cycle to bequeath these resources from one generation to the next has been going on without interruption. Should anything greater than a stock market collapse threaten to foreclose on this situation, there is an expected aversion. It is a normal impulse to shun the possibility of moving from a position of having immense wealth and resources to a position where that is threatened. Are *poor* people more ready psychologically to accept the realism of cosmic cataclysm? Are the rich perhaps more ready logistically? The announcement of an apocalyptic scenario seems to trickle through to *poor* people more readily because for the *poor*, there is simply nothing to lose. The psychology of forfeiture on a grand scale is intimidating. For any of the projected scenarios to be correct, the situation has to be assessed for what it is. We may have to look at a transitional scenario where we decide on what is important to have and what is not. We have to be rational about this scenario no matter how we try to avoid it or hope that it isn't real. Neither the public sector nor the private sectors are prepared for a psychological shift, from having a *total grip* on the levers of the world to being spectators to a colossal cosmic incursion. It is simply impossible for people to contemplate having to be ordinary in extraordinary circumstance. People have always been striving to be in control, directing the way resources flow and the way environmental settlement happens in concord with resources. For this to be threatened would be enraging, upsetting and simply infuriating. What government has to take charge of are the several modes of reactions to this circumstance as it unfolds.

Already in the USA it is taken as fact by the informed public that the scenario of end-times is a real factor. What has not begun though is a practical mind-shift on a scale that would enable a realistic reaction to any changing circumstances. As people throughout the world, we have never assumed that we might have to prepare for risk beyond ordinary *foreseeable* factors. There has never been a subject in school or university that teaches about cosmic cataclysm. The funny

142

thing is that life is the school that is ironically teaching humanity about something unknown about planet earth. The signs are already there for everyone to see and the decision has to be made, of what happens from here onwards. As the story behind this book illustrates, the actions that we take up on being sensitised of the possibilities of imminent cosmic cataclysm have to be legal actions, at-least from the point of view of civilians. The government of course has a broader scope of choices as to how it reacts and acts.

Technically this book has done the work of intimating to government as to the indications of the situation. Most government for the most part have heard the message and would not be totally alienated from the general trend as this period unfolds. The USA is in the lead of scientific work that tallies up with the scenario, at NASA they are noticing anomalous cosmic realities and are first to know if anything out of the ordinary is going on in outer-space or the solar system. Russia had an encounter with the unexpected outbreak of the asteroid in February 2013. It took place over one of the country's territories and thus the Russians were familiarised with the reality of the times we are in. The likes of Graham Hancock and others in the public have done their bit, being the messengers when even the institutionalised sectors of society would not yet commit to anything. Maybe it is a case of the *'haves and the have nots'*, the *'haves'* would never like to imagine the possibility of being *'have nots'* overnight at the mercy of cataclysmic outbreaks. The most pressing issue would be shelving *normal* priorities of *the world as we know it* and take pre-emptive action towards a situation with no descriptive limits.

The psychology of transforming into *reasonable* end-times citizens who do not jumble priorities is most interesting to contemplate. No-one would choose to be a messenger of end-times stories and we know this because it would prove to be a psychological challenge for anyone to *make the story up*. The messengers did not invent this story, they just research and report. How does one find time to conjure up such a genre, even in an attempt to set a morbid *trend...impossible*. Even the most inventive writer of fiction thrillers in literature and film finds inspiration from some real plot. All the possibilities of this story being a crank-call should be investigated and let us see what we come up with. In the mean-time let us keep a keen eye on environmental changes as the *asteroid season* has introduced a different dimension to a *normal* course. What is also valid is that not everything about the planet is known, otherwise all research into unknown frontiers would have closed shop. Once and for all a public debate has to be had between those who say it isn't the end-times period and those who say it is. Let everyone put their evidence in front of the public and let the people scrutinise the data. We cannot have a scenario where people are peddling a non-story at the expense of the public's point of access to information. On the other hand there is enough information that is proving that the planet has reached a point where anomalous environmental signatures are at play.

Could the writer of the script the film '2012', Harald Kloser, have just done a needed social service? Any fictional film potentially explores two or more dimensions because initially it remotely interacts with the senses of sight and sound. This means that the film industry has *allowed* '2012' to be broadcast with the knowledge of the impact that it would have on the public. Well, they have done it by at least steadily immersing the two senses of the viewing public into a simulated environment of the assumed scenario of end-times. The film directed by Roland Emmerich reeled the two senses into a momentarily real and forecasted scene, as the viewer was inducted into the terminal environment that the Mayan calendar spoke of. Now lately, the reality style format like Sid Roth's show are bringing the other senses of touch, taste and smell into the picture. When one superimposes the information that Sid Roth introduced to the public, with the scenario depicted in the film '2012', the five dimensions of human tactile senses are suddenly immersed. In order to make a compelling case, no bit of information should be left out. There are innumerable sources out there that would be embarrassing to ignore. It is just a matter of our state of mind when approaching this issue. We need to be careful not to overload ourselves but at the same time we may not avoid the final encounter with the big picture.

What is possible is to collate the information that is out there in the public space and bring it in front of the people so that they may judge for themselves. The internet is overwhelmed as a source of evidence, if a Court of law was to call for this, in order to make a ruling to compel the State to heighten its awareness.

Will nationalism be a stumbling block in the end-times? Of course, already we see with the February 2013 asteroid over Russia that people did not realise that the asteroid incurred over earth rather than being a *Russian occurrence*. The fact that it exploded over Russia is a matter of environmental positioning, this was an object from outer-space and did not discriminate as to where it would explode. Because the Mayans are South American, everyone everywhere else thinks, well this has nothing to do with us, this is a Peruvian, Mexican, Bolivian or other issue. We witnessed this first-hand when relating the issue to a public official in Johannesburg, earlier in December 2012, trying to highlight the 2012 Mayan prediction. He insisted on questioning how we had reached the conclusion of the *end-times theory* spoken of by the Maya. We told him that we had done some background searches of the issue and that we were convinced that this was an official matter that requires public intervention. His reaction was a display of a nationalism induced perception. He stated that *"we in South Africans have our own tradition of predicting such things"*. On a second interview, it was clear that the official was not entirely uninterested because he told us that he had researched the issue and what he knew of also was that in Miami (Florida, USA), there was a public event where the Mayan calendar was commemorated by the public organised for 21st December 2012. We noticed also that there were events in several South American countries where the Mayan calendar was commemorated.

It seems like national culture, borders and allegiance may obscure a global perspective of what the so called *end-times* means.

145

At the moment, the USA is the only country with a heavy media presence that is asserting an interest even through civilian initiatives and the private sector. The psychology of nationalism is a concern because for as long as we know, nationalism is the ultimate frontier of division and *"apartness"*. People view nationalism as a buffer against the *'other' and* this has been used as a reason to exclude the *'other'* from national consciousness. For a time such as this, nationalism is no viable answer because it limits our scope of the global nature of the time period. For instance everyone thinks that the February 2013 asteroid affected Russia, whereas the reality is that it exploded over planet earth, with Russia being a specific area. National statehood has for the longest time been based on the governments of nations being sovereign and independent of each other. What would this mean in times when nationalism melts in deference to global co-operation? Surely the same sentiments of nationalism would surface with each country wanting to *show-up* the other to demonstrate just how they are in charge or stronger than the other.

Nationalism easily replaces racism as an expression of the inability to be inclusive of even the *unknown* and the unfamiliar. What is even more intrusive is the sentiment that any national preamble and constitution purports, that the nation is strong against all odds and exclusive optimism that will not hold against challenging times. Right now as we speak, the jurisdiction and legal framework of every nation is a sectional instrument that prohibits global unity. In as much as nationalism is a high expression of individualism, the same can be said for individualism. Individualism would not hold in a season purported by the Mayans. Unity of nations, groups and individuals across the globe is paramount in order to have maximum capacity to ride out this challenge. What this tells us is that we have emerged from a mid-epoch to an end-epoch period where the thinking of nationalism that was useful for organising along national lines simply expires.

The paradigm for the end of epoch period is nothing we have ever been prepared for. It might require a complete reversal of a typical *traditional* mind-set, aspirations and outlook. Ultimately what we as civilians say or do in our limited capacity does not amount to a lot. What might turn the tide is what the State is prepared to do about the rumours that have already spread about the end-times. Like any other relationship, we have to forgo one thing for another, should the Mayans and their ilk be proven right at some point. So the State might have to retract its position to acknowledge that civilians have already started to speculate about the end-time issue. With due respect there are governments in South America who took the issue seriously since the anthropological evidence and the message is coming out of their backyard. So we saw in December 2012, on television, events were held to commemorate the Mayan calendar in South America.

It should also not be a matter of big nations being embarrassed. It is fine to admit not having been accurate in information gathering exercises and so have been out of the loop regarding this issue. No nation is above retracting a position and aligning with the temperament of the day. It is safe to say that the psychology of the many is less tractable than the psychology of a few. With many diverse groups, individuals or else, with varying interests, the situation is complex to resolve. There is always action behind the scene where interests jostle for priority. The fewer groups there are, or interests, the more pliable the situation is to resolve challenges and resolve predicaments. This is what we have to reckon with in the period that we are in. Politics is a way for nations to get ahead in the world, but in a time like this, it seems that it is one way of being confounded. The nature of politics is to hoard advantage and to outbid contenders. The world as we know it has been forged by the sometimes belligerent instrument of politics to create nations. Long term expenses incurred for the world to come to where it is today equals a fixed sentiment that is not easy to give up in a day.

With due reserve and circumspection we have to state that this is information that is difficult to cope with. The world is dear to everyone. This is not a moment for trophies and grandiose. We may be called to embrace each other in a way that would make the founders of nations reckon with ideals. This is a moment of reckoning that calls for correct action. Anyone acceding to the Mayan curriculum learns about pending scenarios and all aloofness and bravado recedes. The next thing is a perturbed state of mind, to an extent of restlessness. So who wouldn't reach a point of apprehension inducing an appeal to the State, through the Court, to put the public at ease through an official resolution. After that, a brisk perusal of the public space...groups of several persuasions display variable postures in place of the State does not rein in irresponsible broadcasting. Without much ado...our verdict... the ultimate adjudicator and custodian of citizens' rights is...(drum-roll)....the State. This again is a sovereign receptacle of any matter, no matter how extreme. Already those with platforms have taken the liberty to seize the channels to the public. Not to nit-pick and complain at all, the self-starter messengers were/are *compelled* to tell the story... just to illustrate a point.

Already there should be an outcry and rebuff from the public, who do not generate news, to query why ordinary citizens are allowed to be channels for this information. This has to be a risk in its own right. Isn't it an intriguing question of what type of person it takes to have information like this and still remain within prescribed social boundaries? Society classifies people as a fit and sociable members of the community only when they don't pose injury to health and otherwise. Perhaps it is true, no one would volunteer to speak of the Mayans who are supposed to be forgotten by now. People find it bizarre of anyone who does, isn't it? This is probably a reason why the information is not yet prolific. People fear being labelled for talking this kind of talk. This could be a reason why a lot of people perhaps who might be aware of this information directly or indirectly would not speak. Are there people out there who know what is going on and are just afraid of social attitudes? Besides the fear of embarrassment there is the question of how does one remain unaffected by this information and how does one know this and still commute normally on a daily basis? This is what we find intriguing. Normally in a conservative environment and society, the slightest cough of anything beyond the remit of regular speech transactions, is labelled and branded as absurd. We have to say that Graham Hancock is a phenomenon, for having survived social repercussions due to social apathy when it comes to extra-ordinary realities.

The *right to free speech* has reasonable limits that should protect the public from unintended consequences and this should follow whatever the view of the State is. I mean, what we saw on Sid Roth's show was breath-taking and ironically, the only protection that the more than seven billion people who still have not seen the programme had is the digital divide. People without the luxury of internet connectivity and digital television channels are in the majority, right. People have yet still to be exposed to the vagaries of this information. In South Africa for instance, people who saw the broadcast of the Court application are those who have access to current information, including radio, television and newspapers, the erudite. Another factor is: the interpretation of convoluted information may be an academic exercise. The challenge to government is to simplify the content and make sure that the people see for themselves and make individual decisions. What do we know? The film '2012' is a refined example of an article that met requirements for the public across many information circles to be introduced to the issue.

The South African government and the public are not obtuse. Since around January 2013, we decided not to again speak in public about the issue ahead of the South African government. That means that we are not ready to take media inquiries until the government pronounces on the matter. In the mean-time others have been on television as we have seen. Speaking would prejudice public perception in a way that suggests that we haven't considered elected authority. Government may have looked into this claim or theory and therefore we assume that we shouldn't go ahead of something "that is not established". Either-way, up until now, the story was broadcast in December 2012 on South African platforms and we were informed of the Mayan claims without being short-changed. South Africa showed that it is not a bias society by allowing such a materially intrusive issue to be broadcast. The government put faith in the public to be privy to a worldwide story that challenged our views. It does not matter when the story will swing back into the public arena because it has extensions that anyone can follow up from continent to continent.

Right this moment the issue has resurfaced in the USA and it seems that it has been given right of way to circulate abroad. The 12th September 2013 in South Africa was the technical and official date when the issue re-entered public view. It is just like what happened in February 2013, the media never linked the asteroid story to the December 2012 Mayan calendar story. Right now the media is not linking the 12th September 2013 broadcast to either the February 2013 asteroid issue or the December 2012 Mayan issue. Even though DSTV is only available to as few people as have access to the internet, to say that it has not re-entered the public South African space is inaccurate. So it is a matter of continuity regardless of how many people saw the 12th September broadcast or not. In the USA the situation is different. America is the opposite picture of the *digital divide* as compared to South Africa. Is this an indicator of the terrain as far as the development of the issue? Is there a coincidence between access to information technology and the development of the story?

Putting everything there is to say in a book is the most passable thing. We need to be detached from the demands of verbal communication, this is hardly a comfortable topic. Who wants to talk about apocalypse to anyone, I mean really! The reader has the prerogative to pick up a book, and thereafter to internalise an independent and original opinion.

Depending on the level of appetite for apparently maverick and bizarre tendencies, the reader especially in South Africa is welcome to evaluate this headline presentation. We have to say again that the USA is the most liberated society where there is no holding back when it comes to flooding the public space with every sort of information. Societies in *developing* countries just came out of difficult circumstances, some are still embattled territories and progress at many levels is still some paces overdue. We cannot simply erase entries into the public domain register, the Court application reports in the media, the records of other researchers on the internet...it is more than enough. There is simply no walking away. In fact, there is too much that has already happened around this issue for anyone to retract let alone be reticent. As well as having committed the act of raising the issue in public, we sometimes covet a reality where it would be government instead of us relaying this story to the public domain. We sometimes covet reining in our deposits lest we be perceived to be responsible for inducing undesirable reactions. Has anyone seen what is happening in the USA? There is a whole community of apocalypse conscious people who are reacting through all sorts of initiatives...(see internet). It is a whole new chapter to imagine what the reaction may be in other countries when it becomes clearer that this could be big...Government alone may be in the driver's seat on this one. The private sector can only do so much to subsidise government initiatives. People have a clear perception of the authority of government as their electoral prerogative. The public sector has an opening to salvage a still undefined situation, that is not so obvious albeit having signals and elements of inevitability. Tom Horn's material is in the public domain and there is no telling what reception this entry is perpetuating in households. One should have seen the faces of the audience in Sid Roth's studio to imagine what is possible should a rubicon of sorts be crossed, when the issue is un-retractable from momentum.

A caveat of note is this, that politics may not be the determining factor of how the issue is dealt with because we all know how ideologies and interest sectors are distributed. For a time such as this, oppositional politics is a sure stumbling block and we shouldn't have this as a hurdle. In hindsight will we ask this: Is it prudent to let traditionally reticent governments lead this period or should we the people in partnership with the private sector marshal it all? Since when can government be expected to go beyond its already stretched capacity, to extend over to an unchartered terrain? These are real questions that we may not bypass. On the other hand, this might not be a competitive situation of tit-for-tat between ideologies, the private and public sector or other formations at all. All hands on deck, all feet in through the door! Government should be given the benefit of the doubt in the interest of the people. There are many people across the world who see no value in government and business, simply not trusting government or business. Yes there are people who have not since received even an ounce of benefit from either government, neither from business, so where to from here...proof of this ....Oxfam statistics reports issued in 2015 state that 1% of the world's population control 99% of the world's wealth.

So, the ambiguous stance of government should be treated cautiously, people across the world government to be a cumbersome giant burdened by its own weight. Even at that we still emphasise that the State will help by calming the storm and prescribing reasonable direction. The challenge is not to lose our nerves and people should be advised likewise. This is a situation of the weak and the strong complementing each other through one of the biggest challenges ever. After all is said and done, we will stand shoulder to shoulder, friend and so called foe to ride through these times. Perhaps this moment is the biggest test to this civilization and a test of human elegance. This realism is a test of everything and nothing could be worth holding back. So we have to emphasise that government should say yeah or nay. Without government coming out and declaring whether this is a code red or not, a lot could go wrong. A lot depends on the authoritative directives of government. Up to now nothing has been said and the people are reaching their own conclusions, look at the USA, search Google for apocalypse related topics.

There has to be a point where we find out whether this is it or not, what government should relinquish or not. At what point do we say, alright this is enough, our civilization is facing an impending level five risk and we have to act differently. It is not easy to feign that this scenario is happening and unfolding at this moment, or not. Should

152

that be the case, we should modulate and debrief daily routine in a manner that has never been done before. Realistically we have to still do what we are used to, carry on as normal. We would not want to experience disruption of focus on the reality of daily routine, right? This is a first class conundrum and it calls for the best advice on how to transit from one reality to *another reality*. When will the reality of Mayan injunction reach a point of no return and critical mass? Will we wait for more indicators until we decide to act? Is it enough to reach a decision from what we have seen already? Maybe it is impossible to walk away from a civilization at all. How do we know what is a cumbersome burden or not, in the event that the Mayans and other older civilizations, are right up to this day. What do we leave behind and what do we take with us, right? These are realistic questions to ask even before anything happens, isn't it?

Once we have familiarised ourselves with the details of the Mayan predictions, supporting sources and evidence, we will be able to see the psychology of epochology in everything. For instance we will see how the past two thousand years was just but the beginning of an enlightenment process about the end-times.

When it comes to the issue of refuting the claims of the Mayans, can anyone come out categorically to refute these claims and settle this matter once and for all? Can anyone go through the data and scientifically isolate the valid from the invalid? There is a healthy stream of people who can relate a contrary account. Can this view be given room to show us that the whole claim is baseless? This is the quickest way to get everybody back into a *normal* routine never to entertain this issue again. Can anybody bring as much evidence as there is to prove that this is all imagined? So far there is more information that vouches for the Mayan claims than not, the internet is a repository of this testament. It is correct to interview contrary opinions because of the huge learning opportunity. If we assume or realistically accept that this is imagined, then shouldn't we withdraw these scalding deposits from public perception? Too many people across the world have already been affected by the claims of the Mayans. This genre goes beyond the limits of public access to information and constitutionalism. This is about all and sundry without the discretions of vested interest. Otherwise this wouldn't be a fair process of informing people but a brutal campaign to extort discomfort. The public must surely be protected by compelling a retraction of these statements should it be proven to be a callous literary attack. Or these claims should be rendered to the archives of a fiction genre in film and otherwise.

This is not an opportunity for showmanship and really no-one should be a celebrity for dabbling in the Mayan story, for better or for worse. Anyone who sees self-absorbed opportunities may realise that it is instead a challenge. This is a challenge for everyone, the message from the past is speaking to a whole generation. We should have more than ourselves in mind. This also should not detract people from saying what they should either way.

We should look at beyond more than ourselves in case we are faced with an impossible challenge. We know that it is thought to be impossible to please everyone all the time, but this is a moment when government should. If we can afford to, we should be impersonal and also think of others, even if it costs us more inconvenience than we can afford. Our rational process may not hold in a time of challenges to our way of life. At the moment it is not straightforward to see the curve ball that the future may be throwing.

If the Mayans are right, our rational world organised ever since we have known, may face a moment when even what seems to be irrational will do. Our organised world, designed to make things easier, quicker and more bearable may capsize. The situation may require resolve opposite and contrary to what we have learnt. We may have to accept abstract, obscure and irrational circumstances. Our tenacity may be challenged because we have to *make up* a reality to get us through the day. This realisation is inspired by the film *The Next Three Days* (by Paul Haggis) about escaping from our normal world in order to circumvent our self-imposed restrictions. *The Next Three Days* is about turning logic on its head in order to find our way out of the imprisonment of the norms we have put in place to govern our lives. As unrelated as the film might appear, it is just a typical example of simple solutions that we sometimes need when the going gets tough and the tough have to get going. The story is a modern day account that illustrates predicament and irregular limits and how we have to do extraordinary things to escape sometimes. For something as remote as *The Next Three Days* to influence the times we live in shows that the *psychology of epochology* is broad and everything that we touch is directly and indirectly linked to our modern day predicament. It also illustrates a simple point, that we have to make do with what we have no matter how much it is, in order to get through our challenges in the end-times. When analysing the psychology of epochology, nothing is beyond our scope. The truth is that our way of life would prove to be a trap if the scenario of the Mayan prediction was to be proven beyond doubt, as a must observe status quo. A film like *The Next Three Days* is a recommended guide of how we have to escape the fears that our government might be harbouring by not admitting that the time is what it is and that we have to act. As a matter of curious fact, once the reader is immersed in the Mayan curriculum, every film, story, piece of song and more become subliminal and subsidiary parts of the story. Everything that is happening in recent times across the world become subplots and scenes of a large story unfolding over time...chapter by chapter...I am sure that if I view more films as references they'll reveal the same genre, of interconnectivity to the Mayan story of *termination of an epoch.*

Procrastination on the part of elected officials and government at large all over the world and delaying tactics is a way of leading to untenable circumstances. Will people be liable where people do what it takes to go beyond an official sanction? What does the government deem necessary as incontrovertible and irrefutable proof for it to take decisive and commensurate action? The movie *The Next Three Days* explores simplicity as a more functional choice of action rather than complex contraptions. The film forces us to answer fundamental questions about freedoms. When what we believe in gets tested do we waiver or not? Faith is the highest element that carries us through the toughest of times and the challenge is to find an anchor for our faith so that we have faith in something close to right as possible. This film is a perfect indicator of the psychology of our times. More amazingly is how pervasive the psychology of epochology seems to be...it seems to be present in everything.

After December 2012, we have already experienced reticence from the private sector in the form of the media who will not cover the story because they cannot see the visible advantage it would give to their bottom line do so. When one looks at the attitude of government in the film *The Next Three Days*, one can already predict the reaction of the public sector. The film depicts government as a lumbering giant burdened with an elaborate network of functions and once an act is decreed, it takes forever and a day for it to clear all the levels of red-tape. So whether something is right or not, it will not matter, the government will find a way to observe prescribed norms and procedures. It is not easy for government to circumvent a situation that needs expedience. The private sector finds it so hard to react to punctual opportunities, then what more of the government's reaction to emergencies. This is just a side-view of the possibilities of the psychological paces that might be in for showing. I never thought that I would find compatibility in the film *The Next Three Days* with the *psychology of epochology* but there is a lot.

 The film also teaches us that it is human nature to always have foresight in hindsight, always. We always see things better after they have happened. We seldom pre-empt, foresee or predict correctly, ever. In the plot of the film, *The Next Three Days*, the government finally got to see the picture, way after it was relevant to. We have departments that are dedicated to investigating incidents after they have happened and we do not have as much to investigate things before they happen. That is just the way things work and we have to factor this in when we make decisions about the Mayan predictions. First we have to take time to filter the information.

For the analytical purpose of this book we have used a few films as a sample and more importantly films that we have seen amongst others. Objectively, what becomes clear is that Hollywood is an important reservoir of information. The film industry in the USA can be summed up as a metaphorical book similar to a book spoken of in *Fingerprints of the Gods* called the *book of Thoth.* The films screened by Hollywood through the years have a valuable source of insight into some of the topics that we may classify as epochology. Hollywood has been obsessed with a genre of 'apocalyptic fiction' to an extent that a scholar of *precession* would be forgiven for thinking that Hollywood has been on some exercise to sensitize and inform the public about the effects of *precession* without overtly stating this fact. Hollywood has informed people of the most volatile topics that even government would not admit to. So we can credit the government indirectly because even Hollywood is within the ambit of public administration to the extent that it is an expression of arts and culture, for which there is a regular public sector department. Besides there is no government that would allow any sector to go beyond a legal constitutional mandate right in front of the public, not even Hollywood. Government does monitor and regulate what the public is allowed to access, doesn't it? So in a funny and ironic way, government is in the loop...whew! this is an exhausting logic.

The momentum required for the academic subject of epochology to stand alone has matured well and a case for such a proposal is viable. It might take more than a lot for the official record to recognise an emerging science in the form of epochology, it may be worth the wait for its own merit to be subjected to review. For example Graham is a proponent of *"precessional science"*, that we view as a subject of a general umbrella discipline that should be epochology. The book *Fingerprints of the Gods* is worth its merit in the founding and assertion of an emerging science to be reckoned with. Epochology may be summed as the study of the several periods in an epoch that is defined by the information alluded to by *"cosmic precession"* and the amount of years reasonably classified by the Mayan calendar amongst other data, as an epoch. Part 5 of the book

*Fingerprints of the Gods* is in the order of textbooks that should be the basis for the science of epochology. Epochology is obviously a polymath discipline that draws on on-going research as any discipline does. Epochology as we see is made of the many subjects that form part of the research established in the content of Graham's book. For this purpose it is not far-fetched that we should propose an academic degree for epochology. The challenge comes when deciding on whether the degree is a humanities science degree or a natural sciences degree because of the complexities of synchronising the several areas of research and subjects that make up *epochology*.

The challenge of figuring out what it takes to establish an academic degree is "visitingly" real. I am not a serial author myself but have since engaged the process due to circumstance. So the idea of an academic degree known as epochology is not a result of some academic ingenuity but of a compelling circumstance. Having no other description for the discipline of collating the content for a book such as this one, we revisited an old idea. We had written outlines of such a discipline on a mobile phone that got lost. So we had to start from scratch to refill the gaps in the preamble and preface for this discipline. So now that the opportunity to collate the idea has come around it makes sense to put it out as a proposal.

There's less doubt that such an academic degree is necessary in order to reconcile the various events that are outlined by many authors in the form of speculative sciences. Reasonable ground for such a basis of inquiry and tuition is well established. Enough sources to call on exist to establish such subject. The final idea to propose the establishment of an academic degree is solidified by what we find in *Fingerprints of the Gods.* Besides the fact that there is more than enough material to justify a stand-alone academic subject, there are just as enough people to interview on this content.

*Reasonably*, it is logical that the subject should also be established as a "universal" subject that may be given in school or as a feeder topic moderated for several learning levels. We do in this regard require a curriculum designer, to defer to, in matters that call for expert input and due process. We would like to credit authors of the several topics and subjects in this *learning area* for the purpose of a degree and the privilege of this proposal. Outside of peer review, it may be possible to do so only when something substantive and innovative is endorsed of this proposal. For the larger part the areas are already laid out in *Fingerprints of the Gods* and to some extent *The Johannesburg Formula*. There are many other proposals that we look forward to as a basis for embarking on design. The question to be answered is: how does the area of speculative science that forms epochology fit into a regular scope of academic inquiry? Does the topic qualify or have unquestionable merit for the purpose of the times we live in?

When engaging the question of careers that this field entails, we may start with authorship, research, teaching, applied epochology, government policies, private sector (risk analysis), industrial innovation (in terms of precession proof technologies), legal principles of epochology and more.

Graham's book is more a research reference than a travel-guide. The research in this book is far from unilateral. So an opportunity emanating out of *Fingerprints of the Gods*, is the participation of more researchers and scientists from institutions in more countries. There is scope for partnerships with the leading institutions in the field of precession research. So far, countries with academic and research departments involved in precession science are Egypt and Southern American countries. This presents an opportunity for more countries to participate through institutions of higher learning and research.  A role for countries like South Africa is extended through questions asked by the author in *Fingerprints Of The Gods.*

*Prophecy* says, *'the first shall be last and the last shall be first'*. Could this edict be referring to the role that nations may play in the end-times? The so called *First World countries may* be the last to accept the implications of the forecasts of Mayans. It is well known that the so called *Third World* nations are amongst the *poorest* on the face of the earth. Ironically this means that the 'poor' nations are in a position to act without attrition. The burden of considering built-up industrial complexes and other national treasures may well be an albatross.

Once we started looking at everything through the eyes of the *psychology of epochology*, nothing was the same... Flashbacks of things seen and things heard throughout, some unsettling... some clues of the time spoken of by the Maya. It dawned as a culmination and realisation of what we learnt from Graham's book, that all life has been 'coded' and programmed for moments like these. No matter what we would have liked it to turn out as, it was just one of those things that we could not avoid. Why we ended up in this situation or position where we are writing *The Johannesburg Formula*, after the deposit at the court. I stopped trying to explain to myself and have accepted that things are just the way they are. In a relatively 'conservative' society due to the digital divide, it is hard to freely express inclination to issues like the Mayan calendar. We did not sweat the reactions to the December 2012 court tender that appeared online, because we knew that it would be a miscellany of reactions. We were only exposed to a minimum range of reactions that we could not avoid. People in South Africa are relatively conservative, especially the older generation. It is one of those societies where outrageous expressions are easily frowned upon. In the post-1994 South Africa more institutions have developed at a faster pace ahead of the flowering society. Most people were surprised by the way the officials dealt with the matter by not censuring or rebuffing it in public. That was extraordinary and worth a commendation. Now South Africa is rightfully at the precipice of venturing into ground-breaking avenues in precessional science because the notions of end-times are known of. This doesn't mean that *developed countries* are not as conservative especially in light of the central message of precessional science. There is no public endorsement by government in *developed countries* of research into precessional theory as espoused in *Fingerprints Of The Gods*.

This was a turning point in South Africa as the country opened up to the possibilities of even an overt display of its attitude to the psychology of epochology. Now after the 12th September 2013 screening of a follow-up from a USA channel, whether we know it or not, SA is re-immersed as a country that broadcast and published the Mayan story in December 2012, even when it was a maverick thing to do. It dawns now that the story is again making its way across the globe, as digital channels are available in most developed countries. This is one of those things that the internet was built for, global networking even in the face of hard realities. The inevitable link to outcomes of approaching Court in December 2012 is coupling with extended reaction across the world, even being linked to media reports like the September 2013 Sid Roth show aired on DSTV and many other programmes and films that we have not seen. People with access to pay channels like DSTV are exposed to a lot more material directly linked to the Maya, directly or indirectly, even up to now and going forward. The media will not look at anything that is not an obvious bottom line story. We tried to link-up with the media to highlight to them that the USA has retaken the issue as they have punched a hole in the obtuse veil that is obscuring the public's view of the story. It didn't really matter much because the viewers of DSTV, even in South Africa were privy to this development in September 2013. Moreover, the viewers of Sid Roth's show around the world saw the Tom Horn interview in September 2013. More than this, all this data is freely available online twenty-four hours, seven days a week...this is hectic...We are by no means saying that anyone is trying to conceal this information, it just hidden by the digital divide...now that is exhausting...whew!(#wiping-sweatbeads-off-the-forehead).

Seemingly, the public in the USA are ahead of the information curve on this, as well as the current affairs curve in so many other ways. We don't know what it would take for the South African media to do likewise, maybe another Court application? Thankfully the Constitutional Court of South Africa is ahead of everyone. All in all this is an indicator of the *psychology of epochology*, the reticence of the media sector to issues that do not apparently have investment return signs written all over them. The reluctance of the media (post-December 2012) makes us even more thankful that the Constitutional Court of South (in December 2012) saw it fit to register the deposit of the Mayan claims. Otherwise the media would have unintendedly declared a total "roadblock" on channels to public perception and public interest, through clamping the information pipelines...

So, here goes...#WelldoneConstitutionalCourt-of-SouthAfrica.

...There would have been a total blank-out on this issue and the South African public would have been out of the loop, in December 2012, so to speak. Had that been the case, then by now, in September 2013 trying to procure the issue would have been untenable because there would not have existed a reasonable basis for doing so, nor any interest for the media. That's why the psychology of epochology is heaving, considering the motives for actions that we all take and especially when viewed from the vantage of the Maya. It feels as if the Mayans are watching from the distant past...well, doesn't it? Surely, if information could have reached a critical mass of the number of people who are sensitized to the realism of Mayan injunction, then we would have commensurate action and reaction from more directions. People are in all sorts of mind states regarding this issue...*time-out!*...{Fast-forward to 2015...through manuscript edit...Google: apocalypse (followed by adjective of choice)...view search results-whew!...*back to manuscript*...}.

...(okay, *back to manuscript*)...Without information, people would be putting pressure on organisations, government and the private sector to act correctly. Isn't it they would be hearing rumours on American media... So it boils down to critical mass as would be the case with any transaction in the modern era. This shows us clearly that it is because the issue has not reached a critical mass and momentum for it to be treated as seriously as it should or could be. It must be a matter of time before this happens and we have no way of pre-empting what the cause of non-returnable momentum might be. After looking at what makes people do what we do and why we act on some things and not on others, we realised that the media or private sector is acting out the protocol code of leaving things to chance by saying "what will be, will be". I mean! Don't media houses *et al* have investigative capacity? Shouldn't they have been on the ball by now (or back on the ball?)...In December 2012, the phone never stopped ringing over the days when the media wanted to interviews regarding the Court application (#amazed). We realise that is just how things functions, you do your bit and the rest will follow. There is no point in chasing after a non-responsive media, they will act according to the code of inevitability, so we wait and see. This...is what eludes the quest for logic in grasping the psychology of epochology. Maybe it is just enough to know that there is such a thing. Trying to know what it is and how it works would be like chasing the wind, or ether or signal to connect to anyone in the fourth estate...who is listening anyhow. We decided that even after what we saw as a glaring material movement in the curve of the Mayan story, on the 12th September 2013, we should *chill* and not be agitated by a general attitude that represent something so fundamental and worthy of learning from...#lesson...the private-sector is reluctant where there are no signs of a bottom-line. After all, this is the psychology of epochology at work... it is difficult to grasp. For now, we only observe how it works without seeing into the box to see how the machination functions.

Judging from what happened after December 2012 i.e. January 2013 and beyond, it is visible that it is the perception of the media that this is an important story because it was a Constitutional Court matter, probably the only reason that it was covered and broadcast. Proof of this is that South Africa is the only country in the world where the matter was tendered at a Court of law. Now it is baffling that the situation is the same in the USA in September 2013, the story is only re-emerging on a television show rather than the fourth estate. The government in the USA has not responded to the September television show on Sid Roth's where Tom horn reignited the issue in the public domain, nine months after the 21st December

2012. We know that this is the machination of what *The Johannesburg Formula* terms as the *psychology of epochology* in action. Thanks to activists, the USA is ahead of the public interest curve and by default the logistics curve. *Generally*, people in the USA have been *liberated* for long, this and the fact that the US public is reputed to hold-no-bars, speaks volumes.

The *psychology of epochology* curve looks something like this: awareness, action, and reaction. So this is the direction that everything is taking. First, critical mass of awareness will have to develop, then interpretation and then debates about who is right and who is not, will follow. Then action will be taken. The form of action that will be taken varies from party to party depending on what the interpretation of the facts is.

Then there will be reaction to the action, in the form of responses of various kinds. One thing that will not change for anything is the stakeholder list, the private-sector, government, households, organisations and individuals across the world. All what is variable is the social definition of each of these stakeholders, some are *rich,* others *poor* etc. This process is far from being a full-blown international commission, because there is still the hurdle of the digital divide to surmount, coupled with official reluctance and outright private reticence, period. If ever there was a country prepared and ready it would be the USA. *Ready for what*? Well, ready to accept the realism of the Mayan predictions. There is in the USA, the most information in the hands of the public than any other nation in the world, followed by South America where the Mayan calendar story originates. Many films that deal with the genre of apocalypse and cataclysm have sensitized the American public to the issue of end-times.

The biggest point to make is that Government all over the world should sooner realise that this matter has by now after 2013, long past being a civilian issue that can be unofficially pronounced on in the public. With all due respect, Government needs to rein this matter in as a matter of urgency so that the correct statements may be made in public. Government alone has the requisite capacity to deliberate on this matter sufficiently because of the sensitive nature of this issue. After February 2013, September 2013 and still as public perception and official opinion would have it, December 2012. (#tentativecrowd....). It should be clear that alarm bells are going off and the State is being called on to ascend to the position of leadership on this matter. For now, the public has said enough, especially in the USA and including us in SA. The onus is on Government to intervene for reasons that may only be clearly visible from the enhanced vantage position of the State and prescriptions of the public interest. There is more than enough information for the government to collate. It takes the joining of seemingly disparate dots to see what any government will and should see.

The more we ruminate on the idea of an end of times, the more we realise that being adult is a limitation. Adults have settled views, opinions and premeditated decisions. Adults will never believe that the earth is where it is in time. We saw this in December 2012, when adults just kept quiet and no one said whether the Mayans were correct or not. Adults chose the safe plate in the *game*, silence. Adult disposition just chose the option of waiting it out. We don't know what we were all thinking in December 2012 when we couldn't or didn't even flinch at hearing the information of the Mayan claims. This already indicates the attitude to anything incredible, according to the summation of adults, if it is not logical, then it is not real. Children on the hand are the safest end time crowd....Children have the "stuff" of end-times flowing in their veins. It is not a matter of belief but a matter of knowing. Children have a way of knowing and once they know something there is no going back. Adults are susceptible to long terms of ingrained beliefs and this is where the challenge comes from. Adults will react at the last or latest moment to something that children would have long been sensitized to. This is the psychology of epochology in a nutshell. *Adults are like university students who always submit assignments at the very last moments, even always asking for extensions…*

As a result of engaging the precessional theory through the claims of the Mayan calendar, much insight has come to the fore. *The discipline of epochology, theory of epoch psychology, the theory of the oblate-round dichotomy and the Johannesburg Formula* have been explorations into variable possibilities about what we know. Astro-anthropology is also a focus subject of this chapter as a way of linking astrology and anthropology. It is clear that we may have to weld together the discipline of anthropology and the field of astrology as combined tributaries that focus on the science of epochology and precession. Otherwise we will run around with too many variables that are separated at conception, making the task of interpreting data all the more difficult.

Afterall is said and done, we take our hat off to the South African government, the Constitutional Court of South Africa, the media (of 2012...#lol) and the citizens for having allowed the invasive issue to pervade in December 2012. This was an unexpected turn of events that ushered South Africa into the frontline of cosmic awareness and will to take the future as it comes...salute Mzansi! This shows that South Africa is an emotionally developed country. South African is known to be endowed with a high order of emotional intelligence, these are the people who walked away from apartheid without feeling a thirsty need for revenge. This could have just been one of those precessional moments. This means that according to the times, South Africa came out of apartheid just in time to be ready for a crucial role in the end-times situation. This figures! The end-times story is the biggest online story right now as we speak. The internet is a cache of endless information about all the possible scenarios and reasons for the times we are in being terminal. We cannot fathom the overwhelming preoccupation of thousands of people across the world with this story.

Far from end-times mongering and wanting to sound paranoid, we are strictly heightening our own awareness as part of a legacy of generations that can face reality about the tenure on the earth. Far from foreclosing on the illustrious gains of civilization and the benefits that many experience as the course of the human enterprise

166

advances, we have also to be aware that the earth has its own cycles of renewal and rejuvenation, and that these we may experience relatively as environmental incursions. The earth is also part of a wide external solar environment and this too makes the earth susceptible to cycles of renewal. We are part of a greater scheme of a cosmic realism and this we will feel and experience from time to time, whether in a calm way or indeed a turbulent way. Sometimes the earth is part of a season where comets streak across the sky and sometimes, asteroids breach the atmosphere. This is a reality that we may not avert, even as we go about our own preoccupations that may seem insignificant in the greater scheme of things. Nothing is insignificantly less important than any other thing that is found in the union of the experience of living.

Also interestingly, is the fact that humans have been programmed to win, to beat the odds, to overcome adversity and to circumvent misfortune or danger. It is simply in our DNA. The human species has overcome incredible odds ever since civilizations have been coming and going. This means that we have to keep going, keep doing what we do best, even when we know that there might be a callous inevitability that lurks in the domain of the unknown. Humans have even survived cataclysms before in the past, as we all know, the deluge of Noah's time is an example. Humans are wired to survive. Part of survival is about knowing the threats and risks. A SWOT analysis was designed for humans to overcome challenges. Coming face to face with the possible truth of end-times could be just the thing to get the human species through a difficult moment. Humans are what planet earth is known for, one of the most indefatigable species on earth! Survival at all costs is a must. The Bible as a whole can be read as a survivor manual that the kindest Creator has bequeathed to us. The Bible is also a cataclysm-watch guide that warns the human race of impending changes in our circumstances. Humans are so ingrained with survival that we have even developed a way of knowing before a cataclysm happens. The Bible and the Mayan calendar are but a few of such early warning systems developed for humans. Somehow I get a feeling that everyone knows something about the cataclysmic reality of living on earth. This is one of those global challenges that is going to test our mettle and make us prove that we are humane first and for most. We will show yet again that we are more inclined to put others ahead of ourselves when times get tough. This is what makes us human. Time will tell.

After a storm, there comes a calm...we felt this feeling of calm towards the end of the editing read that we took of the book now in October 2013. We were overcome by a feeling that it is okay to be immersed nose in first into the keyboard and getting around the script of this book. It is sort of like this, someone tells you something and you are listening and then you react by saying: "what?...you did not just say that!...really?". We realised that "hey" anyone in this position would have done the same. Who would not after hearing that the earth is in a period of epoch closure, not react the way that we did? Who would not think that this is a matter of public interest, let alone national importance, a matter of international importance? We bet anyone would react the same. Or is it a matter of listening and hearing? This is what was going around in 2012, remember the screening of the film titled: *2012,* in 2011 and things like that...we heard this... *"the Mayans say the world as we know it is coming to an end in December 2012, through some sort of cataclysm".* (This was the general talk online and in newspapers remember?). Would this not cause anyone to get into a no joke mode? Sure the difference is that I had prior encounters with a similar account from another perspective, but had long almost thought that it was an open-ended issue...Things took a heated turn in early 2012 for anyone who was watching this issue anyway, so we went for it...off to Braamfontein, Constitutional Hill, where the Constitutional Court is located.

Anyway, people like Graham were right to write books for the world to know about the Maya, the Hopi and other almost forgotten people that once walked tall and some still tall to us today. Even now as we speak, it is right that we should be perturbed at the prospect of a terminal epoch, whenever it may be. To be sure that we are not in a twilight zone of some sort, we all need reassurance so that we can still carry on doing things as normally as we always have. The reality of the world as we know it is here and present with us, so let's carry on. We have to carry on. No-one has knocked on our door and said "yes, we are taking you away to an institution to be observed" yet, right. So we are not a case for observation at a facility after all, just because we said, hey! ...*here is information that the earth has reached a critical terminal point of a cyclical nature*. This could have been the case, maybe if this was 1938 or so, just maybe. We were privy to the information and heavily interested in the topic. We had the space and we took it, no regrets. We feel relieved when it finally dawns that we did what anyone would have, to raise the alarm. It's not as if we went and screamed "Fire!" in a packed movie theatre, now, right?

Instead, as a compliment, the South African public did not say nay. They observed without judging. Graham Hancock is not a maverick afterall, he is a balanced person who did what anyone in his position would have done. He said, here is information that needs to get out and he got it out through his book. This is it, we moved from the position when we were pacing up and down, to and from the Court finalising the submission, to feeling like err...maybe we should not have....and then to, well that was fine, anyone in my position would have done exactly the same.   When we woke up on the 22nd October 2013, it was like, hey we are okay, this is how things work, media gives preferment to stories *that they like*, everyone reacts, some feel apprehensive, etc, this is normal. So keep on writing...  Besides, the realisation that we are discovering things we wouldn't have had we not started this whole thing, is a source of relief. Somewhere in the middle of a sitting, while typing, we realise that the next book that we need to get hold of is *The Sign and the Seal.* This book should be re-read. Why? Because lights are going on...the link becomes remotely visible... hey, there is a link between the message of this book central to answers that are going to lead humanity in the direction of *Fingerprints of the Gods.* This book *Fingerprints of the Gods* should in and of its own right be reckoned with for what it is, an early warning tool. Hold on, we just realised that this is actually

169

the biggest, oldest and most intriguing story ever. The story of precession or end-times is an old story that has been with us forever.

This story has its roots in the oldest traditions, the Bible and modern day classics like Graham's. Moreover for someone to put themselves in line of social diatribe is an even more intriguing curiosity. We all want to see a curious and exquisite showcase once in a while, right? The story of end-times is one of those, it is a self-fulfilling parody of these days.  Today on the 22nd October 2013, we realised that the Grand Union Theory is a valid truism. Everything that we have done and everything that is happening all around us is part of one story-board. Every song when listened to closely reveals an undercurrent of the psychology of the times we are in. Everything is linked, every action, every outcome has a psychological twist that speaks of the times we are in. Observe closely and anyone sees that everything is programmed to our future, whatever that may be. Humans are amongst champion species on earth, a precious lot to the Creator. Where the future goes or takes us, we all have something to do with it. For the purposes of the *end-times*, we have some (even if just a bit) control and it is also up to everyone to do with the future what is possible. One thing that is for sure though, is that value systems are forever changing. Some things are dear, some replaceable and others not. Is it possible that everything has been preparing people at large for the *end-times*? The vast amounts of the wealth of nations and built up environments stored up by today's generation could have been just what the doctor ordered... Fact and fiction have a funny way of melting into each other.

By the look of things, we would say that somehow uncannily, the generation of today is ready for anything. We have to make the call... We just have to look at ourselves through the spectacle of psychology to see that whatever we may want to think, the people of the world are ready for the end-of-days. Just have a look, listen to the music in your collection and you will see that this has been part of an uncanny algorithm that has been talking in song for the longest time... The psychology of music is evidence of another dimension

170

that is communicating an independent message. The psychology of music enables us to see other messages that are embedded in the subconscious of the world. Analysis of music reveals an innate strength that people have to deal with a *hard cold* reality. What we learn from music is that it teaches us to observe and to realise that the longer we look at anything, the more we see aspects of it that we never saw before. We have heard instruments that accompany lyrical music that we only noticed on repeated playing of the same song. We have derived meaning from a topic in a song that we never saw a connection with before, on listening longer. Literary analysis of the art and science of music, through interpretation, deducing metaphors and figurative meaning may reveal more than the obvious. Any song has more than one literal meaning because meaning can be subjective or objective depending on a function of purpose. On listening we find that we have been bequeathed a future that to grapple with. Music has the ability to talk to a higher aspect, so music is an essential tool that is crucial to cosmic transition or transformation.

Everything needed to meet challenging times head-on is in the hands of the people. The government and the private sector should look closely and hear the people in order to accept the reality of the times. There are eight billion perspectives out there. It is nearly astounding to imagine that everything created is programmed to behave the way it does. Nature could be a "programme" with a high level algorithm intended to behave the way it does. If this is acceptable then, it means that every action no matter how small or seemingly insignificant, may be programmed to do just what it does. It is possible to think in terms of the state-of-the-art as a reflection of this natural design. Then defect in the grand design could be compensated for by inbuilt mechanisms of nature correcting itself. Could everything in the past 100 years be part of *precession*? Let us objectively examine a case study of the most gruesome behaviour that humans have been engaged in over the past hundred years, wars. For example, could the world wars of the past 100 years have been fought as part of the psychology of epochology? It seems as though this is indeed the reality. All the events or actions of everyday are part of a *precessional* outcome. We may deduce that the last two world wars and indeed all wars that humans may remember, were part of the psychology of cosmic precession. These wars were a career to the end-times period that has taken definitive shape ever since the times of biblical figures. How pervasive is the psychology of epochology, even? The outcomes of all major wars have only been noticeably quantified in terms of the triumph and vanquishing of either of the parties. This is the psychology that our generation carries into the future. So, there were victors in these wars that shaped the tone of things to come right? It seems possible that the triumph of the wars have actually been a triumph for the course of precession. This could be a symptom of the effects of precession on the course of humans over time.

So we are saying that it is possible that if the vanquished forces were not and there was wholesale enslavement of the human race into the present, then the Mayan prophecy would have found a different world void of the developments that have taken root ever since the triumph of freedom and liberty due to the forces that triumphed in the past two world-wide wars. This is a portent for the end-of-days, it just illustrates the propensity of humans for foresight and propensity to act in their interest for the long term and for posterity, ahead of circumstances. It seems as though there is an algorithm in operation as the future intercepts the process of the present unfolding. It seems possibly that we are in a precession time machine that is determining moment for moment as it unfolds.

Another case study is the triumph of liberty over colonialism and slavery. The past 100 years in the story of humanity is intoxicatingly filled with events that we would say are linked only through a hyperbole of joined dots. The liberation of former colonies is a major aspect that we would attribute to precession. As well as the two world wars still in the memory of a lot of people, the liberation of former colonies was a stringent purpose that had to unfold if the theory of precession and the end-times is veritable. There is no way that precession would have been clearly identifiable if colonialism had persisted as virulent as it was at its onset. People would have still been caught up in the loss and gain politics of colonialism. If colonialism could have been perpetuated into let's say 2012, the gains for those who benefited would have been much too luxurious to forgo. There seems to also be something more compelling that made colonialism to buckle. Towards the end of colonialism, the colonisers had more military and tactical power than when colonialism begun. It was possible to continue with colonialism through armed resistance and vested interest due to a roadblock of backward ideas. Colonialism seduced colonisers who benefitted erroneously and led to the outcome that caused the two world wars to be fought, with progressive luminaries vanquishing the evils of the colonial era. To a precessionalist, it seems cogent that these wars were fought at the behest of collapsing colonialism and that the collapse of colonialism was itself at the behest of precession. We wouldn't comment much about the major wars fought before the eighteenth century. These were also part of the possible precession theory. The pressure of the knowledge that the end-of-days was upon the world is a probable force. More recently, the knowledge of the end-times has been propagated for over two millennia in our current and recognisable context. More so, the Mayans had knowledge of the end-times over five millennia ago. In the mean-time, colonialism was a strong arm game and logically, the colonial forces had the nerve and arms to continue. The beneficiaries of colonialism had a pretext for perpetuating colonialism longer than when it expired. What force of knowledge collapsed the idea and franchise of colonialism until it was rendered obsolete even in front of the eyes of the former colonial nations who were so full of steam at the beginning? It seems plausible that some deep seated foresight was operating over the past 100 years to dismantle the tragedy of colonialism. All those who acted could have been unaware of precession as the fundamental driving force. The world simply had to be in a position where it would be ready for the precessional due dates.

To a large extent, the two world wars were fought as part of the campaign to bring colonialism to a halt. Those who would have supported colonialism to be perpetuated would have been the agents of blundering devastation in the end-times. The plaintiffs in this case were unaware agents of proprietary action in the end-times. The serendipitous foresight that has been playing out is only visible after a long search of fundamental reason for some actions that have marked the story of humanity in the past 100 years.

A possible theory is that the vanquished colonial extremists lost to a force of precession that was rolling almost in stealth mode, invisible. The windfall of the two major world wars is a direct factor to the relentless disbanding of colonialism in its entirety. Could precession be a psychological current that dominates all life without announcement of its prevalence.

This is the most plausible theory that is related to why the past 100 years have been so feisty in the run up to the end-of-days. It follows logically that if the theory of end-times and precession is veritable, then the 'world wars for precession' theory is also a valid summation. This is what the psychology of epochology approach is asserting. It more plausible, everything is inked to precession...proof: a civilization as early as that of the Mayans could see the clear trend of cyclical cataclysm and variations in consistent solar system patterns. The Mayans knew that notions of eternity are variable (or cyclical) rather than fixed. They made it their business to warn us.

This is a valid observation and credible answer to the question: Is the end of colonialism related to the end-of-days? If this is indeed an inscrutable truth, then it follows that all the Armistice Day commemorations ever since the Second World War have been a process of induction into the action that would be required for the end-times. If the two world wars in the past 100 years fit the bill of being fundamental precessional processes, then the people who fought in the liberation struggle all over the world will be pleasantly surprised to learn that theirs was a struggle to be free at the end-times moment.  What this should tell us about the reality of the end-times is that it is a hard won process for the world to come into the realisation of the period we are in. it is possible that it is going to take militant campaigning to make the powers that be realise what time it is. In South Africa it was shown just what an arduous process to put the end-times issue on the table is. The Constitutional Court received an application in December 2012 and the public were privy to the story of the Mayan prediction. It was even made clear to the public that, this was the beginning of the period and that even if nothing specific happened on the 21st December 2012, the process was unfolding.

What may be interesting to state is that it is a logical conclusion that Africa and South Africa specifically should be so forward looking regarding any outcomes of the cosmic transition period. The science of tectonics tells us point blank that the African plate is the most solid plate. It is well established, and accepted as fact that Africa is a stable geological environment in terms of severe activity, so Africa should be the hot-bed of stability should anything extreme happen on the planet. Africa is then supposed to be the place where the people of the world look to in times of extreme geological consequences that may occur as a result of a verifiable cosmic transition that is characterised by environmental upheaval. It should then not be strange that Africa is a credible plaintiff and worthy respondent to the claims made by the Mayan prediction that the cosmic transition is due to take place within the time period that the planet is in, generally and as it were the tentative 21st December specifically predicted by the Mayan calendar. It is reasonable that the first Court related response to the claims of the Mayans comes from South Africa as a way of saying that the world community is one and should anything be said to be happening on a global scale, Africa is first to recognise the duty that is incumbent on all.

One definitive aspect of the end-times debate that we have learnt to accept is that there are no guarantees. Whether the Mayan prediction of end-times is a real event or not, is not the actual point. The opposite is also true, just because some people say nothing will happen, does not mean that the end-times will not unfold. This is a reflection of the world we live in, it is just as precarious as it is secure. So just as risk analysis functions, expect the best and be prepared for the worst.

What we know is that the people writing about the Mayans are envoys and that the Mayan calendar exists of its own account without the embellishment of researchers and writers. With or without researchers, writers, commentators and the media, the Mayan issue lives on its own accord. We should not confuse the message with the messengers. Anyone may go straight to the source of the story without relying on researchers and writers who are extending the story to the public.

Finally, why is shock therapy so valuable? Maybe that has to be how the mind functions. The shock therapy value of December 2012 media reports of the Mayan story is something that won't be discounted. We are yet to deduce the effects of this psychological process of "shocking" people into awareness. If the Mayans intended to shock us into awareness of their predictions, well it worked! People all over the world have been shocked into awareness...in fact the August earthquake in South Africa reminded people of December 2012. So, were Mayans apocalyptic "terrorists" of note or not? If that's the case then they sweep all stake of the title for all times. If their "terrorism" is meant to warn the future of a horrendous fate, then it has a strange efficacy. Surely Mayans didn't mean to scare and terrorise people of the future, otherwise they would have bequeathed nothing or said nothing, now...that would have been the last degree of psychological terror.

# CHAPTER EIGHT

## THE BEGINNING OF THE YEAR 2014

According to the seven candles theory, the year 2014 is a second candle of seven candles, with 2013 being the first. It is our view that the years may usher in somewhat of a spectacular inning that we have not seen in a while. Long before even searching for and finding suitable means to be published, the hypothesis of the *Johannesburg Formula* has taken an even headier turn in outlook. It is with a fair amount of trepidation that we have to admit that the very quality of hardiness that the human species is known for is probably the biggest risk. The theory that the strongest point of any system is its weakest is again making landfall as 2014 has proved the claims of the *Johannesburg Formula* to be within a range of the credible. The 19th February 2014 and 05th March 2014 dates make for cosmic history on a recently unprecedented scale. These two dates are ominous as they are dates on which the planet earth is proved to have had close encounters with asteroids that happened to pass by within a distance of 400 000kms. This is not a negligible fact as it seems to be mirrored by the tabloids and newspapers in South Africa, that only dedicated less than five lines to each of these near earth encounters, on both occasions the incursions being played down by the amount of attention they received. To avid watchers of this recent subversive trend, this is too close for comfort, because as it is today on the 08th March 2014 as we add this paragraph, there is an asteroid known as 2003QQ47 that has the avid community divided about where this asteroid, that is reportedly supposed to make some sort of incursion on the 21st March 2014, will end-up. Arguments are raging online (the only prolific environment where these issues are being discussed) and it is anyone's bet as to what the likelihood of this asteroid breaching the earth's stratosphere is. One thing is for sure though that the earth has entered a period where the asteroid-belt that is lodged between the planets Mars and Jupiter is experiencing a meltdown of sorts due to a solar flare (gripping the entire solar system neighbourhood), not experienced in centuries. What the *Johannesburg Formula* is correct about is that this is probably going to be an annual occurrence and it is not known what the frequency of asteroids being dislodged from the asteroid belt is going to be and how this is going to affect the earth from now on. Today, as we write this paragraph, it is the 08th March 2014, three days after an asteroid known as 2014DX110 is reported in a South African newspaper (THE NEW AGE), in three sentences with reference to the source as *metro.co.uk* and the article points to the Virtual Telescope Project and Slooh websites for footage of this incursion. "The New Age" report states categorically upon reporting about the 05th March 2014 asteroid, that the world is open to uncertain danger due to the recent realisation of asteroid incursions. We have to say that by now, if the world has not realised that outside of human civilization having a credible and known cosmic early warning system, the three asteroids from February 2013, February 2014 and March 2014 are signals that the world has entered an unprecedented temporal zone and we should have by now been acting differently by interpreting these as timeless warnings of note. So far in early 2014, we wouldn't say that there are conclusive details about what is happening in the solar system. We can say this determinably because the asteroid incursions seem to be surprises that have not been foreseen, from what we deduct in the reports of early 2014. Our own table-top hypothesis is that there is an unquantified meltdown occurring in the solar system. Any object "small" enough to be susceptible to a viscous and chemical gas that suspends objects as large as planets in the solar system, can be dislodged. We have seen this now for the past two years, stories of asteroids being reported to be hurtling towards and around the perimeters of the earth.

...Today on the 12th March 2014, we are reeling because we would by now have wanted to be published as this would have enabled readers to participate in the hypothesis of the *Johannesburg Formula*, live as these stories unfold. Nevertheless, even as the public domain, especially popular tabloids in South Africa are reflecting on the 2013 asteroid issues...it is worrying that there is no linkages to the Mayan prophecy, similar to the dots that are joined even theoretically by the claims of The Johannesburg Formula. Here the anecdotal theory is making links between the recent spate of asteroid incursions and the Mayan prophecy in general. Recent realities in the asteroid belt could even prove that the Mayans knew something about long-term periods in the solar system, that modern science is overlooking. Could the end and/or beginning of a pre-calibrated period of 5125 years be a period of definitive "solar hyper-activity" and the attendant melt-down in the solar system resulting in all sorts of categories of *end-of-the-world* scenarios on a cyclical basis? We would like to put this question to Mr Graham Hancock, an unassailable authority on the Mayan Prophecy. *Fingerprints of the Gods* focuses specifically on a 21st December 2012 scenario of what the Mayan *end-of-the-world* theory entails, astonishingly, 2014 is redrawing the picture as a climax of the scenario painted by the Mayans culminates. Remember *Fingerprints Of The Gods* was published in 1995, so more credit is due to the prolific description and historical account painted in the book. The reports of asteroid related information in the public domain now in March 2014, finally ushers in something that for long has been relegated to the fringes. Finally the curriculum pioneered by the likes of Graham Hancock is going to be a reliable and formidable scientific platform. Precessional science may even be recognised and accepted by the world as a forerunner in explaining the recent anomalies unfolding across the world. The ground has been well prepared to highlight the connections between seemingly unrelated dots.

We don't know what anyone else thinks, but it is a state of emergency on planet earth when two asteroids whizz past the earth in a period of two months of each other. If anyone especially in government doesn't see the threat, then we  don't know... the 19th February 2014 and 05th March 2014 are phenomenal dates on the planet, objects that are more ruinous than all the nuclear bombs put together are showing up at or near the circumference of the earth's stratosphere and everyone is muted? This is the psychology of epochology in its most unadulterated form.

...Today is the 11th March 2014, and after listening to a meteorologist being interviewed at mid-day on Talk Radio 702 by Stephen Grootes (if I recall properly, her name is Janine). The meteorologist admitted on radio that they could not explain the cause of the 'unusual' rain. It was day number ten of the incessant rain and Stephen struck a chord with me when he was asking the meteorologist about whether the polar vortex or 'climate change' had anything to do with the weather trend as South Africa is perplexed by the 'unusual' weather patterns ever since about ten days ago...

The sun has many characteristics and activities of which we don't know much (as people on the planet), most of us only know it as a life giving inferno. From what recent reports associated with the recent behaviour of the sun, the sun is said to switch its poles every eleven years. What is not known for sure is what happens on a longer term. On top of the eleven year polar switch of the sun, there are long term but *fixed* periods that also culminate in changes that affect the tempo of the solar system. For instance, it has been widely reported online that the sun is flaring up and excess plasma ejections are the order of the day. For all we know, the compounded effects of the solar plasma ejections, could build up and eventually a once-off solar heat wave may or even will envelope the solar system and disrupt the current civilization as satellites and other orbiting space objects from planet earth may melt due to a searing rise in heat temperature.  Please be warned that this is theoretical conjecture in the absence of official empirical research from the State anywhere in the world. After all hypotheses is the basis of accepted theory and later may be refuted or confirmed based on shifting positions.

Listening to the radio and people explain the recent unfolding situation where South Africa is smothered by heavy rains that the Weather Services have admitted are unusual, today is a...err..what shall we say... *"frustrated"* day (yes we are saying the day is frustrated...*a bit of literary licence here and there*). We want to put it on record that there has to be an explanation for *what is going,* someone out there somewhere. Someone may explain it all. For now it may be an "official" source or not even... Our own summation as a newly forged *astro-anthropologist* and *paleo-astronomer*, is that we will find answers in inter-disciplinary forums. The future is just that, new occupations are bound to be forged if you are wondering what an astro-anthropologist and paleo-astronomer is. There is no-one to be found anywhere to make known our now anxious suspicion that the planet has entered into a time-zone of no return, an imminent global melt down.

Meanwhile back on earth....the rain in South Africa is throwing an epic tantrum...On top of stories about unruly asteroids, there are reports of collapse of low set bridges in some provinces due the tenth day bout of the rain. Is this signalling a beginning of an integrated meltdown that is happening in the solar system in general and washing out as out here on planet earth? Are we feeling the opener of this phenomenon that is going to end in a total collapse of this civilization as we know it in the coming years? Q*uestion: how does this all tie up? Well a hotter solar system could result in a warmer planet, depositing more moisture in the atmosphere and a huge stock of rain that results in floods...*This unravelling state of affairs is happening with compounding effect and the end of it will not be quantifiable nor graspable. Right now as I write, I hear a radio announcement by a presenter that "the government is slowly *scaling up to a state of emergency* even though it has not yet been declared". Don't be alarmed just yet, this is regarding the incessant rain that has been pelting Greater Johannesburg and neighbouring provinces, causing unprecedented medium flooding.

Can you imagine, as the author of this book there is room to sometimes over-react, especially when reporting real time events that may turn out as damp squibs later...Anyways lets carry on. The test is whether we can maintain calm nerves in the face of big data and high suspicion of the whole metaphysical notion of *climate change*, it is forgivable to be on a constant stake out... It feels more like the plot of a movie where an investigator is on the heels of a shrewd villain. Only in this case the investigative team is on the heels of *climate change* as it is known...( #sounds of accompanying soundtrack in the background...imagine that...eerie..). We wait it out, while springing to action from time to time, when the subject moves. While building a profile of the *subject*, we know what we know, the rest...we leave it to time and space to bare. It beats having to wait it out until an opportunity reappears to tell someone about this bizarre picture we are looking at. This is real, no matter how long it takes to write this book, we will wait it out. We are persuaded that we are looking at real time evidence to the dossier that we expressly relayed in the application to the Constitutional Court in December 2012.

So far in our investigation, our hypothesis is that from now on, the planet has entered a temporal zone (time zone) that coincides with a (mega) solar flare of note, causing a meltdown throughout the solar system. Accordingly, this will impact the planet in ways that have not happened in millennia, roughly equivalent to the *end of the world as we know it.* The asteroid-belt is a solid indicator of what is happening in the solar system. The recent behaviour of the asteroid-belt and the apparent melt down reflected by the distinct dislodging of three asteroids so far, one of which have caused injuries to people on the planet and the other two having come too close to cause real concern and sound warning alarms.   Honestly, by now we would have thought that this book would have been published, but means withstanding, we are still typing additional material...today, the 11th March 2014.  Nonetheless, from here on it looks like the installations and the built-up environment around the world will tear like a garment, stitch for stich, as has already been seen, earthquakes have struck in China, Barbados in the Caribbean and now lately a magnitude six earthquake in California sent 300 000 people scurrying. All this is happening in 2014, from here there is no predicting where things will go.

One thing that we are sure of is that, what we are about to experience will fast *roll-out* from the ambit of the State to handle. This like a run away train...eventually even the State will be overwhelmed. Because this is a global realism, covering the entire planet, people are reluctant to deal with this aspect of the temporal zone we are in. The "rains of March" in 2014 here in South Africa, may relent, but this is only a lull...the system will migrate to another place on the planet and this may be over the sea but sooner it will make landfall elsewhere on land. All what the Johannesburg Formula is confirming is that instead of the planet-centric view that is focusing on High and Low weather systems, that are the apparent cause of the "Rains of March" 2014 in South Africa, there should be a wider net cast beyond the planet and the sun should be looked at as an additional culprit, because the asteroid-belt is registering unusual behaviour. The asteroid belt is a main indicator of a rampant coup playing out in outer space but all the same headed for a *landing* out here on earth...

One of the developments that we would curtail is attributing the recent and culminating incursions to astrology and cosmology exclusively. These are also components of pure astronomical realities that can be traced for causality. Even ancient societies had glimpses of a broader plot and coded the science in cosmology and astrology for preservation and transmission to the future. So now this big data has strong aspects of empirical accounts. Look at Graham Hancock's modules to follow the trail...this is a good start for all of us even.

...Today is the 12ᵗʰ March 2014 and as we look at some newspapers from this week, we realise that there are indeed newspapers that are supplying the public with some of this so-called *fringe* information. For what we could get hold of, a South African tabloid called "The New Age", copies from the 10ᵗʰ March 2014 and 11ᵗʰ March 2014. These papers reveal a *wealth* of information though in tit-bits for the eager theorist in the face of the recent reality of an asteroid-belt that has gone awry. Most people in emerging economies do not have much uninhibited access to internet

183

resources and some even do not have access to newspapers due to cost and other factors such as the digital divide, product compatibility and outright unaffordability. For all that its worth, for the times when we have been able to access newspapers...we have been surprised. Today we learnt that a newspaper called "The New Age" is carrying summaries about meteors and asteroids, even reports on NASA, in a section called "20 STORIES IN 20 MINUTES". These bits of information reveal that a spectrum of scientist have proven that there are periods in the distant past when asteroids pummelled the surface of the earth, proves the "asteroid-belt volatility" hypothesis proposed by *The Johannesburg Formula*. For the benefit of the public this is proper information that supports people who have been saying similar things long before the media was forced to report this information because of the recent spate of encounters with asteroids headed in the direction of planet earth. The Johannesburg Formula theory is finding a fertile basis of supportive data. Primary sources cited in "The New Age" (South Africa), in a section: "20 STORIES IN 20 MINUTES" goes a long way to shore up *The Johannesburg Formula's* suspicion or tentative hypothesis. Because at the moment the spotlight is on South Africa due to the notorious case in the media, people across the world might have discovered by now that South Africa is going through a rain down-pour that is being labelled as unusual. This rain has so far lasted for more than ten days, the 12th March 2014 being the 12th day. The spotlight shifted this way mostly because South Africa has captivated the attention of the world as the Oscar Pistorius trial is making headlines across the world. The Oscar Pistorius trial story is coinciding with the "Rains of March 2014", that makes it a ground for cosmological hypothesis and speculation...only if you happen to be simultaneously looking at the recent activity of the asteroid-belt and sun for that matter...

@editingmanuscript#FastForwardto2015/03/21st : now that we have an account on www.createspace.com/5331085 it is a relief that we now have a self-publishing account, it is a different venture to what we felt back in March 2014 when we didn't know how it would

184

happen as the reader sees from the diary style entries...back to @2014#editingmanuscript...

...Sitting here typing in what we hope are final inputs to the book before getting a viable opportunity to publish, today on the 12th March 2014, the weather is displaying signs of the rain clouds opening up. Somehow we know that these are fleeting illusions of weather that could clear as most people would like and also the Weather Services announcing that the rain might abate. What we surmise is that there is no telling when the "Rains of March" 2014 will clear because the hotter it gets, the clouds clearing (during daytime), an even bigger chance of the rain returning later at night is greater. In lay terms and observation, as even we have not realised that the heat will simply rise to the sky and then again condense to form more rain that might fall at night when the colder air is trapped beneath the hot air. This is because I have not yet detected that the cause of the rain is more the result of a hotter solar system at large that is pumping more than usual heat to stream to the interior of the earth's atmosphere, even though the reality is that atmospheric systems do migrate. The theory or hypothesis that we are advancing is that the atmosphere below and above the stratosphere is being heated up in a very unusual manner because of an unusually hyper-active sun, spewing out higher than usual densities of plasma.

Interestingly we saw in "The New Age", a report that appears in a section called "20 STORIES IN 20 MINUTES", with the heading "Earth has a plasma shield". This two sentence article proposes that: *"The sun can wreak havoc on Earth during its more active periods, leading to radio blackouts and geomagnetic storms, says ibtimes.com. Fortunately, Earth has a plasma shield in its already-protective magnetosphere, which researchers have discovered acts as another protective barrier."* This article appeared in the issue of *The New Age* published on the 10th March 2014. Although indirectly related to this article, comparatively, to the point of linking dots between other articles published on other days in the same publication, is the fact that an asteroid may breach a plasma shield. We are saying this based on a comparison between this article and the article that appeared on the 11th March 2014 issue, that talks about asteroids pummelling the earth in the distant past. Even at that this plasma shield appears from description to be a layer built up from the sun's own plasma ejection, so deposited, that eventually coated the stratosphere of the earth over time. Also, it appears conclusive that the shield may be breached if the sun increased volumes of plasma ejection as is the case when the sun reaches a cyclical peak, that results in hyper-activity. So we are virtually at the mercy of the great inferno that is the sun and roving space object of all types.

Simultaneously, after much exasperation at what we thought to be a flagrant discount, by the State (anywhere in the world), overlooking glaring signals as the asteroids of 2013 and 2014, this year on 12th March 2014. The newspapers on the 11th March 2014 symbolise and reveal that there is a retraction in public and probably governments across the world. This is thanks to scientists and researchers who are researching and reporting on climate and solar occurrences. Formerly, maybe even due to past attitudes smothered by the pre-industrial mind-set there is a change. Before this, everything was pinned on hope that the world would be normal and that things will proceed as usual. The sweeping change is evident, an article published in a South African newspaper "The Star" (published on the 11th March 2014), titled *"Earth's ruin by acid rain"* signals the changes. If this information is being published at this moment, then there is some awareness that coincides with the notions intimated in *The Johannesburg Formula* and the hypothesis about what is going on in the solar system recently. This article speaks about "rocks" that crashed into earth 65 million years ago, unleashing sulphuric gases that caused acid rain, and the acid rain drops that brought the dinosaurs to their end, in what is known as the *Cretaceous–Tertiary* period. All this speaks to the recent behaviour suggested by The Johannesburg Formula. The recently observed asteroid-belt behaviour indicates that the "glue" that is keeping the asteroid-belt together is apparently dislodging asteroids that are being *randomly* hurled out of orbit towards planets in the solar system, including the

Earth, putting the Earth in recently unprecedented risk. We suspect that the coming weeks will see a more heightened and concerted effort to report on this aspect of life by popular tabloids as there is an awareness of the reality of the recent "anomalous" temporal zone (time zone). Increasingly worrying, as we were yesterday on the 11th March 2014, based on recent reports in the media, is the fact that a picture is emerging, overwhelming even at a personal level, to culminate in a *Mayanesque* scenario. As everyone can glean from media reports available as public data, dinosaurs were wiped by asteroids 65 million years ago. Recently, 2013 and 2014 have ushered in a period of asteroid-consciousness as the world is experiencing close-encounters with asteroids. Could this be exposing a cyclical anomaly that we are now re-encountering, in the form of an asteroid super-season? Nobody knows if there is real cause for concern because of the huge numbers. The 65 million years record of the relatively recent *Cretaceous–Tertiary and* the assigned 15 billion years history of the earth are huge numbers. Naturally a question arises as to how many times in 15 billion years has the earth been bombarded by asteroids, changing the world forever? By now, even a table-top researcher may conclude that this is a cyclical scenario. Through and endeavour to learn more about the broadening topic, The *Johannesburg Formula* is painting for itself a picture of what is going on, collating data with the "official" accounts that are making their way into the public domain through the media.

#2015edit...since radio reports in 2015, our view has changed it is reported that orbiting satellites to monitor solar flares are being launched by joint operations. #back-to-original-script...Up until now in 2014 it was easy to deduce from the priority of government across the world, focus on tangible issues around the planet. Not much due focus on what is causing the anomalous behaviour of the weather, for example phenomenon that is admittedly being classified as "unusual", as the "Rains of March 2014" in South Africa, on a wide scale. Even after twelve days of this "unusual" rain, the focus of media reports is on the damages that have been due to the rains. Admittedly, the rains have come unexpectedly as the Weather Services have announced and many people have lost properties and as well as lives have been lost. On the 12th March 2014, in Mamelodi East, Pretoria, South Africa, three boys are said to have drowned in storm water while playing. Elsewhere reports of swelling dams and rain soaked coal that led to the shortages of electricity supply are abounding. This past week of the 03rd March to the 10th March, black-outs have occurred due to electricity shortages because the state electricity supplier is receiving wet coal from suppliers because of the "unusual" rains. This was a totally unforeseen circumstance because of unusually prolonged rain that wet coal stored for delivery to the electricity utility. To us these are but indicators of all the things that can be affected in a *perfect storm* and chain reaction. Let alone a mild suspicion that this could be a beginning of a terminal temporal zone, that will run to where nobody knows. A frustration can emanate when someone wants to alert authorities of this possibility. At the same time one has to accept that it is not always possible to raise credible alarm without credible evidence. Let alone have access to the right party contact that will even take this story seriously. A dispassionate reality is that nobody will buy a story that the world as we know it may end, it is simply incredible in the true sense of the word. What kind of person really believes this stuff, one eventually introspects and starts looking at themselves really awkwardly. Humanity is by nature optimistic and it may not be possible for anyone to accept the realness of such a debilitating possibility. So we decide to leave it alone until the Mayans speak for themselves... Also when the possibility avails and until this book is published we propose that it goes out as a report. A report to enable public awareness, as well as insight into our perspective for established researchers and precession scientists.

We are more inclined to now estimate that the Mayans had sufficient data and statistical knowledge that warranted them to peg their period to 5125 as a definite cyclical measure. They knew that every 5125 years the sun peaks with hyper-activity, that is followed by drastic changes throughout the solar system, that is why they knew that at the end of 5125 years, the world as we know it does end and some long term evolutionary mechanisms kicks in with planets in the solar system experiencing cataclysmic upheaval. This hypothesis is gleaned from the information from palaeolithic and archaeological evidence that suggests that dinosaurs were wiped off by incursions of asteroids plummeting to the face of the earth.

Wow, it is becoming clear that was dubbed the *polar vortex* at the beginning of this year (2014) in North America, is in fact the beginning of a "global temporal vortex!" (GTV). North America was swamped with snow, reminiscent of storms that enveloped the same location with storms in 2013, at around the same time...

Today is the 13th March 2014 and the weather is not relenting over Gauteng the home province of Johannesburg in South Africa. South Africa is becoming a case-study for the global predicament that has been developing since 2012 onward. On the news today reports are rampant that a province to the north of Gauteng province called Limpopo, an area known as Bela-Bela, is experiencing unprecedented flooding... *(interruption...#on edit now in 2015 I would like to qualify this as medium flooding)...anyway lets carry on, back to 2014...*Also, thousands of people have been rescued from a highland after they moved there to avoid drowning in floods around a farm in Limpopo. As we sit here on the thirteenth day of the "Rains of March 2014", a South African experience for the past thirteen days, our theory that something else is happening across the world in terms of the recent "solar peaks" is taking hold. We are hoping that an episode of *fatal optimism* doesn't become a bane to fate. Many people in the know, would be quick to dismiss the theory that we are advancing, for the reason that humanity has become so used to the comforts and trappings of a way of life, to a point of refuting that the earth could be slowly unpacking into an unprecedented "global temporal vortex" as we choose to call it. It is a reasonable observation that we are alleging, of the fact that it would be difficult for the world to declare an international state-of-emergency, especially when a high level of optimism is a way of life. The order of the day is proceeding at any cost. To us it is an incongruent anomaly to be sitting here reading news reports about how well the world economy is doing, while at the same time the other pages of the same newspaper bear news about unusual weather, unusual asteroid incursions and other uncomfortable reports about human behaviour as nations are at each other's throats for control of the world. Well, this is a picture of the world today, the various sections of a thick tabloid tell varying and conflicting stories. Just take a look at a usual Sunday newspaper and compare the sections of news and see what comparative picture emerges. For today, we are advancing caution and awareness of *fatal optimism* which may cancel out any foresight of a possible terminal "global temporal vortex". This for us exposes a *fatal aspect* of the phenomenon of the *psychology of epochology*.

A rudimentary explanation is that the recent *solar bursts* are exposing the world to heightened or peaks in solar emissions of heat, that eventually reach the earth's atmosphere and are inducing this "unusual" and recent development in weather that has manifested as the "Rains of March 2014" in South Africa. A sceptic will obviously retort that a weather system that has developed over South Africa cannot be transposed to be a global experience. We say for sure, but note that the weather system migrates and we foresee that the system that has enveloped South Africa will migrate to another position else-where on the planet. Even at that, there is nothing wrong with speculating outside of an official report or investigation into what the cause of the "Rains of March 2014" in South Africa is, a month after North America was smothered by a snow storm, something that we venture to say is also unusual. The only reason that we are adamant, is so that the international community may take action to mitigate the possibility of a long term " global temporal vortex", if this is what it is. It is frustrating for citizens to be disposed to this kind of behaviour, what we are engaged in, high suspicion of an asteroid and solar-peak besieged or threatened world. Evidence of what an asteroid threatened world is likely to run into, is reinforced by a recent Japanese study by astronomers, where they proved that the Jurassic epoch was obliterated by a high asteroid activity period, (see: The Star of 11ᵗʰ March 2014- a South African tabloid). Put the Mayan scenario into the mix and you have reason for high apprehension and suspicion that something cataclysmic is unfolding. Sohsuke Ohno, a Japanese scientist at the Planetary Exploration Research Centre in a place called Chiba, has put riveting data into the public domain about how the Jurassic epoch folded. This shows that a definite cyclical period where the earth is exposed to extra-ordinary circumstances is a reality. What nobody seems to know is when such a typical period is bound to be defined. The Mayans might be vindicated after all. This might not be the time for fatal or unbridled optimism that would amount to governments across the world firmly planting the *world's head* in the sand. In South Africa, we know best about the behaviour of ostriches.

...Today is Friday, the 14ᵗʰ March 2014, the weather has defied all optimism and pleas that include complaints from people all over South Africa, for the "Rains of March" 2014 to abate. At the same time I have been monitoring a report ever since the 20ᵗʰ January 2014, after going online and learning about asteroid-2003QQ47. It was said that this asteroid would reach either the earth or possibly whizz past on the 21ˢᵗ March 2014. Various debates were had about whether the asteroid would impact the planet or not, and people gave their various motivations. For the purpose independent social awareness and research, we have learnt not to be reliant. For example, dare we say, before the 15ᵗʰ February 2013 asteroid explosion in Russia, no astronomy observation stations, or anybody at that, actually informed the public definitively about this possibility. This was a complete and unexpected surprise! So from now on there is no definitive determination of how any asteroid may behave. Although there was knowledge about the asteroid, as it is said that it was being monitored prior to that, no one warned the public of the 15ᵗʰ February 2013 asteroid explosion. This is our conclusion because there was no broad-based information about this possibility. Also we wouldn't really blame anyone because these things seem to be astronomical accidents that are almost incalculable and unpredictable. It is also a reasonable case study to determine whether there is a connection between the "Rains of March" 2014 and the asteroids that are showing up on the brink of the earth's stratosphere and atmosphere for that matter, as was proven by the Chelyabinsk (Russia) asteroid in February 2013. Nothing is impossible when dealing with unknown and undeterminable scenarios. Today on the 14th March 2014 the clouds are still covering the sky and occasional drizzling through the morning. This is possibly the fourteenth day of the "Rains of March", and more damage is being reported in another province of South Africa known as the North West, where two more boys are reported to have drowned in floods. The costs to lives and property as a result of the "Rains of March" 2014 is still to be quantified, through a report of how many people lost their lives as a direct cause of the rains and estimations of properties destroyed. Our own theory is that the "global temporal vortex" is a reality. I have a feeling that the "Rains of March" 2014 will be the measure through which we judge the "global temporal vortex". We should test the "global temporal vortex" hypothesis for its mettle as a veritable outlook. We have to observe what the "Rains of March" spate, so far the effects of the rains have been a devastation-trail that started in Johannesburg's Westdene, went on to Soweto, ravaged the Northern Suburbs by leaving tarmac turned upside-down, overwhelmed the Vaal Dam, *broke* the banks of the Vaal River, went on to drown children in Mamelodi- Pretoria, ravaged farms in Limpopo and up to so far on the 14th March the North West province saw some children being drowned. All this has been over fourteen days and we are still counting. While we have made direct connections by now, we don't know when the direct link will be made to the Mayan prophecy by others like meteorological services and space object monitors. As the general public across the world at large, we remain relatively flat footed because only if professionals pronounce on something to be fact, is it is accepted. Organic or social anecdote is highly frowned upon. Experts have unfettered rein over the domain of public perception and public information. The problematic challenge with this is that it takes forever for organic opinion or pronouncement to be accepted.

Throughout this week of 10th March to the 14th March, it has been pure estimation, without anyone being able to supply the public with credible and reliable weather forecasts. This is because the rain has indeed been unexpected and unpredictable, that is why it was officially declared as unusual, it is no-one's fault. On the afternoon of 14th March 2014, a Radio 702 weather forecaster, Simon Gear admitted to Xolani Gwala a presenter, that it was not possible to state when the weather would abate.

At the one side of this organic theorizing, it is overwhelmingly reassuring that there is no science that does not start off as inference and speculation. It is all equal to hypothesis before being declared as theory. Many conditions and circumstance need to be fulfilled before a theory can be declared to be valid, even at that, a theory is not written in stone and after many years of passage, alternatives emerge or are discovered, so a theory may be proven to be transient. The *psychology of epochology* and the *Johannesburg Theory* follow the same. We have tried all through this book to present an objective hypothesis, that considers that in any investigation or research there are sides, "for and against" the veracity of the proposed theory. Let's resume then, let us put our arguments forward in support of either proofs of the binary sides of debate. Let's debate whether the Mayans are correct or not, it's the only way to resolve this matter.

What we foresee as a matter of realistic objection to the notion of a Mayan prophecy, are issues of jurisdiction. If a scenario of a "global temporal vortex" should be a truth, then it becomes *frighteningly* clear that the question of jurisdiction is the undoing of all notions of nationhood. In South Africa, the "Rains of March" 2014 reveal something telling regarding the issue of jurisdiction. No country hurries to declare an impending risk before an actual disaster and all state-of-emergency declarations have been made only after the fact. As for natural disasters, a state-of-emergency is rarely declared based on forecasts of risk. This means that internationally, a state-of-emergency is only declared after a natural disaster risk incident has played out, and by that time it is too late. On the 14th of March 2014, after three provinces experienced battering from the "Rains of March" 2014, officials were saying on the radio that a state-of-emergency had not yet been declared. *Note that this is not intended to cast aspersion but to illustrate a point about governments all around the world...*This means that it is a matter of practice for governments across the world to declare a state-of-emergency only after the fact. What this tells us is that if a scenario of a "global temporal vortex" were ever to be true, there would be a conflict based on who may declare a global state-of-emergency. One country may find it un-strategic to declare a state-of-emergency outside of circumstances that are perceived to warrant such a call. This means that the need for a global declaration is a point of disagreement. Simply put because a state-of-emergency has never been declared based on forecasts and predictions necessarily, then accordingly, speculation of a pending calamity is not enough. For governments all over the world to deal with natural incursions, is more like the disaster first has to happen then we deal with it. Yes it is also true that there have been a lot of disasters that were simply unpredictable and unstoppable.

Today on the 15th March 2014, 08h00 bore prospects of a day filled with sunshine and a blue sky. The sun was out although clouds held their own all around, with sparse troughs for the sun to be partially displayed. Two of the biggest teams in the South Africa are playing at the world famous FNB stadium near Soweto in Johannesburg. This is a sold-out ticket affair as a crowd of 90 000 people is reportedly headed for the face-off between two of the league's top football clubs, Orlando Pirates and Kaizer Chiefs. So naturally every soccer enthusiast in South Africa is optimistic about the weather opening up after two weeks of a non-stop rainy bout. Far from the football pitch way above the stadium up in the sky, it seems as though this is a tall order as this is no ordinary weather. Unbeknown to the football organisers, the rain this March is another brand of "serious stuff" as we reckon. What we noticed is that the openings along the seams of clouds in the scenic episode of the "Rains of March" 2014, is a lull of note. Any heat that ends up escaping the cloud cover to be absorbed by the surface of the ground and any sunlight is ironically just a perfect condition for more rain later on in the day. The surface cools due to the sun setting and the atmosphere getting colder as the hot air that accumulated earlier in the day rises to the top where clouds are reinforced and cool overnight conditions let off rain, as has been happening through the two weeks. The point is that the phenomenon of the "Rains of March" 2014 has to be watched carefully because it seems as if this is an affront to security. These rains have already assaulted South Africa in ways that no one would have foreseen. Several people have lost their lives through drowning, private and public properties have been destroyed and damaged as the "Rains of March 2014" have had a free reign. The loss of lives due to the "Rains of March" 2014, is a measure of 'belligerent' times. Without being aware to the fact, the time period 2013/2014 has perhaps been a turning point that we will only quantify after the fact, as the "Rains of March 2014" have shown us. The 1 pm news on the radio reports that locals of Bela-Bela, Limpopo have requested that the area be declared a disaster zone. If this happens it will herald something exponential about the assault that the "Rains of March 2014" have had, and without hesitation I would venture to say that this has an extended bearing on the "global temporal vortex" guess. 13h00p.m. of the 15th March 2014 in Johannesburg is a change of tune from the totally engrossed week before today, where the days were definitely suffocated by a total cloud cover and unselective downcast of rain through the days of the "Rains of March" 2014. Our estimation that the "Rains of March" 2014 and the "global temporal vortex" are somehow linked, is the capital instalment of the proposition towards the end of this chapter.

15h00 of the 15th March 2014, is a game change. As we look at the sky, there are hopeful gaps that have not been seen for over twelve days ever since the "Rains of March" 2014 started. This is a condition overhead in Johannesburg, as we have no idea of what is going elsewhere. Although still overly cloudy, it hasn't rained this whole day and the reprieve seems to be a boon for all soccer enthusiasts who are probably going out to the FNB Stadium in Johannesburg. The 15h00 news report on the radio informs us that a high alert for Free State (a province in South Africa) has been imposed by the provincial administrators and the Weather Services announces that on the 17th Monday 2014, there is a high chance that the rain will return. The news report also states that two hundred households were left homeless in Gauteng due to the rains, while seven hundred households were temporarily housed in community centres in Limpopo. The weather forecast announced on the 15h00 news say that showers and thundershowers are expected on 17th Monday, less than what we experienced in the previous week. Our view based on the GTV assumption is emboldened towards a big picture that includes the Mayan prophecy, something that will as we foresee, unfold with compounded effects through the period post 21st/12/12.  By 16h00 on the 15th March, the sky had cleared so much that the blue sky seemed to be winning against the clouds, the lingering few being the only sign that by evening everything could change.  At 16h40 the sky is all around blue, with the only clouds being visible in the distance of the horizon. I know that this is illusive because it does not mean that the "Rains of March" 2014 have gone and we can close the chapter, because elsewhere in the country the phenomenon is well heeled. This is exactly the point of the global spread of the GTV, while now at 16H45 the sky outside would not be telling evidence that the "Rains of March" were supreme force to be reckoned with for the past two weeks.  The only residual evidence is elsewhere in other locations across the country where rivers are overflowing and people are reeling from loss of even scant properties. The municipal services are now beginning to do a measurement of the damages and loss.

The experiment of monitoring the "Rains of March" 2014 is essential because it is valuable data that feeds the "global temporal vortex" scenario, something that by now we are persuaded is a reality.

These notions are broadly affected by the 2013/2014 asteroid intensive exposure that the earth has experienced. This tells us that as a modest estimate, even if the asteroid-belt is too far for our naked eye to see, there is some kind of commotion happening out there. This, according to us, is billed to usher in a milestone for the earth, enveloping the place in indiscreet and unintended repercussions as the solar system *revamps*. Here is a sum of what the "global temporal vortex"-(GTV) hypothesis is. The GTV hypothesis assumes that the sun is going through a moment of hyper-activity, based on cyclical behaviour. It assumes that there is a higher than normal electromagnetically charged ejection of heat plasma into circulation around the solar system. It also assumes that the asteroid-belt is an indicator of what is happening in the solar system. It assumes that when asteroids start 'flying off the hinges', it's a sign of cosmic risk to the planet. The GTV also assumes that indicators on the planet can be tied up to and traced to the general hyperactivity in the sun. The GTV assumes that the Mayans have an irreproachable message that the future should heed. The GTV assumes that the solar system has entered an extra-ordinary temporal zone that requires and will impose a differentiation in how everything in the solar system behaves and evolves through adaptation. The GTV assumes that the earth will be co-opted into a point of no return where ordinarily everything "disintegrates" from what we are used to, especially an impact on the built-up civilization on the planet. The "Rains of March" 2014 is the proverbial *smoke* to the "global temporal vortex" *fire*...

This is a reflection of a 'volatile' period unfolding throughout the solar system because of a generalised solar flare. This is where *relativity* is important, because for all we know, this is a 'normal' cyclical eventuality and we *appear* to be on the *receiving*-end when the solar system is going through a *renewal*, "cleansing" or evolutionary routine.

This is a difficult illustration...but hold-on... here we go: the whole process is like when a person has a shower or a bath, the dirt on the skin is washed away before it starts to develop into body odour...

Dirt loves to thrive because it is a bunch of bacterial-microbes that lives on the *dead* skin cells and anybody who washes deprives the dirt of a thriving livelihood... This is the closest visually coherent illustration... the dirt is in fact a cocktail population of bacterial-microbes and other micro-organisms that would otherwise have loved to be left alone without the host washing the dirt off. While the dirt is living off the skin of the host, it has no idea that the host washes everyday and that the time of living on the *juicy* skin will be up when the host washes... The body of the host represents the solar system and the dirt represents the organisms that are thriving throughout the solar system. The only way to reckon with this eventuality is to be aware and to rely on collective knowledge and take pre-emptive steps if and when it is time for such.

The claim of the GTV is that the "Rains of March" 2014 is/are as a result of the recent hyper-activity of the sun, that we deduce can be confirmed from the index of the asteroid-belt's recent behaviour. This is what is happening...the hyperactivity is depositing extra-ordinary heat that is causing the asteroid belt to thaw. Nonetheless the sample of the city Johannesburg, as an observational area is sufficiently proportional because the "Rains of March" 2014 is something that is gripping four out of nine provinces throughout South Africa. A reprieve over Johannesburg is not enough to start concluding anything about when the phenomenon will bow out. Something very important for readers who are not in South Africa is for you to note that this phenomenon has been reported as an unusual trend by the Weather Services and this is why it has relevance to the globe as a whole. We are also putting this out there so that others in other geographical locations can see if they won't string the dots and extract a big picture. It is important because we are interested to see how other phenomenon elsewhere across the globe are being reported as unusual. For one the rain in March 2014 occurred in autumn and this is said to be unusual.

On the 16th of March 2014, radio reports from the South African Weather Services announce that the entire week that began on the 12th March 2014 is soaked out, so far it is has been raining throughout the week. Interestingly, as reports of the referendum that is held in Crimea in Eastern Europe or Western Eurasia (whichever way you choose to look at it), it is said that it is raining there as well, while people make their way to the polling booths. It is 15h00 right now and a day that started as a sunny day in Johannesburg seems to have already given up as clouds *muscle-out* any traces of blue in the sky, peppering the air with a cold tinge. This is worth a case, because it is essentially a continuation of rains that have been occupying centre-stage for a strong two weeks. This is a case because in as much as rain is a usual custom, these rains have been billed specifically by meteorologists as 'unusual', making the point of singling out the "Rains of March" 2014...a feasible exercise in weather forensics.

These rains coincide with a case at the High Court in South Africa where the world famous Oscar Pistorius is being tried for the life of Reeva Steenkamp, his deceased and erstwhile girlfriend. The business of society and day to day procession on earth is competing for centre stage and attention with cosmic issues of disproportionate measure. For example, the coincidence of the Oscar Pistorius case with the Russian asteroid is a moot point albeit the case rightfully and totally eclipsing the asteroid story. Notions of *conspiracy theories* hover around because at the same time of the threat of an asteroid incursion looming large, even unfortunate and fatal issues are proceeding to the bench. Gross issues that are transpiring seem also to be obfuscating the looming scenario of substantive cosmic issues. This is a slight but dis-shelving logic, procedural state-of-attention diverting long overdue focus on the "global temporal vortex".

...Today on the 17th March 2014, at 11h07a.m., the clouds above Johannesburg at this very moment prove that there is nothing that we may be sure of regarding how the weather behaves. The Weather Services are advising that it is expected to be "partly cloudy and light showers are expected". This is accurate, but to an *uninformed* person living and surviving on the often wild urban streets and member of the public, the bright display of the sun this morning

199

with the heat would have led one to believe that the "Rains of March" 2014 was a bygone. This did not last, the clouds came back with fervour and as I type this paragraph in, the sky is completely creamed by clouds, something of a contrast to the conditions at 08h00 this morning, when anyone would have dressed for a hot cloudless day. Before I could even finish this sentence, it starts to drizzle outside. The issue is that this is no ordinary rain, it is a continuation of the "Rains of March" 2014 bout, there is no clear winner between the clear blue sky and the upset clouds that are harbouring rain. As we know now, the rains have been declared as unusual by meteorologists and the Weather Services, this according to the GTV hypothesis, indispensably makes the rain part of the precessional global phenomenon. Seemingly the causes are not explained as ordinary local causes that are known of rain in South Africa. The third week of the rain bout is giving credence to the theory of extra-ordinary exogenous forces as responsible and culpable. While we tarry, a sound of thunder makes its way through the atmosphere, indicating a tension of charged ions, explodes on impact and collision, releasing rain ...mingled in the sky is a thundering boom and within a few moments, at 12h19 midday, it rains. This is a moderate to heavy downpour that sends anyone doing anything outside packing indoors. So the "Rains of March" 2014 are/is still firmly here over Johannesburg specifically. This extends our civilian study of this phenomenon that was vetoed by the meteorological services when it started, being identified as unusual. The disclaimer issued by the Meteorological Services that these are unusual rains, makes this a global issue because the rain has to be traced to its logical and real cause. Later on in the afternoon, on Radio 702, one of the presenters Jenny Crys-Williams is asking people what they did on Sunday 16th March 2014, because as she says "the rains opened up for four hours". All sorts of interesting people are phoning in. This rain is definitely worth a headline in the news because it is an unusual incursion that clearly disrupted many communities at large. By now, at 13h23 I have given up on the blue sky winning the day, it is afternoon and my guess is that the cloudy sky will win. A report just came in at 14h30 on the news that the Cooperative Governance Department has announced that the total of people who have lost life due to the rain these past two weeks is 32. This is a siren of the culpability on the part of this rain that has declared what amounts to an assault on South Africa. The total of provinces that are reporting being lashed is five, Gauteng, North West, Mpumalanga, Free State and Kwa-Zulu Natal. By now, there is a remarkable game that is on in the bout, the rain might not be incessant but the strangulation of clouds is without a challenge.

Our hypothesis further intimates that the avowed solar riot is multi-factoral. It constitutes geomagnetic and thermal components that contract the plasma ejections as a vehicle of. So it is not only heat that is projected, it is also an electromagnetic wave emission that is indexed by the dislodging asteroids. This will be proven when the effects built up and a critical mass is reached, something that we have already observed to peak in February (annualised), ever since we made issue with the Russian asteroid in 2013. The month of March seems to be implicated as well because of the asteroids of 19th February 2014 followed by the 05th March 2014 window respectively. This period seems to be the period of high volatility based on this observation and I am eager to find out what the specific circumstances are out there in space, where the sun and asteroid-belt are positioned and how they affect the earth. I would say that this hypothesis warrants further investigation and resolution. Our firm suspicion is that February and March of the years 2015, 2016, 2017, 2018 and 2019 will be highly volatile in terms of the outcomes of the GTV hypothesis. A side issue is that we are also monitoring our state of mind and we vouch that we are of a normally functioning cognitive disposition and process so we are not inclined to doubt the validity of the hypothesis entailed in the Johannesburg Formula at large. This is important to state because it is a new terrain of inquiry of psychology, as many people would ordinarily doubt the veracity of the hypothesis, let alone the soundness of a person purporting it. I am not a qualified psychologist to warrant a self-diagnosis that would pass a legal test and outside of that process being in-hand, I have to keep-up this organic assessment of self. For instance, is it an unreasonable allegation that government across the world is wholly liable for the loss after 21st /12/12 due to any incident that may be proved to be as a result of the resolved GTV, as well as after being informed of what the Mayans warned of? Surely, action was taken to warn governments of the world and no recusal may be proffered in this regard. The challenge we are facing at the moment is of access to the correct legal channels to bring unfettered accountability for disasters that ensued since December 2012. The degrees of liability are in direct correlation with primacy, the more *powerful* and logistically coherent a government is, the more capacity it has and therefore the more the liability attributed squarely is.

The announcement that the state in South Africa will assist the families of those who were affected and who lost life will be assisted is a ground-breaking precedent. As soon as governments realise that the string of causality goes back to the Mayan prophecy, then the governments of the world will see that something else is going on here. We reserve the right to take the matter on appeal so that governments may be compelled to align with this realism, as was the intention of the December 2012 application at the Constitutional Court of South Africa as the only *available* point of access. As we sit here, listening to the Mayor of the City of Tshwane (formerly known as Pretoria) in South Africa, committing a budget to repair damages caused by the rain this year and storms in 2013, we are anxiously wondering if anyone has a view of the GTV hypothesis. Accordingly, instead of repairing the damages caused by the rains in March 2014, the whole world should be migrating to a GTV paradigm and a long term readiness for a high grade eventuality of cataclysmic reality. What this scenario would demand as early as now, would be for governments to abandon unilateral development and embark on collective pre-emptive action of preparing for the extremities at worst. This would include mobilising the citizens to become survival agents, the government redirecting budgets to *readiness* infrastructure, that factors the prospects of 7 billion people. This requires a more than militant or radical shift in mindfulness and capacity analysis. Government across the world may realise that the people are primary to the prospect of surviving the GTV reality as is assumed...(#)...Instead of viewing the 7 billion strong people as passive recipients of strong-arm resolutions of executives, the collective strength and stealth of 7 billion minds may be unleashed... (#2015editorialmusings).

...The morning of the 18th March 2014 is a show of a cleared blue sky in Johannesburg. Ever since, anyone who has not had the benefit of the dapper sun to dry their laundry is all over their washing line, taking their clothes out for a long-lost air brush. The only damp thing is the news that the province of Kwa-Zulu Natal reportedly saw one person lose life due to an overnight storm. This is the trail of the now notorious "Rains of March" 2014, that is on a wet rampage. Even as a reprieve, the hot breeze in Johannesburg is an unreliable contestant as it might lose to the cloudy threat at the end of the day, because there is no strong indication that the "Rains of March" 2014 have officially declared a ceasefire and pulling out. For someone who is elsewhere either than South Africa, it is crucial to provide an account of what has been happening throughout the "Rains of March" 2014 showdown. For instance today on the 18th March, Johannesburg has been experiencing scattered rains, where an area of several hundreds of square kilometres has been hit by sporadic and stop-and-go showers that register as mild. The city-centre of Johannesburg has been hit with mild rain, while areas to the north have been cloudy without a shower necessarily. Nonetheless, the radio reports about the east coast of Kwa-Zulu Natal leave little to desire, because of loss of life that is reported as places like Bergville were attacked by violent storms overnight. Also, as repairs on the N14 highway in Johannesburg have resumed, huge sums of money are said to be what it will cost the provincial administration. Limpopo province to the north of Gauteng province is said to have suffered the most damages to roads that have in some cases been swept away by the rains.  It is as useless as going to war with a pen-knife against an assailant armed with a machine-gun to try to predict the point at which the "Rains of March" 2014 will halt. The Weather Services have given the 20th March 2014 as a likely last day of the rains in and around Gauteng, but I am sceptical. These rains are on a war path, more than military strategy is needed to pre-empt any conclusive trend in its behaviour. The declaration that this is unusual rain is more than enough information about our own ineptitude in its face.

*#side-issue...The delays in getting this book to market due initially to financial and several constraints have allowed for the further furnishing of the GTV and the "Rains of March" 2014 input that was a matter of having the manuscript in hand and having this perspective while waiting... After attempts to source publishers and emails to one of the reputable publishers whose information we got online, we were not able to contact the ideal parties but only got outdated contact-info. Our email bounced. This acted to enable us to further furnish the book with even the end parts of this chapter. Also we were looking for a publisher who would take our book based on a payable fee that would mean that we are not hostage to the penchants of publishers who might refuse us based on their own preferences of the kind of books that they are prepared to publish. Organic art is at the end of any literary compilation and this is how we want to keep the book. The procedural process of editing seems just too laborious to embark on, when faced with raw need to go to market for entrepreneurial reasons. We hope to use this book to diversify into other projects that make up our extended outlook. As the details and small embellishments suffer in the process, all that stands glaringly exposed is the real rigours of commitment to the requirement for quality while providing products on the market. The learning curve pervades the process of even writing this book because it has been a mechanical act of the storyline that emerged organically. This is an act of redeeming self from the gross mental space of the Mayan prophecy. We never thought that we would write a book for any reason otherwise. #housekeeping.*

...This is how bad things got, some of the road got affected by the rain, potholes were sprouting all over the place. There was a *pothole protest* that was blamed on the rains recently, one of the headline stories of the day on the radio. Officials said that the workmanship of the road was at the behest of service providers who built the roads in the province. The cost of repairs of the roads forced by the rain was announced. This is a sign of old architecture collapsing under the pressure of the "Rains of March" 2014 another heavy metal incursion at the hands of the rain. The 18th is another feather in the cap of the emergency budget financial stats. The damages caused by the rain, were added to the cost of building the roads and for the repairs. This is ironically the first trickle of entanglement in the GTV scenario. The ultimate frontier in emergency budgets might be tested even in simulated conditions of the GTV scenario. The "Rains of March" 2014 *forced* a state of emergency preparedness test and these tests indicate *natural* reflexes, a crude picture of the real capacity for a GTV scenario. Almost all day long, every weather news bulletin announced *"another partly cloudy day with showers"* as a slogan for March. This has been the case over the past two weeks and we are now in the throes of the third week as the rain holds the blue sky hostage. Ladies and gentlemen, this is the "Rains of March" 2014, the longest lasting inning in more than 14 years. No doubt this is more about the beginning of autumn 2014, for as long. Autumn has never had it this good in over fourteen years, unusual rain.

This has been a case of simply observing a captive cycle of cold and hot air displacement that has ensconced in the clouds. We moved towards an early end of autumn in South Africa because a rained out March means that this is an enmeshed and swift sprint to winter. This however is fertile because it is a gateway for a comparative analysis of other regional trends. Based on the declarations and announcements by the meteorologists who featured often on the radio, March 2014 seems to be isolated coming to the fore in a specific temporal domain, as well as incomparable to past years. In case nobody in public noticed March 2014, the book will be a channel to highlight these unique weather conditions in future and bring the experiment to bear.

The two-in-one question of why is it raining and how it rains, is a unique opportunity to this part of the world at the moment. It has rained for so long that it has been impossible to ponder the process. Besides the bare fact that it has to do with the gas hydrogen forming clouds and oxygen rich heat combusting the gas into rain, the question is more about the so called normal patterns of rainfall. On pondering some more...so seemingly it is a process of simultaneous combustion and condensation...

At 10h00, the morning of 19th March 2014 is an ambitious condition of a blue sky that is quickly shouldering the clouds out of place. Wow, this has been a match of wills between clouds and the clear blue sky with us here on the ground being the unsuspecting referees... This follows on a clear night sky last night on the 18th, where long last seen stars were holding their own. At 10h30, Captain Chris Mangena, a ballistics expert in the SAPS (South African Police Services) is being cross examined in Court as we can hear from the radio broadcast of the trial of Reeva Steenkamp's ex-lover, Oscar Pistorius. The testimony of ballistics science is intriguing the listeners as it is the first time in South Africa that the public is listening in to a real case broadcast in real time. While our preoccupation with the manuscript ensues, we are forced to see that the Mayan case is no less, we should be applying the same rigorous framework of interrogation to the case for GTV. Based on the explanations of the ballistics expert it becomes possible to explain the circumstances around the explosion of the asteroid in Chelyabinsk that injured close to 1500 people. Also a forensic and expert explanation is required to bring the fatal trail of the "Rains of March" 2014 to book. These are issues that we encounter as we have nowhere to run to except mount an investigation into the veracity of the Mayan claims. This book should be a start towards such a process. The forensics witnesses were questioned last week in the trial and more evidence that flowed from the case would serve the inquiry of this book to apply similar circumstances. Outside of the Constitutional Court having put the application on the burners, the broadcast gives us an opportunity to adopt the Oscar case as a study for application to the GTV hypothesis. For any diplomatic or other reason, if there is no government that is prepared to mount the case of the Mayans, then we have to leave the judgement to the reader to issue a verdict as to where we should go in terms of the recent asteroid realism. The Oscar case is in its third week and the public has been immersed without a chance of escape even anyone tried to avoid it for anything. It is everywhere. The decision to broadcast the case is a windfall for other cases in the wings. People have said that case received prominence because the people involved are themselves prominent. This may be the case but this case highlights the possibilities for other cases to be treated with efficiency. The Mayan case is one issue likewise that may benefit from such an environment because public interest, public participation and public opinion is paramount.

10h00 of the 20th March 2014 is the bluest sky draped day for the longest time now, after Johannesburg was cordoned for two and a half weeks.   The predictions of the Weather Services that the rains would seize on the 20th March 2014, was spot on as far as we can see and should there be a cause to indicate otherwise we will let you know. It seems that the last of the rain has gone its way and we have been relieved of a threat that left a trail of nearly 12 000 potholes in Johannesburg alone at a repair cost of R60 million or roughly US$5.5 million. Today people were seen doing laundry with unbridled confidence as the blue sky looks like it could last until the clothes dry. A "partly cloudy day with a chance of scattered showers" is the radio weather announcement, a brooding repose from the past two weeks. The Weather Services predict that Friday, 21st March 2014 will be a rainy day. This is after a blazing day that was hotter than even the summer days of last season. This is a suspicious condition because things can go either way where it rains because of the heat that may rise. We will see if this happens as a test of whether the conditions of the "Rains of March" 2014 linger and as a test of exactly how long this phenomenon is looming. More than this tomorrow is a day that according to some reports on the internet, it is said that an asteroid would either hurtle earthwards or whizz somewhere past the globe at a distance, as did the March 05th and 19th February this year. I have heard nothing of this asteroid in the media and this is proof that this specific issue is not that important. For some the issue is important. Look, for instance based on the internet report, there is uncertainty of whether the asteroid may hurtle earthward or not. This means that there is no way of determining what kind of physical force or velocity an asteroid requires to breach the stratosphere and atmosphere. Sometimes it may skirt the circumference of the stratosphere and head elsewhere.

The 22nd March 2014 is a historic date, announcements on the 18h00 news about fighting in Baalbek, Crimea flaring up between Ukraine and Russia comes on the coldest Johannesburg day this autumn. Today is as cold as any winter day and this is a contrast to Thursday the 20th March 2014, that was hotter than all of summer put together here in Johannesburg. "The search for the missing Malaysian plane in the South Indian ocean has led the search crew into the eye of a cyclone" booms the radio. It is reported that a cyclone is unravelling in that part of the world over the sea. These are the features of the year 2014 that had asteroid watchers on the edge of their seats as the 21st March 2014 was billed to be fatal day as an asteroid was sighted earlier to be heading to the earth and was expected to show up near or around the earth. This entire conflagration is a sign of the times even to the avid optimist cum denialist of what is unfolding right in front of us. The irony of it all is that in true human style, after the radio news pronouncing the tensions in Baalbek, the music carries on as if everything is normal, when people know deep inside that something is wrong in the world. This has to be a positive irony because music is a salve for the world on the brink of multiple sweepstake disasters and a total disintegration with no winners...

The truth about behaviour is that it is a mystery of proportion. Right now as we speak, Russia and the West have started to flex muscles at each other by proxy. The airbase at Baalbek is the site for what could be a runaway conflict that most have said is a stage for the beginning of a world war. This is merely because economic and military interests are thin and in-between. Both America and Russia are armed to the teeth and all it takes is for a wire-crossing of the ego and this could flare up incrementally. We put it to cosmic forces, the sun for one influences everything on planet earth, from growth of energy sources to how humans are wired biologically. This means that as alleged by the study of astrology, all other objects in the solar system have a bearing on how humans and all sentient beings behave and evolve. The now caustic sun in its height of cyclical upheaval could just be a recipe for a full-scale barbed conflict that would be a last before an unprecedented asteroid downpour. Human behaviour may just be laid at the door of planets in our solar system and this hypothesis has to be advanced as a collateral aspect of the science of human behaviour at all. The Mayan prophecy is overshadowed by an even more graphic apocalyptic prescience recorded in the book of Revelations at the end of the bible. The scenes are not dissimilar.

Russia drew first blood as a report of a journalist being injured came in on radio and the claim of consolidation of Crimea being the pole assertion. The 20h00 news broadcast is a sound of a mounting stand-off. It is said that Russia is adamant that so called foreigners are being emptied out of now ratified Russian territory. It is now in the hands of the USA and Europe to respond and Sunday should be the day where we hear what these powers say about Ukraine.

On the 23rd March 2014, from a perspective of a cosmic news starved member of the public, we have not heard or seen anything about the asteroid named 2003QQ47 that was said to make a show on and around the 21st March 2014. We will make means to follow up on 2003QQ47. All what we can say at this point is that we have observed a pattern and we bet a bottom dollar that this trend will intensify in 2015, 2016 and onwards. Asteroids will make living on earth a challenge beyond our most advanced technological achievements. The industrial and 21st century industrial outlook has not prepared the scientific community to factor in the upheaval of the asteroid-belt and the unannounced dislodging of asteroids that may depending on velocity and trajectory hurtle earthwards. There is not defence system that claims to be able to deal with an asteroid incursion, nor is there a curriculum that is proficient in mitigating an asteroid incursion. The observation of 2013 and 2014 as asteroid flushed time periods is not negligible and more public engagement on this issue is warranted. Other probable events are in the order of the polar vortex induced snow storm that attacked North America in January 2014 have developed a pattern like recurrence that almost makes it predictable that either January or February of 2015 will see even worse or intensifying phenomenon around the same part of the world. Given the migratory nature of weather systems and phenomenon it has been noted that Zimbabwe (a country to the north of South Africa) also suffered floods after the "Rains of March" 2014 seem to have cooled off in South Africa. It might be a worthwhile guess to assume that the intense system migrated northwards after wreaking havoc in South Africa for the duration of mid-March 2014. These are not issues that we can toy with lightly given aversion to the reality that the earth and the solar system are open to irregular natural anomalies. The loss of life that the "Rains of March" 2014 in South Africa and the Polar Vortex in North America wrought is something that should stir government in terms of preparing society for an unchartered future. Other anomalous weather events have been recorded like Palm Beach County, Florida in the USA on 11th January 2014, where deadly torrential rain was recorded, even at Boynton Beach that was reportedly lashed by 'what was called "historically heavy rain". This was reported by the National Weather Service (NWS) in the USA. Two people reportedly lost life in this heavy downpour, and this is the reason for us making a call to governments around the world to be more circumspect.

On the 24th March 2014, reports of the previous night on the weather was something intriguing, the weather system seems to have migrated westwards over the country (South Africa) as it is said that by Tuesday 25th March, the western side of the country and the western Cape will be wet. This is particularly odd because the system does not seem to have a simple and traceable path, it has also affected Zimbabwe to the north of Limpopo, a province that was drenched by the two and a half week rains in March.

As a matter of weather watching due to the result of the "Rains of March 2014" peak, we can say that today's is a mildly windy and brisk inning. As an amateur weather watcher it is safe to say that it looks as though the system from the middle of March has waned and the rains have moved on to the western side of the country and we await reports of how the saga will settle. Today was hot though and we have to submit that this is noteworthy because we don't know how this could be a factor of the system that brought about the exceptional "Rains of March" 2014. On top of that the temperature is supposed to be declining to definitive winter conditions. At some point we have to conclude on whether the system has gone or not, because if it rains again later on today or some days later it will be difficult to compound the subsequent rain with the specific "Rains of March" 2014. As an amateur weather investigator for now, I submit to you that March has been a weird month in terms of vagaries. March 2014 has all the features of a winter and summer put together and yet in South Africa it is certified autumn. Now at 16h56, there is a brisk wind that is competing with a hot and dry condition that was dominating at around 13h40 earlier on. At this stage of our investigation, we are using the observable conditions displayed by weather as an indicator of a condition on a bigger scale in outer space in and around the solar system environs, while chasing the theory of the recently hyper-active sun and an asteroid-belt gone ballistic.

Outside of the weather and the environment rioting, human behaviour is adding to the 2014 toxicity basket. Today it is reported that today, in Ukraine, there is a meeting of the Western side of the conflict to see if they won't impose further sanctions to be targeted at Russia. The conflict is an indicator of the vagaries of human behaviour, nothing else. It is further reported that Russian tourism figures in London have slumped by 17% in the month of March 2014. Also, it transpires that apparently the Ukraine forces have been routed out of Crimea at the Black sea base and Kiev has withdrawn admitting defeat for the day. We will have to see how Kiev rejuvenates their campaign for Crimea and the air-base around Baalbek. Russia has slapped a ban on Canadian officials in return of the sanctions imposed by Canada on Russia as part of a western front. This is the story up to so far by the 24th March, where these bits of actions and counter actions will eventually snowball into an ugly picture. This is the story of 2014, a brooding year that has seen the asteroid hypothesis being reinforced and the Johannesburg Formula's seven candles being given legs. Safe to say that this is only one quarter of the year and it is a chilling imagination gateway to the possibilities of an angry year should it play out.

As the Oscar trial in South Africa carries on, with spin-offs of public education, today the question on Talk Radio 702 is what a *statement* entails. A statement is taken or made for the purpose of going to court in the case that a legal matter drags on. A statement is supposed to stand the depositor in good stead at a future date, so that consistency is maintained and dependability may be established. This was debated on radio because the open-justice principle exposed the machinations of court matters to the public. In the interest of bringing the matter of the Mayan prophecy we decided to listen attentively so that we may compile a statement for the allegations we are making to the effect that there is a legal basis for the case of the Mayan prophecy being a reality.

On Xolani Gwala's show on Talk Radio 702, advocate Manovitz said: "for a witness or accused – you report to an investigator, the investigator takes down the statement, you take an oath, later on if you are subpoenaed you go to court. During cross examination, you may read a statement while being led on the evidence in chief where you outline what you saw. The cross examiner tests credibility and powers of recollection. It is important to ensure that the statement is consistent. For example when reporting on a shooting, the date and place have to be right if one is a witness. The prosecutor will lead a witness and it is important to stick to one's version of what one saw or heard. The basic facts should be set out carefully. Specific incidents should be recalled. The power of observation and witness evidence is crucial while in court. The evidence in chief should be concise. Reliability, dependability and accuracy are crucial". A caller from the NPA (National Prosecution Authorities) Karen Tusson, was interviewed on radio, she said: "state witnesses may be prepared by the prosecution authorities to enable members of the public to perform accordingly". Court etiquette and mannerism was also addressed. All this was at the behest of the Reeva Steenkamp murder trial.

Based on this process of court procedure, we are of the view that the case as explored in the Johannesburg Formula is viable for review. So outside of that, you the reader should be the judge in this matter. From what we see, there is a strong case of constitutional breach on the part of government throughout the world. Ever since we made contact with the court in 2012, we have argued for government to be more cautious. Many people have lost life through what we leave squarely at the door of anomalous times and manifestations throughout. We dare say that no government may revoke its responsibility to familiarise itself with the Mayan notions.

Take the 25th March 2014, it is a weather maze, the sky is whitewashed with a thick and creamy cloud cover as early as 08h00. There is no chance of the blue sky showing even trace. We have to wonder what this is all about, is this a continuation of the "Rains of March" 2014 phenomenon. If this is the case, then the phenomenon would be going on for close to three weeks to a month, with negligible intermissions. This is based on a sample of the sky above Johannesburg as an observational square kilometre area. The Western Cape was issued with a warning of flash-floods for today. The Western Cape is not new to this condition at this time, where they even see a rainy, windy and sometimes snowed winter. Our main inquiry is based on the "Rains of March" 2014 and the mixture of effects on everything else. By 10h00 it is a dance between peeking blue spots that swear not to be outdone by a throttling group of creamy clouds. This is a recipe for a generally cold day splattered with sun streaks that struggle to convincingly pierce the shield of the clouds and even when this happens, it is an obvious fight. By

14h30 today on the 25ᵗʰ the clear blue sky over Johannesburg has won the fight for space. Even an amateur would suggest that the phenomenon is a goner and that it is a closed chapter. One may assume safely that the phenomenon that saw March send emergency services in the province of Gauteng stand on alert is a closed chapter.

A top-up is the announcements that the G8 group of nations will meet as the G7 indicating the deepening isolationist stance adopted by the mainly western influenced position aimed at addressing Russia's audacity. It is now G7 because of the expulsion of Russia. This is part of the rolling commentary and reflection of the developments in Russia and Ukraine, a situation that people say is extended beyond the two nation's interests, influences and alliances. So it is expected that should the G7 be acting as part of the pro-Ukraine bloc, then the pro-Russian bloc likewise has the right to reciprocate and exchange insults, blows, downright punches and pot-shots.

True to all things 2014, the Crimean issue is the biggest international and political event that will forever be marked as such. It is said that the population of Crimea are jubilant and are by now moving to adopt the Russian currency and mobilising other essential services and businesses to adopt a Russian modus. The Crimean issue is significant as an event of 2014 that is coincidentally mingled with the cycle of a world that is an immovable firing line of the asteroid-belt. 2014 is indeed a toxic year that was preceded by the 2013 asteroid that blasted the airspace above Chelyabinsk. The year is unique by far and it will be enthralling to see it through because it only brings the year 2015 closer and we have much to look to in terms of the possible upheavals in weather and the solar system. The Americans on the other hand are said to be mobilising the western bloc to act against Russia, just as well the supporters of the Russian bloc are silently in the camp by association, with formations like the BRICS being a silent partner. So it seems as though the camps are two ways, the G7 and BRICS on the other hand. The definition according the BRICS/G7 divide is something that took a while to form as a modern chasm in world affairs, and so everything and anything will follow this not so obvious stand-off. What we know is that the people who lived through the first and second world wars were no more different by any measure to the people who are alive in 2014. What is for sure is that the asteroid-belt is a challenge to all camps and there is nothing that either would do if there was a code-red of the order of anomalous cosmic incursions. While the G7/BRICS camps flex on earth, a larger conspiracy is unfolding at the asteroid-belt and the sun, that has the propensity to flatten any military prowess that both camps might possess at the edge of any cut. We have stated our case and the leaders may choose between what is important or not. It might seem that bickering over oil, gas, platinum, gold, food, land, political power and else is the most correct thing to do. Meanwhile the constitutional rights of 7 billion people is possibly being violated in advance, by a handful of headstrong leaders, all of whom are supposed to represent the interest of the people at large...this is appalling all over again. So what does this amount to? When we specifically know from now on that everything has to be done to get people out of harm's way and the poker-faced civilization stands still, with disregard. The account of how many people have lost life due to weather in the period from 2013 and 2014 is nothing short of violation of human rights by the governments who have nothing on causality. No one will even glance at the fact that the asteroid-belt is awry and what the actual cause of this might be, nor even regard for putting this information in the public domain for the people to decide on what the general action should be. Government has been the principle decider of what people can do, based on the arbitrary boundaries established by history. Our view is that Africa is the future of humanity if anomalous cosmic and weather is to be avoided. Africa is known to possess the most ancient relics from the distant past. So Africa is essentially a safe-box in the event of an end-of-days scenario, that seems to be looming behind the asteroid-belt realism. Only 2015 will be the most conclusive index, in terms of the hypothesis of escalating dangers, that have made a debut through the incidents of the polar vortex and the 2013 storms in North America. There are countless amounts of people who may speak more on the Africa's endowments and position as a primary safe-zone, more than we can in this book. This will become apparent at some precipice, when it becomes clear to all that Africa is the safe-house of humanity if and when an apocalyptic reality should become irrefutable. In African tradition, the Elders are the ones charged with leadership in this regard and we may not presume to speak ahead of the Elders on matters of the ancient and revered relics and objects endowed to Africa. This tradition has been alive for as long as forever and it will come to the fore when a time arises. We dare to say that the asteroid realism that has been a recent part of the world's story is an indicator that something else is going on here.

Anyone would venture to say that 2014 is a year of surprises as the Malaysian story of a plane that went missing and the various theories involved is another wide-ball. 2014 is the craziest inning, with just a quarter of it being spent. At this moment we would strongly endorse a wholesale evacuation of the world, all to Africa. This is a deeply held right of expression that we won't spare for anything. Anyone is welcome to refute this suggestion, with one condition, bring all the facts to the contrary. This book has said enough for now...let us wait to see what 2015 will present and take it from there, that is also only if 2014 does not go off the hinges on its own. Alright, before we even close the page for the day, it is reported that Egypt is running amok. Morsi and 600 plus members of the Brotherhood are standing trial and this has brought another riotous situation to the city of Alexandria, Egypt. 2014 is a strong-arm affair. Just put everything in a basket and you have a planet splintering at the seams. Egypt is a country of genesis and so much of the world is hinged on what goes on in Egypt for many reasons. For one, the Mayan hypothesis of the end-times is partly anchored in Egypt, the pyramids at Giza, a site of one of similar cyclical scenarios. For as long as 2014 has been, we have heard only shivering stories about the world. Every other story is pensive, what do you call that? Where does that leave 2015...? Oh wait we are telling you what you already know. This mission is done.

Do what it takes to research the possibility that this book is intimating. The reins and endorsement to acceptable and veritable data about important issues and matters in the interest of the public is with the people at large. Elected representatives and officials of the world should also represent the right that people have put with them, to do something that they would not ordinarily do regarding existential and veritable data relating to the Mayan prophecy. Look into this hypothesis of the Mayan prophecies coupled with the scenarios outlined in the book of Revelations and the recent reality of the asteroid-belt revolting out there in space with repercussions on this civilization. This could be related to what the book of Revelations says and a reason for its existence at all, we all have to ask this compelling question at around this time. Can we afford to set the book of Revelations aside as a source of scientific, cosmological and astrological data? There is reasonable cause for the scenario caused and outlined in the book of Revelations. Then the world should be ready for the prescribed scenarios that are outlined in this auspicious book, as a matter of a source code for referencing things that are going on beyond the remit of the human experience in the neighbourhood of the planet.

This is an issue that may only be directed at government as there is no civilian or citizen with authority beyond the august institution. At the moment the world is gripped with elite institutionalism that holds meritocracy as a standard to the exclusion of billions of people. The reticence and fear of those who hold the keys to wealth and perceived power is stupendous beyond belief. Vested interest and built up notions of convention and habit may be an unimaginable prison in a time like what the Mayans speak of. Whichever way we may imagine ...otherwise the people instead of the governments retain the right to liquidate the espoused stores of values that this civilization is built and based on before any apocalyptic realism may halt it all at a booming screech.

It is startling that the 2012 application to court has such renewed allure. There is no limit to the amount of times that we may call the reader to take the mantle of judge and jury decide the merits of this appeal. By now in March 2014, there is no amount of traditional protesting or civil action that will stop the advent of the asteroid era even as a way highlighting this fact to the powers that be.

It is 18h33 on the 25<sup>th</sup> March 2014...the collective straw of the world just broke as we heard on the news that a mudslide in Washington, USA, induced by rain, is sweeping through the big capital. What? Rains are sniffing lives across the world and government doesn't read the writing? "Then Give the people the right to encounter this reality.... Surely there is a time when the situation comes square on the street of the people to see to finish. Government is notorious for red-tape and the inability to make decisions on the spot. The year 2014 is rampaging through sensibilities, threatening to turn into a bizarre fiend in broad daylight. Due care is a responsibility attached to rights even all what people entrust to government. The time may arrive at anytime when the people have to talk to the powers that be. People and *leaders* shouldn't only meet at cross-roads. As outrageous as it might transpire to be this is some form of reality. The government and all should facilitate for end-of-days forums and discussion once and for all. What is happening up there in the high offices of power should coincide with the reality on the streets. This system of a civilization is facing a challenge. The power resourced presidents of this world ...all of the leaders with a collective franchise, should have to always evaluate positions in relation to the moving sands of time, complete with alignment to the past, present and future as an observable continuum. This is the people's world! People may have to act when necessary and take back responsibilities and rights! The rains across the world in the year 2014 compel the people to ask questions? Many circumstances are crossed vertically and horizontally and just now civil rights and well deserved constitutional rights coincide and intersect by a literal and linear reading of the situation as is...People bear the right to consider all what is possible to do regarding what is transpiring. People should have to reflect on what this situation is. It's easy for leaders to be captured by shenanigans in a world of ideas, the domain of issues of economics, finance and *interest rates* preoccupying big business and government beyond the interests of the people at large. It is easy to infer right now that with or without a properly constituted forum of judges and executives, the people are prepared to cross the Atlantic Ocean if it comes to that... Dear Sirs the silent diplomacy of the world leaders may very well be a slowly sinking titanic if we don't mind. Release the ships and airplanes for the people to escape the anger of an apocalyptic disaster. It is a lucid plea to ask the *authorities* to bring all the people to Africa as the end-times milieu plays out. It is incoherent for elected representatives in government to ignore the reality as followed through by the Mayan injunction. The past is an important part of the time continuum, so by virtue of due regard to the 2014 realism witnessed by all, it is now a challenging test of the psychological verity of the assertions of the *medium* of the beginning of 2014.

Anything is possible....It is possible that at the moment, the world is experiencing a severe alteration of reality and perception induced by change in atmospheric pressure due to hyper sun activity. Afterall perception is influenced by chemical changes in the body and this is not far from non-fiction. Have you seen the latest truncheon of movies from Hollywood in recent times, everything is high voltage twilight viewing. Who is to say that these series and films from Hollywood have not altered the perception of viewers by now already...On a more serious note though, habit or convention is as strong a drug, we are simply used to a specific way of life and if extreme change should happen we wouldn't detect it nor adopt. Reality is made of a multi-levelled continuum of events that are unfolding in sequence in all domains. Right now we may even just be immersed in a situation where everything is changing, even time and space. Here is a dose of fictitious reasoning from a parallel dimension....average dilution of quantities of everything (quantum) that has happened in the first quarter of 2014 as a picture of past, present and future... How is that... #laugh-out-loud.

But seriously let's get back to business.... #here is to more complaining... It is possible to be bamboozled by the numbers, millions and billions of dollars that the stock markets and stock exchanges rage and rave about ahead of reports, of daily news and the rank and file of priorities. This should not obscure the objective of bringing the people home if there is ever a need to do so because of a level 5 warning that emanates from the asteroid realism that assumes that there is a high activity window in February/March of the beginning of any year after 2013. This is an order of realism that has been bequeathed to 2014. The focus on the erstwhile indelible reverence for rule of law overrides any logical aversion to asteroids, apparently in a sphere of reach of the earth. Rule of law as an existential and substantive institution, should also meet the people half-way, things have changed...and listen to the complaints of the people at a time like this in the first quarter of 2014. Procedural institutionalism is another subversive and subliminal prison, executives and officials take cover behind procedure when the going gets tough and it is impossible to resolve administrative and political issues...this does happen. A recent example in the news if we remember is the case of a woman who set herself on fire in Syria, for food...This is a graphic expression of the volatile state that cities are in across the world. National jurisdiction has an element of restricting people from voluntary movement because nationality unintendedly also leads to captive geographical space, especially in the case of the *poor*. Common reach and access through travel is a challenge because of physical remoteness across spans of ocean. Economically poor people simply cannot travel or participate in the aloof habits of economically wealthy people. This is an element of geographic seclusion and virtual imprisonment, isn't it... The leadership in political and economic circles should also accept it as a reality of several challenges faced by many across the world.

People accept that sometimes government runs into trouble, dilemma and difficulty, example... when natural disaster occur and government is unable to cope with relief and disaster prevention, the people who elected the officials ironically suffer like people drowned by rain across the world in early 2014. People are not wrong to then sometimes ask questions about whether government is not able to put measures to prevent natural disasters sucking vitality out of people. In the age of broad-based access to social media, silence is something that sometimes eludes the public sector and the private sector also can't keep things quite, especially when risky events engross or encroach on daily routine unexpectedly. Businesses also have something to lose whenever something goes horribly wrong. The public sector outfit simply becomes a real challenge to officials in a time of hyperbole like inexplicable natural incursions. The public sector is a tricky place whenever a natural challenge has its own way, regardless of how armed a State or government is.

The challenge to people in such circumstances is that presidents around the world are answerable to the houses of cabinet and parliament, experiences that are sometimes far from the regard of common experiences faced by people. The real thing is that when natural events or disasters take centre stage, character is demanded from high office and from people in cities, even people who have been left with nothing have to rise to the occasion. We would all run for the nearest cave should an asteroid pummel our cities. In moments like these we are all challenged for what we are made of. The man in the streets of cities whether homeless or not is as important as the other. Our normal manicured and pedicured comforts as opposed to the rough existence of many people in the world's cities make everyone indispensable. Reality is that the world belongs to people who have nothing to their name as well as the people who have everything. Everyone is duty-bound to accept that people are equal in challenging circumstances beyond normal daily experience. People everywhere realise that it is everyone's business to visit this reality without fear or favour. The highest office should lead the charge. Natural incursions prove that no one is above the vagaries and harsh realities of a sometimes wild earth experience. People at large should realise that they are so important and should not take any position for granted. We the people have to sanction ourselves. Those responsible for the office of government, should also commit to the dutiful obligation that says "should one more person lose a life due to rain and floods in 2015, 2016, 2017 and beyond, then it is on the hands of government, this is what is called for of the highest office. Government is becoming a highly charged responsibility and an even more onerous occupation. Government should adjust to these variations and deviations from traditional stereotypes and convention. A challenge to readiness in a fast evolving end-of-days scenario is the fact that the rich people should also put a shoulder to the wheel and employ the resources of this world to a pre-emptive and mitigation of a full scale GTV. Ladies and gentlemen we should not leave things to time and chance, at the moment is cyclones, landslides, floods and incessant rain, do we only want to listen when it starts raining meteors and asteroids start pummelling the face of the earth, wiping out satellites and government installations from earth... By the way in case anyone thinks that we are making anything up, do a Google search...these are news reports that are archived for all to see.

Without insults being thrown around, for now, it seems that the most care is leveraged on the interests of the already rich people and this has been proven for all time by the way that the interests of the poor are slow to resolve. Unfortunately, as seen in the news, of the Syrian woman who set herself alight, there are still people who lose life for food. Irony of ironies, this is an indication of the readiness for eventuality, there was no way government could uphold the woman's right to life, government couldn't be everywhere all the time. Critical resources are still overly focused on guarding the status quo that entails entrenched interests. There is a general perception and perhaps reality that mostly people comply with anything that does not offend their interests and good standing. Without offending the powers that be, there is a perception that this is what presidents have been forced to do and been known for throughout. There are sometimes sporadic riots and protests in cities and this as a yardstick of the readiness of government around the world for extra-ordinary circumstances. The fact that there are riots and protests means that the governments are far from being ready because clearly there are still immediate challenges like satisfying people who are protesting and rioting. We may not claim not to know when we are challenged by even cyclical medium to long term events like an end-of-days scenario (as the Mayans said or are still saying, it is not the first time that this happens). We might be distracted by the illustrious achievements of modern civilization, reality is that there are still immense challenges around the bend. Well, we shouldn't wait until we have no option one of these days to hear what the Mayans have been saying for all so long. We shouldn't wait for libraries and stores of value to burn (by extraordinary incursions like an asteroid bombardment). We should see what is going on sooner than possible, what we see going on is a steady deterioration of the solar system's space integrity. People should find out what the truth is about the solar system. The information is still fairly convoluted and limited to scientific circles. We may not afford to perpetuate perception that leaders are more prepared for extra-ordinary eventualities...already people are asking why people are secretly building bunkers. We can't blame people for conjuring and entertaining conspiracy theories due to *skewed* thinking about the elite being of higher net value than people in general. Up to now, the collective actions of governments across the world have been relatively inadequate and short of substantial gains for the general population. The people might not accept that "government tried", public office is more demanding in volatile times compounded by sitting poverty. This should not be interpreted as a typically scathing attack, the people at large have endured more than what is fair to. Government's assertion of accepted jurisdictions and territories of nation states, unintendedly trump the interests of the people and public perception is that resources are siphoned for the rich only. The world has the capacity to be a school and we are slowly learning, that the people who have nothing to lose are part of the lessons we have ahead of us when the need arises. The situation in the Democratic Republic of Congo is a blatant case of the world being flat-footed while genocide ensues.

We put it to the Court of Law that the people may not be hostage to the shenanigans of appointed officials and private sector peers in authority across the world. The technical and strategic obligations that resonate in long and convoluted speeches, often circumvent simple matters. For anyone in leadership to claim non-interest is non-realistic, the world has been more connected than what is passing off today. Developed economies benefited wholesale from the decline of Developing economies in the past. So Developed economies and Developing economies will find that these countries are more interdependent than the current status quo admits to. Administrative obligations and things like that sometimes prove to be unnecessarily complicated for 7 billion people all around. It will be a heady day when the entire world realises that once again Africa is at the centre as the world as we know it folds.

The resolution to heed the signs of a disintegrating natural environment will put the people outside of the continent of Africa in an advanced position. We strongly hold it to be an affirmed reality that it is better to head for Africa before even time and space force this action. This way the environment in Africa could and should have been built up in time to preserve the integrity of people as much as possible. From our own conclusion now we realise that Africa should have been highly developed by all the countries building reasonable installation to house people from all over the world. This did not happen soon enough and now that the situation is dire, arrangements should be made.

Wow everyone can see, ever since 2012, unusually, there have been volcanoes erupting in Europe and South America, more earthquakes erupting around the world than before, erratic and anomalous weather with an unexpected mudslide in Washington USA. Anyway more importantly, the announced meeting of the African Union and the European Union in Brussels on the 03rd April 2014, should have also been about the realisation that the world is in a volatile period that needs timeous action and preparation as items on the agenda.

For the purpose of this topic government executives have done less than enough by prioritising laws that imply that the rich are entitled to hoard resources by virtue of their power or strength. It is not enough of an argument to say that the rich have become so because of their own intellectual prowess. We submit to common sense that this is an abrogation and dereliction of duty, because ethical discretion should override this status quo. The biggest threat to the world is that everything is monetised, risk is monetised and outlook to risk is measured in terms of monetary value. For anything substantial to happen there has to be a monetised framework activated. An emergency circumstance of an earth-wide proportion would be bland in the face of a monetised system...Monetary value cannot be placed on an earth-wide emergency.

For instance, the insurable risk of natural disaster is quantified in terms of the monetary value of replacement and risk cover. This will not suffice when the world as whole is threatened by risk emerging out of the recent developments of an asteroid prone world because the potential damage is beyond monetary valuation, this is wholesale collateral risk that the world is faced with. A further risk is that only the powerful or well-heeled and educated seem to be entitled on a whole to reap the benefits of the resources of the earth. This is an element of risk because naturally the well-endowed would resist any suggestion that the world is facing a recently unprecedented risk that could wipe out all the value imaginable. The first casualty in a high risk environment is perception of what is valuable and worth fighting to keep. It is unintendedly our own institutions that prevent people from achieving likewise and this is a risk. The risk outlook and risk profile of the planet in the face of meteors and asteroids does not easily pander to the audacious bidding of power and wealth. We have to activate a colossal sense of stewardship in order to countenance a pre-emptive response towards the now more obvious and impending risk. Harmed in the future due to asteroids and floods is in the hands of elected leadership across the world. The Mayans have warned this generation through bequeathing scientifically veritable data.

A moratorium on further isolation and alienation of resources away from developing economies and Africa in particular is necessary for the whole encounter with the Mayan injunction. Reason for course should restrain the already risky behaviour that has put people around world at risk. The one-way-ticket of unfettered accumulation and consumption inclined to more and more resources unintendedly shying away from real risk could blast the modern civilization out of kilter. All the conferences of governments and industry should by now have been geared towards encountering the eminent risk outlined by illustrious legacy communities. Efforts will be derailed by tilted and unmitigated optimism that defies the reality of the asteroid and hyper-active sun circumstance that is visiting the modern generation right now. The waste of opportunity in the past 50 to 500 years in retractable colonial enterprises of suppression and domineering economics and politics have unintendedly derailed the focus of the modern generation from global risk due to the recently unfolding reality across the globe. Well trained armies of sophistry wielding analysts touting rules and laws as a defence in volatile situations is unintendedly inclined towards keeping the status quo and tilted interests of the wealth and power grid. The typical argument that business owners should earn more than the workers because the owners take risk is stale in the face of imminent cosmic risk. The farce becomes even more denuded when the value of people as bearers of economic rights and other sophisticated social rights, is threatened by extra-ordinary risk elements. This is the bane of modern world value systems mingled with real risk from sun-spots.

Economic exclusion has marooned people in places where they are not even able to travel to other countries even as bare minimum tourists, what more of emergency evacuation circumstances. Agreeably, the wealthy will gladly jump onto airplanes and ships to escape an apocalyptic scenario. Precession denialists will defend the status quo, speaking against the assertions of the end-of-days scenario. It is no wonder, the politics of economics won't allow beneficiaries to imagine a global risk bearing on deeply entrenched career ambitions to high office and so this realism may realistically be a source of defensive resistance to apocalyptic aversion and risk categorisation. Generally as a secular forecast it is highly possible that the younger and new generation is more inclined to take over the world's key points and power-centres in order to perpetuate "traditional way of life", and aspire to do as has always been done. Alternatively the new generation may see the responsibility to lead the risk burdened apocalyptic realism.

As far as this argument goes, the burden of proof is with the State in any country. Let's proceed right here and now with the argument, to either agree or dispel the claims that the earth is vulnerable to an asteroid attack right now as we speak. 2015 may further illustrate and extenuate the risk and show everyone that the world is in for a high-jump.

The 26th March 2014 is a day for keeping calm, after yesterday's ranting at the powers that be. Today we happened to see an article published in the *Saturday Star* (March 22nd 2014) in South Africa, on page 11. The article titled *"Nothing paltry about hell's chicken",* is about a discovered dinosaur Anzu Wyliel, a 3.35m-long, 226kg bird-like species from the Cretaceous period, about 68 million years ago. What drew us to the article is the mention of the word *asteroid,* that struck the earth near the Yucatan peninsula. The dinosaur is said to be a member of a group called oviraptorosaurs. This dino-bird was discovered on a ranch in North Dakota, Utah by amongst others scientists from the Carnegie Museum of Natural History. The mention of the word "asteroid" is becoming more frequent in tabloids, using South African as a field-sample. This is an indication that the phenomenon of asteroids is proving to be accepted information and now for the purpose of the Johannesburg Formula, in relation to this time period. The article is a purposeful informer about the reality of a 15 billion year old world, and the real last and recognisable period that was thwarted by an end-of-the-world scenario, that saw a dominant life form succumbing and replaced through evolution by species that eventually careered life-forms of this time period. This is not a weighed debate about whether the *creationist* or *evolutionary* school of thought is valid or not. This is about weighing scientific data for dependability and veracity for the purpose of presenting a credible case in front of a court of law from anywhere in the world to balance. We find that the creationist and evolutionary data are both credible for the purpose of explaining short and long term realities about the world and tenure through time. The debate seems to be over, we find a logical sequence of events based on credible data and it makes incredible sense that creationism and the theory of evolutionism, co-depend as a super-theory. We appeal to sectarian views that see a chasm and irreconcilability between creationist and evolutionist scientific outlook. A side issue, that for us is quite ingrained, is palaeontology and evolutionists debate on whether these Cretaceous creatures were herbivore or carnivores. We are more inclined to think that all dinosaurs were herbivores, the modern school has just assumed by the size and appearance of the Cretaceous species that they were carnivores. Bizarre anatomy does not translate to carnivorous behaviour, physical and dietary requirements. Conditioning is a big determinant of survivalist behaviour. The Creationists view should also see the linear logic in adaptation and continuation of species because of elementary commonality with other species. Personally I don't see a contradiction between Creationist and Evolutionist explanation of the earth as we know it...it all makes perfect sense when looked at together as a continuum.

Sectarian views are based on prejudice and discrimination against other species. A superiority complex makes it unimaginable that humans and other species have a common Creator and DNA bacterial pool. Humans share many physiological similarities with other species. A show stopper is that all species occupy a common environment, the planet. Because of cognitive development humans may show discriminatory tendencies against other species. That is all the differentiation there is, cognitive and lingual abilities, nothing more. Nutritional requirements are similar across all the species how do we explain this common requirement with other species. We all eat the same proteins and minerals out of the same vegetation, this is an astounding common physiology characteristic. Difference humans and other species is over-inflated. Because of the aesthetic achievement reached by humans it is possible to shun a common environmental genesis, even if it is based on a 15 billion year record of specie development and various periods of physiological changes and adaptation summed up as evolution. Deep seated prejudice is at the bottom of aversion to the divergence between the Creationist and Evolutionist outlooks. Creationist and Evolutionists should accept the inviolable fact of the earth being 15 billion years old and contemplate the events of a developmental trajectory, that is not even foreclosed up to now. Ironically, the ability for cognitive processing ability, has enabled humans to be belligerent towards other species and the environment. It is on a permanent and indelible record that enslaved each other as a vogue, humans are known to hoarded resources to the exclusion of other humans. This is a contradiction to the specialised cognitive and physiological ability that humans have achieved since. Even recently, racism and discrimination based on physiological characteristics is still something that defies logic. It is not enough for humans to claim to be superior to other species based on arbitrary criteria. This has been an excuse for humans to act out high and extreme prejudice. Other species on the planet have been saved from being absolute marauders by a simple switch of design, the inability to convey data through linguistic adaptation. The fact that other species are non-lingual has been a blessing in disguise. Humans teach children the same behaviour that was ruled to be unacceptable... racism, greed, war etc.

 How do we as humans claim sophistication and civilization without accounting for the destruction to the environment and each other in pursuit of a livelihood. We are decrying human behaviour regarding other cohabiting species because humans have even behaved worse towards their own seeing nothing wrong with economic slavery, economic domineering and economic discrimination, at horrendous costs. So we wonder how humans are behaving towards each other in times of apocalypse.

For anything at all we are prepared to submit a memorandum to the Constitutional Court of South Africa to review and investigate the claims contained in the Johannesburg Formula. From our point of reference, we strongly support a review or appeal of the matter including a fair hearing at the International Human Rights Court. The process of legal recourse is based on affordability to activate, we strongly advise that *ordinary* people struggle with access to legal recourse because of ludicrous costs.

Back to the weather and other things, okay now, to close one meteorological chapter once and for all, the 27th March 2014 is a cloudy but warm day with prospects of unveiling the blue sky. By now the trend on the "Rains of March" 2014, seems to have made way. The belligerent rain in the middle of March is something that is somewhat of a has-been. Even an amateur may weigh in a penny for a thought and venture to say that the weather system has moved on. The fact that there is a lingering cloud cover today here over Johannesburg is not serious information enough. We could easily deduce that this is due to the hyper-active sun being deflected by a constant cloud cover that has been hovering and hoarding the airspace for all the remaining days of March until today. The tie between the clear blue sky and brooding clouds is what anyone can see in this unpaid for heavyweight division match, there is no clear winner. Even the most of capable referees would not call this day impartially. We do not have a final order of when we will say the phenomenon is gone because clouds still represent a tentative threat. The only stubborn remnant of the "Rains of March" 2014 is a band of reluctant clouds at 13h50, 27th March 2014.

An inescapable but ironic puzzle is that next year, 15th February 2015 will be the second anniversary of the Chelyabinsk asteroid. We may not discount this fact and for the purpose of being alert, we observe this day as a day that asteroid history was made in recent times. The close to 1500 people who were injured in Russia took it on the chin for the rest of us, this could have been anyone and the asteroid could have done more or less damage depending on capricious factors like time and space. No one wants to even raise the issue for due consideration of aversion and wanting to wish it all away and hoping that it doesn't happen again, but we have a reason, the reason is to educate/inform and to make others who may not have even heard of asteroids before aware.

230

...It is the 28th March 2014, around 02h00a.m., it is early on the pensive morning with news about Ukraine across garrisoned airwaves. The announcement on the news is shocking to a recently ardent observer of the Ukraine issue. It has just been announced to a raucous background of Ukraine paramilitary, that a Ukrainian was shot earlier in the week. Everyone including the American president who was in Europe this week made public commitments to the effect that the West has no intention of a military confrontation with Russia. In other words, they have not prepared anything either than economic sanctions to level on Russia and that was the promise. What the public did not hear is that by virtue of supporting Ukraine, that if a Ukrainian was shot as one is reported to have been by Russian forces, then the West is even if not vicariously but certainly involved by proxy. So if in the beginning of the week of 1st April 2014, more Ukrainians should be shot and others were to retaliate, then the principals would be adjoined through agency. We take it for granted and think that because the United States of America President stood up in Europe in the last week of March 2014 and said what he did, to the effect that West does not seek military confrontation etc. This is what it would translate to on the streets, the world is not wired like that at all, people don't take official announcements as gospel, not when there is discrepancy between the rich and the poor. Often poor people are left to their own devices and to defend themselves against the elements. In the news on the 28th March, it was announced that a Ukraine was shot by a Russian soldier, regardless of what the president of the USA said while he was in Europe. The point is this, after making all the commitments of a non-military positioning, what would the President do if an American was shot at in Ukraine or a person from the West was mistakenly shot at, would the President be able to stop people from getting into a scuffle from the remote location of an office? We have all seen and heard of many predictions about future conflagrations, these are also insightful... On the other hand it is noteworthy how all the predictions about the future relating to technological advances are expectedly accepted as infallible, but the predictions about the end-of-days scenario is ignored wholesale.

Another thing, our theory is that if cyclical deterioration of the world environment is true, for instance that the apocalyptic scenario is non-fiction, then we have it that deterioration in human behaviour is a result of whatever cosmic energy forces plying on earth. For instance behaviour at an end-times period, is typically going to deteriorate without humans being able to explain why there is irrational behaviour on earth, at such a specific time.   If this theory does not hold water for intellectual antagonists, then will someone explain why super-powers are armed to the teeth with nuclear weapons pointed at each other. Why are countries having more money committed to military budgets than other departments ever? Currently the world is experiencing the most heightened levels of social unrest and some of the most frightening scenes are carried across the world on social media for all to experience the trauma.

In western Ukraine a trooper named Alexandra Mutsichko was killed by Russian fire and....now a back and forth between the Russians and Ukraine is heating up. Russia is said to have more ambitions for territorial annexation to enlarge Russia to its former state. How is a speech by the leaders of the western alliance going to stop people in the streets of Ukraine and Russia from exchanging fire, retaliating and maiming each other? At which point will leaders change their minds about the intentions of Russia? The world is not made only of speeches, the streets are not made of speeches from heated and guarded chambers. 2014 has already taken the trophy for the most toxic year ever. Within three of the first months, two asteroids have whooshed past the earth, a country has been annexed, a polar vortex has paralysed cities, our own "Rains of March" 2014 have robbed South African of more than 45 lives, a mudslide swept Washington up, more than two earthquakes have registered a record on the Richter scale (see California, Chile and China respectively).

All of us have a duty to defend our little *corners* across the world regardless of where we are in the social ladder. By 07h30 in the morning, it is a deeply cloudy day that favours the conditions from

232

mid-month. What brings these clouds to close ranks in this manner has us thinking that it a defence. If this cloud cover was not there, the earth and area around Johannesburg would be sweltering. 08h36 there goes, the rays of penetrative light substance has breached the clouds and light has just streamed into the airspace below the clouds all the way to ground level. Window panes and trees are throwing shadows while rustling in a light breeze. It is a hard won breach of light streaks and one gets the sense that the earth is a fragile body that is cooperating with the clouds to protect its own face. It must be too early for the ground to be hit by heated sunrays. Wait a minute, how about this, if the "Rains of March" 2014 were said to be unusual, then what about everything else, the almost persistent cloak of clouds and the bias towards the mid-March conditions? Admittedly it looks like winter is coming early as much as summer *lingered* longer than usual. This is a confusion all on its own. The last week of March has just been that, a wrestle between post-dated summer and pre-dated winter, autumn has not held its own, it has undoubtedly been bullied. This is a tinge of 2014, unpredictable and indeterminable, only the markets have held up optimism, but the rest of the outlook is on the brink of the unexpected. No amount of preparation or foresight could do for 2014, she is not an easily impressed year.

In the afternoon, the DJ plays a song at 17h 55, with the lyrics... *I'll send an SOS to the world, I hope someone gets my, message in a bottle* for a refrain... quickly saw this as a reflection of even what is coming across from this book. The rock group: Police's *"message in a bottle"* struck me as being a momentous message for the day. It is clear that sending an SOS to the world is exactly what the doctor ordered.

# CHAPTER NINE

## THE 28th OF MARCH 2014

The 28th of March 2014 is a day of reckoning, the radio report on the news at 20h00 announces that Russia has militarised the eastern border of Ukraine. The number of soldiers posted is said *easily* to be more than 30 000 and others report much more. The western bloc that has been drawn by other means of association is put into a fix by destiny. The Russian bloc is connected to the situation in Crimea by proxy, this is going to be the final verdict should Russia go for gold and impose a military affront. At the moment it seems as though they have just posted army personnel and ramped up a presence nearby. Anything that Russia does, has the tacit touch of consent and association that implies that Russian allies are part and parcel should things get out of hand. No one has a firm finger on what forces are controlling the world as the two sides are already implicated by virtue of today's reality being that the silent war is way ahead on. The things that people say about each other behind closed doors and the things that people think of each within the recesses of their minds and chest's keeping is more telling that what plays out as actions... No one knows what dreams people are having. This is the world in 2014. No one is born desiring the worst for themselves or desiring the worst situation. Surely even by mere signs the rubicon has been crossed, even long before Crimea was annexed. This story started even before Crimea was given to Ukraine after the last world war. The rubicon was breached before world war one, the situation in Crimea is a continuation, this is part of the story of the world in 2014. There is no way for anyone to rein in time and space, every so often it is time for what will be and what will be, will be. As other situations unfold in other parts of the world like in Egypt it is a fray by association. Any war anywhere on earth affects the world including DRC, Egypt and anywhere else. The world is more connected than what our collective behaviour is letting off, it is welded together by time and space. There is only one world, the here and now, everything is of the world. There are no chasms as the recent conflicts may allude to, at all. Geographically the world is one, politically the world is or should be one, economically the world is one or should be one, and anything else outside of this is happens to be a state of embattlement. Even a fight between two people anywhere in the world affects the world because everyone everywhere is connected by virtue of living in one world. Put all these things together and what do you have. Every bad news report about any category of crime is part of this a subliminal and compounding war. Put all the reports of the world into one world report and you have a horrendous picture. That's all.

The weekend of the 28th March 2014 is the worst weekend so far in 2014. This weekend is a weekend of confrontation in Crimea, the stage is decked. The world is deteriorating into an organised confrontation. The confrontation has been looking for a point of entry and it has found a critical point at which to enter the veins of the world. It matters little what formations have changed and reorganised since world war two, the subjects of embattlement remain the same, land, oil, gas and whatever else you have. Nothing else has changed but alliances, loyalties and interests. This is the frontier that confrontation is thirsty for and we fall into the trap one by one. Confrontation is laughing at us by now. This book has been done for a while and at this moment it is writing itself just as well as the situation in and confrontation that is pushing into Crimea is doing so on its own. People are accessories to the confrontation, the dispute is fighting itself using people as responsive agents who take sides. It does not matter what we do, the confrontation started long ago. Many of the things that people are fighting for or over are things from the past. World war two continued in so many ways that is why the confrontation is resurfacing at Crimea, you may call it what you like. What about all the other regions where conflict is continuously flaring up or threatening to flare up...People are likely to fight as they did in world war two, the same thing that made people fight in world war two has not disappeared. People fought over resources then and are fighting over resources now. Welcome to 2014. The

28th March 2014 is the day that the confrontation crossed a rubicon and engulfed more than what is required to blow out of scale. One just has to consolidate everything that is going on everywhere in the world to see that this is a state of broken world. The casualties are just too many, casualties of disease, casualties of weather, casualties of human confrontation, casualties of selfish decisions, and more than this. Nothing has changed and everyone is following suit. The confrontation is going on household for household, street for street, town for town, city for city, state for state, province for province, country for country, state for state region for region, bloc for bloc, this is a confrontation over ideologies, philosophies and outlook. Who can stop this confrontation, come out to the frontlines and put an end to this confrontation. The boundaries of civility have long been discarded, colonization and slavery were the ultimate beginnings of this confrontation that is continuing today, today it Crimea and tomorrow it is every street in the world, every nook and crevice, every jungle, every sea and all airspace. An illustration that the confrontation has not been doused is that there has been no appropriate apology for the enterprise of colonialism and the damage caused to economies has not been rehabilitated, so this simply means that the fray has not ended, the subliminal battleground is ablaze. This is just the way humans have behaved. It will be a miracle if anything else happens. The superpowers are ready for a confrontation, armed to the last and there is no commander in chief to be found willing to desist from the fighting. No journalist or amount of talking will stop the armed and thirsty mongers bent on dispute and skirmishes. The armies of the world are dressed for confrontation each wearing camouflage. Every country is armed for confrontation. Ordinary people on the street have no say to stop the thirst of armies being quenched. The fights of yesterday and the fights of tomorrow all have one thing in common, these are all for the supreme control of the world economy. With all this thirst for war being in the corridor, beware of the Mayans and their ineffable message. This is exactly the kind of circumstance of behaviour typical of the predictions of the Mayans.

The 29th March 2014 is a cloudy Saturday in Johannesburg, last night, 28th was a cloud-covered day that innocently did not know that in a land across the seas, Crimea, the situation was deteriorating. It is like a chess board, any piece that is moved has a bearing on all the other 15 pieces, a pawn does not move innocently, it portends the destiny of the rooks, bishops, the castles, the king and the queen's fate. The war for airspace that started with the "Rains of March" 2014 was fought over the skies of Johannesburg by clouds and the clear blue sky, it drew casualties of over 40 people that lost life. Today *climate change* is being observed with the *Earth Hour* theme that will see people across the world switch off lights and that sort of thing. This is aimed at making people aware of issues that are related to the degradation of the world's energy sources and the behaviour of weather phenomenon and the likes. As for the Johannesburg Formula, our view is that there is a gross miscalculation and misunderstanding of symptoms like the *polar vortex* and the "Rains of March" 2014, where these anomalies are being put at the door of global warming. What we purport is that global warming and resultant symptoms that are being labelled as climate change are as a result of the cyclical GTV that is a summary of what the Mayans have warned about. In other words, this is the end-of-days scenario compounding and confounding the world. If we had the audience of *climate change* proponents, we would debrief and brief them of this reality. We have however not spared a word or action to get this message out there, in the form of this book. For us the clear picture is all about joining the dots that include what has been labelled *global warming* and *climate change*. In fact for us we are doing it right here in the pages of this book to literarily *hijack* the *Earth Hour* event as an all-out end-of-days scenario rather than singularly *global warming* and *climate change* assertions. The only forum that is available to us right here and now is this book. The outcomes of the *Earth Hour* will be that, a global event of collective action to heighten awareness. Add the claims of the Johannesburg Formula to the mix and another picture emerges. We are officially annexing the event of *Earth Hour* by the declaration that this is in fact an unconscious appraisal of the end-of-days scenario that is compounding as we speak.

Also we hereby annex the *climate change* and *global warming* assumption and expression here in the book as actually being precessional expressions in total. We realise that there is no amount of mud that we may sling at the climate change and global warming pundits that will persuade this lobby to realign with the end-end-of-days outlook. On our part it only makes sense to annex the global warming and climate change paradigm wholly and to realign it to the end-of-days paradigm. It is now up to the climate change and global warming school of thought to accept or refute this position on condition that there is an un-scalable advance in scientific data that is presented. So do you blame us if we allude to conspiracy in a desperate attempt to highlight the urgency of the end-of-days realism. So readers, do we now see how the world is organised? We have the entire academic and scientific community committed to the *global warming* and *climate change* paradigm. This is either optimism with the hope that industrial action is responsible and therefore corrective industrial pull-backs on the industrial-assault on the environment will fix everything in time. The enclave that purports industrialism as the main cause assumes that economic and industrial policy alone is responsible for the effects of environmental degradation. This to us is a gross mistake. What of probably unintendedly obfuscating the real and original causes of the symptoms of degradation to the environment and changes? The real situation is too gross to contemplate let alone communicate to stakeholders so that correct pre-emptive action may be embarked on.

In any case as people on the ground we have no recourse in this regard and we have to mount our own research to challenge more than a thousand researchers and professors to cajole them out of this tilted outlook. Also it is an uphill battle in front of entrenched economic interests from the past that purport the view as infallible. The only reason industry would support this view after retracting a denialist stance, is the implications of wholesale precession on vested interests. Winston Churchill asserted that *"we shall fight on the beaches and we shall fight on land"*, we henceforth purport that we shall fight on the pages of books and we shall fight on the internet pages, where information exists to prove and highlight views that are contrary to established norms. For all intents and purposes and for the benefit of the 7 billion people across the world, we hereby and formally annex the climate change and global warming line of thought and the entire enterprise of purporting, researching and broadcasting of this view. We hereby attest and assert that the end-of-days outlook and hypothesis is the correct view in this regard. This is then a formal annexation of the global warming outlook and reassertion of the end-of-days outlook that claims that the cause of these effects catalogued as global warming and climate change is inclusively the recent state of hyper-action at the sun due to a cyclical and temporal realism. The sun is self-diagnosing and modulating the solar system as a cyclical process of house-keeping at all. We hereby in our capacity as the citizen of South Africa and rightful citizen of the world side by side with 7 billion people as the rightful stakeholders and interested parties, declare that global warming and climate change are not the pen-ultimate scientific assertions and diagnosis of what is happening to the planet Earth. In addition to the established norms of global warming and climate change as pen-ultimate phenomenon, we put the end-of-day realism in the mix as the supreme cause of the observed anomalies in recent times. We do not however discount the findings of the global change and climate change school, only thing, we hereby abridge the findings of causality as being those asserted by the end-of-days school.

Back to the news....On the 17h00 news on radio, President Obama has unequivocally asserted that they (the west) will do everything to protect Ukraine in the event of Russian aggression, while the Russian Foreign Minister Sergei Lavrov, has reassured the world that Russia has no military intentions in Ukraine. These are words that give little reassurance to the reality on the ground. The leaders may say what they say and the reality on the ground will be something else as usual. Presidents seem to think that their words will rein in and halt the actions of people on the ground. People on the ground are the triggers that may escalate national responses. Up to so far, we wait to see what will be. At the moment we are only monitoring the situation from the vantage of radio broadcasts and the tweedy pages of this book and whatever happens, the people on the streets will be there to pick up the tab. For far too long the leaders of countries have discounted the agency of the citizens, for crying out loud, there are 7 billion of us here and if you trample our rights in favour of your interests, we will meet you half-way. We have reason to compile a "2014 toxicity dossier" that includes Crimea, the Polar Vortex, earthquakes (in Chile, China and Barbados), the "Rains of March" 2014, the asteroids of 2013/2014 and the GTV as our findings of an escalating and compounding environment that will only be encountered when it is too late, welcome to the-end-of-days. The Johannesburg Formula chapter titled *THE 28th MARCH 2014* is a signature chapter of the "2014 toxicity dossier".

If I didn't know better the last day of March 2014 seems to be either signing-off and closing a chapter for all or it is a signal of what April is going to be. A report that it was pouring (rain) in the middle of the city of Johannesburg was somewhat of an enigma because we don't know what other anomalies are in store as 2014 makes her mark. The rain on this last day of the month, the 31st is a definite stop-over and March is leaving an indelible reminder of what it was all about. At 18h00 on the evening of the 31st March, the clouds are closing ranks around the skies in and around Johannesburg in all directions and somehow the remnants of the "Rains of March" 2014 looks as though it is announcing a departure through drenching and soaking the ground for a last time. It hasn't started in this part of the woods yet, but the rumbling roar of thunder and a charging rain is audible. The flashing of far –off lightning and sound of thunder is a sign that the night will be a long drenched affair that is pre-empting April, a yet unknown future that is one day away. It is the end of March and the first quarter of the year, a milestone of worth for such a notorious year. The thunder is getting louder and closer and within an hour or two it should be dripping and pouring. This is the only way to send March off into the irrecoverable past. One thing that is foreclosed is that the last day of March and the evening in particular is an unusual affair, at 18h15, the air is already electrified with a flash of thunder and it promises to be a blistering illustration of lightning. The radio is crackling with the interference of the electric waves from the thunder. As it starts to rain at 18h20 on the last evening of March, the month itself seems to be categorical that the "Rains of March" 2014 should never be forgotten as the rain takes on all what was a dry atmosphere and drenches it all. The night will see to finish because this just about shortens the time as the ambience and mood changes to a rained in state of mind. Rain is rain anywhere one goes, but this is another thing, this rain swept through South Africa taking more than 43 lives in March, alone.

The 1st of April 2014, is a declaration of an early winter. This is supposed to be autumn but there is no such sign on this day. Today is as cold as a mid-winter day and this is probably due to the disastrous month of March in terms weather. Sporadic clouds and a brisk windy rush is all but a show of the strong arm tactics that March brought through. The first day of April is information of a probably sliding condition and we don't expect a well behaved month at all. The weather is not showing an appetite for April 1st gags and it looks like we are headed for surprises. We hope that April does not warrant a stand-alone feature in this book but from the texture of the weather today, we leave it all to chance. The behaviour of the first day of April is an informant to the effect that this year as a whole needs to be watched because the weather is taking on a persona of its own.

...If the 2nd April 2014 is not a declaration of anger then nothing else is, we just switched on the 8h00a.m. news bright and early and we hear of an 8,2m earthquake in Chile. Mind you for 2014, this is a second earthquake in Chile, in either February or March there was a 4m earthquake that was one of a few around the world, including China, California and Barbados. This is no ordinary earthquake, it triggered a tsunami warning that was later withdrawn. Most of all when this earthquake is factored into the toxicity index of 2014, then we have something else to think about. Our hypothesis of a melt-down could just be about to be put on steroids, and a blistering highway. Today's theory or hypothesis is hinged on the fact that the sun is experiencing a state of hyper-activity.

We have to be careful that this earthquake is not an index of a further rattling of the earth's sub-terranean range and a chain activation of earthquakes and volcanoes because of an extraordinarily heated atmosphere that is baking the crevices and chasms and weakening the integrity of the earth's surface and immediate crust. This goes back to an earlier chapter called *THE EARTH WAS ROUND (Chapter 6).* Frankly we never thought that April would show a colour and probably set a trend for a month long tension. As part of the Johannesburg Formula outlook and the "2014 toxicity dossier", a measurement of the level of toxicity of the year 2014, amplifies our concerns for critical circumspection. 2014 is muscling in on the prospects of humanity and we probably won't see it until it is too late. March was a rained out month and April has just debuted with an 8.2m earthquake accompanied by fears of a tsunami. We don't know what else is waiting to explode underneath our feet. The Chile earthquake is a bully of note, it has released aftershocks and generally terrorised the people around South America with warnings of evacuations being extended to as far as Peru. The weather over Johannesburg on this morning of the 2ⁿᵈ April 2014, is almost standing in solidarity with the people and region of Chile, the brooding and moody showing is indecisive but more in favour of cloudy hostility. This is a season for alertness and awareness as far as weather and other natural phenomenon. This is beyond normal, the reality of a hyper-active sun that is exerting temperature pressure on everything and inducing a meltdown seems to be more real than we may speculate. The news report is that the M3 road in Fernwood, Cape Town in South Africa, is flooding due to rain, so we may conclude that the phenomenon of rain and floods has lapsed into April as is the case in the Western Cape. If a picture of 2014 were to be put up so far, it would be clear that there is some sort of problem, this is tantamount to a red alert. As it starts to rain at 10h11 on the morning of the 2nd April 2014, this is a signal to us that April may be a deteriorating extension of March 2014. This is not light rain over Johannesburg, it is noteworthy rain in the order of damaging natural incursions. We submit and put it to the judge and the jury that the earth is cooling off from a hyper-active sun. The rains and polar vortex is a result of a hyperactive sun and the earthquakes so far in 2014 could very well also be as a result of a meltdown. This means that there are several causes of earthquakes and rain, but the general source is singular, the sun is at the centre of it all. As far as earthquakes are concerned, it is also possible that outside of the tensions alluded to in chapter 6 as causes of earthquakes, it is also possible for an overly heated crust that may give way to earthquakes because of heat induced displacement. This is a plausible explanation for the overly cloudy March and opening of April, the rain and clouds are a shield from extreme heat being ejected from the sun. Nobody wants to admit that a toxicity index is essential. For instance if we were to be faced with a situation where, weather, natural disaster, war or threats of war, social unrest, long standing  poverty, terrorism, coups and more known risks we all to unfold at the same time then we would be in a dangerous spot. This is what has been happening in just the beginning of 2014 on an incremental basis and this needs attention.

I just heard a penny drop, coming to think about it, the admission by the South African Meteorological Services in March that the "Rains of March" 2014 was *unusual* is also somehow a supportive statement to the hyper-active sun position and postulation. If the meteorological services out of their own admitted that they did not have a plausible explanation for what caused the rain in March, and they are not looking at the solar system at large for the effects of a hyper-active sun, then there is a possibility that we are blind-sided and that the climate change and global warming proponents are also blind-sided, just as the meteorological services could not take an explicable responsibility for the "Rains of March" 2014 at all. What this further illustrates to us is that the weather of March was an observable symptom of a larger phenomenon that is unfolding in the solar system and we had the view from here that manifested as the exchange of blows between an extremely hot sunshine and grumbling clouds cover that led to irrational rain in March 2014. In just one day (especially since the rain in March) it goes from rainy to extreme heated sunshine with the two competing for centre stage at any one time. This being the 2nd of April 2014, there is no room for blunders as we have to keep an eye on this trend.

As early as now, it looks like this generation is headed for cataclysm and it is up to everyone to act in order to maintain the integrity of the world as we know it. There is more than enough evidence to support this notion and point of view. The submissions and hypothesis espoused in this book are an entry-point to this position. Nobody should have to encounter this issue, but as the experience of adulthood would have, it is unavoidable. Even the most lounged person can see that this civilization is riding on a time that is critical and the signs are all over. 2014 is a yet unprecedented year that is showing signs of higher attrition than most. On average, the year 2014 is unpredictable and random. Well here's to April as we ride into a point of no return and unknown destination. By the end of this month we should be persuaded in one way or another. What is becoming indisputable is the fact that this weather and the polar vortex are all defensive measures. The earth is defending itself from a hyper-active sun and the attendant effects. Sun spots are not caused by or the result of wayward industrial behaviour and $CO_2$ emissions, so *climate change* and *global warming* are ruled out as the only causes of modern headaches at all. As we speak right now, the clouds above Johannesburg are hostile and this seems to be a continuation from the month of March. We saw a two week hostile takeover of the blue sky in the middle of March as South Africa was left reeling from damages by rain. This goes back to what we talked about in chapter 6, the earth is defending itself from an overly heated solar environment. The sun is the culprit this time around and the earth is defending itself by being "rained" in. If the earth did not come alive tonight then this is not 22h19, Johannesburg is poured in with rain-water, this is an expression of the last vocalization of the rain incursion. This following on the heel of a Chilean earthquake growl and cracking of the bones of the earth. Rain is no longer what it used to be, a grand watering of the greenery. The urban environment is even accentuating the language of the rain.

This rain is even assaulting the built-up concrete with anger that splatters on the surface of paved areas when even cascading from roof tops. The sounds are intelligible and 'protestful'. The damage of the March rains even spread to agricultural and country side known as so called rural areas. The rain has intermittent bouts where it falls and stops to rest. This is a definite refusal by the earth to be burnt into molten stone. I don't know of the trigger that could burn out the ions of the rain making interface of cold ad warm fronts even anything that could stop moisture from being ferried inland by the winds, so the earth won't allow itself to burn without defending itself one way or another. We would read this as floods. Should the atmosphere get dry and hot without reprieve, it could reach fever pitches that warm the seas and heat the surface and immediate interior of the crust to levels that trigger weak spots to jostle and crack into earthquakes. The rain and floods at worst, snowstorms and the like would be a dynamic resolve, or a mechanism for the earth to cool off from the heat. So either hot or cold extremities indicate real extreme circumstances in deeper regions of outer-space even all the way around to the extent of the solar system.

As the news of the day would have it, there is a report, Gazprom (a Russian gas company) and NATO are at it again, they are in the middle of a spat for the future of Russia. Gazprom is at the head of Russian opinion on the future of gas supplies to the west and the shift of power as Ukraine and Crimea are at the centre of the ever ballooning fall-out between Russia and the west. Belgium is the stage for the strategic fight of the future of Russia that is refusing to demilitarise Crimea. The western powers and NATO are meeting in

Belgium to discuss the options to the resolution of the Russian/Crimean issue if at all.

...The 3rd April 2014 is a sunny day that is drying out the wet greenery from last night's pouring rain. It seems like the stand-off between a dry and wet weather is taking a permanence. We don't want to make a mountain out of a proverbial mound. It is a hot morning and this is an almost sure sign that the afternoon and evening are going to be rained out. This is a direct result of the fact that the sun is hyper-active as we have said. That there is a visible trend of a warmer atmosphere is also tangible to even amateur weather observers. Now the trick is that the hotter it gets, the more rains we expect at night of every hot day. March left us guarded as we were unexpectedly assailed by the rain in the third month of the year 2014. This left us more wary of the intention of the year 2014 as a bout to mind. We are left with no sure proposition as to where and how the year would meander going forth. Even though the occupation by the rain in March has eased-off, the threat of a resurgence is lingering because we don't know what turn things will take. We don't know what winter in South Africa will bring with it. Our experiment in Johannesburg is tapering off as the month of March is, when the incursion was rife. From now on we are at the mercy of the vagaries of the weather and we call it as we see it. If the sun is as hyper-active as we suspect and have also verified through some reference publications on the internet that have stated that this is the case, then we don't rest easy.

A presenter on Talk Radio 702, Jenny-Crys Williams, a fellow optimist of note opened her talk-show by celebrating the weather, saying it was a warm and glorious day today. Her show is on at 13h00 and we have known her for her bright outlook and high spirit. I felt at this moment that if I could, I would have called her to highlight to her that what is behind this clear blue sky is a conspiracy of note, because the weather is accentuating an eminent disaster that is compounding on the outer-skirts of the solar space. Jenny announced that UCT (University of Cape Town) is offering summer school (for adult learners) and one of the programmes that was as well booked out, was a course on asteroids and comets. This programme is offered to members of the public who want to do additional learning, while the students are on recess. Jenny interviewed Medy Rahl the director of the UCT summer school who described the courses and lecturers. She gave the address for people to follow up. Email: ems@uct.ac.za, (telephone) 021 650 2888, www.summerschool.uct.ac.za.

We want to follow up this link and speak to Medy Rahl to discover what that they were lecturing about regarding asteroids and comets, especially in 2013. Isn't it amazing the frequency of the word asteroid in circulation recently, this has to be a sign of sorts.

On the 16h30 news, it was announced that Russia has now occupied Crimea militarily with an unknown intention, but NATO and other western air travellers have been warned to stay away from Crimean airspace. No one knows how a declaration of war will unfold here, but the promises that the leaders have made to each other are no comfort to the people at large. We cannot afford to separate nation to nation hostilities from the latent environmental incursions, reason being that the casualties are all the same, loss of human life. There is no difference between a loss of life due to a bullet fired at war and loss of life due to floods.

Acknowledgements and Copyright Disclaimer:

The Book *Finger Prints Of The Gods* written by Graham Hancock, published in 1995 by William Heunemann LTD is referenced.

The reference is made to illustrate theories etc developed in The Johannesburg Formula that are inspired by *Fingerprint Of The Gods.*

Other referenced material is mentioned and accordingly acknowledged in the passages as written.

www.ingramcontent.com/pod-product-compliance
Lightning Source LLC
Chambersburg PA
CBHW070636290526
45790CB00001B/114